INSIDE
HOME DEPOT

INSIDE
HOME DEPOT

How One Company
Revolutionized an Industry
through the Relentless
Pursuit of Growth

Chris Roush

McGraw-Hill
New York   San Francisco   Washington, D.C.   Auckland   Bogotá
Caracas   Lisbon   London   Madrid   Mexico City   Milan
Montreal   New Delhi   San Juan   Singapore
Sydney   Tokyo   Toronto

Library of Congress Cataloging-in-Publication Data

Roush, Chris.
    Inside Home Depot: how one company revolutionized an industry
through the relentless pursuit of growth / Chris Roush
        p.   cm.
    Includes bibliographical references and index.
    ISBN 0-07-134095-5
    1. Home Depot (Firm)—History.   2. Do-it-yourself products
industry—United States—History.   3. Building materials industry—
United States—History.   4. Entrepreneurship—United States—Case
studies.   5. Corporations—United States—Growth—Case studies.
I. Title.
HD9999.D624H657   1999
381'.45683'0973—dc21   98-47998
                                                                CIP

McGraw-Hill

A Division of The McGraw-Hill Companies

1 2 3 4 5 6 7 8 9 0   AGM/AGM   9 0 3 2 1 0 9 8

ISBN 0-07-134095-5

*The editing supervisor was Penny Linskey, and the production
supervisor was Tina Cameron. It was set in Fairfield by Ron Painter of
McGraw-Hill's Professional Book Group composition unit.*

Printed and bound by Quebecor/Martinsburg.

This book is printed on recycled, acid-free paper containing
a minimum of 50% recycled, de-inked fiber.

CONTENTS

ACKNOWLEDGMENTS

As with every first-time author, writing a book presents a big challenge. Certainly, I could not have finished this project without the helping hand, guidance, and suggestions of a few key people.

Karl Weber took on the task of selling a Home Depot book and made it a reality just when it seemed as if those hopes would be dashed. He and I had never met at that time. Yet he quickly found a publisher and guided me through the process of negotiating a contract. Meanwhile, Karl's expertise as a former book editor provided keen insights into the editing and rewriting process.

McGraw-Hill editor Mary Glenn and publisher Philip Ruppel are congratulated for publishing the book. From the first day they saw a proposal and sample chapters, they have had the enthusiasm and dedication any author would dream about.

When the first draft of the manuscript came close to being complete, one person gave it a thorough editing for typos, subject-verb agreement and content revisions. Retired journalism professor Mickey Logue, also my Little League baseball coach, gave this book a quick and thorough edit, filling the pages with his trademark scribble. His wife, Glenda, also read it for another perspective. Mr. Logue is still teaching me a few tricks.

Former *Business Week* colleague David Greising, who had written one book and was finishing another about Coca-Cola Chief Executive Roberto Goizueta when I started this project, became a willing listener to my frustrations, concerns, and questions. He encountered some of the same problems I faced with his book, as Goizueta and Coca-Cola did not cooperate. At my lowest points, David picked me up and told me I had done the research to write a Home Depot book that no one else could. He also read much of the manuscript and offered organization and content suggestions.

Adam Levy, Atlanta bureau chief for Bloomberg News and

my closest friend and confidant, provided counsel as I wrote and interviewed sources, and even gave advice to a few former Home Depot managers. Lastly, Adam also read an early version of the book and helped polish it.

The editors at Bloomberg News have been more than understanding when I might have been short with them on the telephone or in computer messages. I want to thank John McCorry, Rebecca Cox and Galen Meyer for realizing that this book meant a lot to me, and the Bloomberg organization for hiring me. My goal was to give them top-notch stories and reportingeven while working on this book. I hope I succeeded.

Thanks also go to fellow Bloomberg office mates Steve Matthews and Kathleen Sullivan, who put up with me during the writing of the book. Steve, my former boss at the *Tampa Tribune*, also read an early manuscript and made suggestions.

Curtis Coghlan, a former assistant business editor at *The Atlanta Constitution*, encouraged me to write a book about Home Depot, reviewed the initial outline and read some of the first chapters. More important, however, was the confidence he gave me as a writer.

There comes a time in everyone's life when you make a decision that changes the rest of your life. In 1994, I was faced with such a decision. While my career as a journalist was rising as a young, up-and-coming correspondent for *Business Week*, my personal life was going downhill fast. In March of that year, I wrote a letter to a woman I had known a decade earlier, fallen in love with, but for some reason lost touch with. Luckily, she kept the same feelings toward me even though we hadn't seen each other in almost 10 years. We met each other again, and fell in love again.

Today, Mindy is the wife that every husband hopes to have but is thankfully only mine. She is witty, smart, and beautiful and the best mother I could have asked for to our sons, Andrew and Tyler. And she was as determined as I was to make this book a reality. Throughout my entire work, she put up with my late nights in our downstairs office, pecking away at the computer keyboard when I should have been upstairs, going over the day's events as she wound down. She also took care of the house and the children, even scurrying off to Birmingham to spend time with her parents when I needed the house to myself to complete some writing. For her patience that went beyond what was asked, I am eternally grateful.

Chris Roush

THE BEGINNING

Bernie and I founded Home Depot with a special vision—to create a company that would keep alive the values that were important to us. Values like respect among all people, excellent customer service, and giving back to our communities and society. And here is the key—a value means something only when you live it.

—ARTHUR M. BLANK

This is the story of Home Depot, the most successful retailer to come along since Wal-Mart—and one that is more admired according to national surveys. "I think Home Depot is the best-managed retail company in America, ours included," says David Glass, chief executive of Wal-Mart Stores and therefore considered somewhat of an authority on retailing.

This is the story of a chain of stores that has arguably revolutionized its industry more than any other retailer, surpassing companies decades older by catering to designers and rural markets through a relentless, yet methodical, pursuit of growth.

This is the story of two executives who made that happen. Arthur Blank, with his Rhett Butler–like moustache, olive skin, designer suits, and lithe body conditioned through years of marathon running, has the stamina and drive to spend 14-hour days in the office and in stores pushing Home Depot. Bernie Marcus, his graying toupee hair and twinkly eyes, along with his rapier-like wit, used for humor and for chastising, lifts the spirits of thousands of Home Depot employees with his motivational talk and implores them to work harder.

This is the story of how the two executives hit on a formula for success—a huge assortment of goods in warehouse-sized stores, cut-rate prices, and a wheelbarrow full of customer service—never before tried in the hardware retail business. They

1

then found the employees to build the company, whipping them into such a bleeding-orange frenzy that they will do anything to be one of Bernie's Boys—or part of Arthur's Army.

The result: Incredible financial results from the stores and on the stock market.

Home Depot had nearly $30 billion in sales in 1998—with projections of $50 billion in sales by the turn of the century—and more than $1 billion in profits. That makes it one of the biggest retailers in the world, behind only Wal-Mart and a handful of others. Since Home Depot's stock went public in 1981, the price has increased by more than 37,000 percent. In the past 10 years, Home Depot's stock has risen an average of 41.8 percent annually. (It rose 76.9 percent in 1997 alone.) Of the 100 largest companies in the country based on market capitalization, only Microsoft Corp. has provided a better return to its shareholders during the past decade with a 45.6 percent annual return. Wal-Mart's stock has risen just 20.5 percent annually in the past decade. That's half the rate of Home Depot's.

Not a bad performance for a company founded by a former comedian from Newark and an accountant from Queens who were fired from their previous jobs and who begged to find the money to start their new retail venture.

In their early careers, Bernie Marcus and Arthur Blank were solid, but not outstanding, retailers. After graduating from Rutgers University in 1951, Marcus became a druggist at Two Guys from Harrison, an early discount chain where he first caught a glimpse of low prices. In the 1960s, he was vice president of merchandising for Vornado, Inc., whose stores were the precursor of home improvement centers. That's where Marcus first learned about products such as electrical wiring, lumber, and faucets. In June 1970 Marcus became executive vice president of Daylin, a Los Angeles-based conglomerate that owned the do-it-yourself chain Handy Dan Home Improvement Centers, Inc., and a pharmaceutical company, overseeing its merchandising. On September 2, 1972, he was put in charge of Handy Dan, which in two months would sell stock to the public.

Blank graduated from Babson College in 1963 and returned to New York, his hometown, working for the accounting firm

Arthur Young & Co. He left in 1967 and returned to the family business, Sherry Pharmaceutical, which shipped drugs to doctors, drug stores, and hospitals. Blank became its controller and got its books in shape. In 1970, Daylin bought the company. Daylin executives took Blank under their tutelage, making him controller of a discount drug store chain in Savannah, Georgia, called "Elliott's Drugs." Two years later, he became its president and chief operating officer. In July 1974, Blank became controller of Daylin's largest subsidiary, Handy Dan, and moved to Los Angeles.

From the first day—July 8, 1974—together Marcus and Blank made a team. Marcus was a smooth front man, quick with a joke and a pat on the back for a job well done. He was the extrovert who dropped by your office to say hello, and the visionary big thinker. Blank was the behind-the-scenes bean counter, although running Elliott's had given him merchandising experience and the ability to understand how sales and promotions inside stores, keeping items on the shelves, and customer service affected financial results. "We were the true odd couple," said Marcus. "He's meticulous, well organized, and knows exactly where he's going to be at every moment, whereas I'm loosy goosy and unorganized. But our goals have always been the same."

One Friday afternoon in April 1978, Bernie Marcus and Arthur Blank walked into a meeting in their Handy Dan offices in southern California. Marcus, the company's chief executive, walked in first and was shocked when no one called him Bernie. Even then everyone called him by his first name. "Mr. Marcus, will you please sit down," said Sandy Sigoloff, the chief executive of Handy Dan's parent company Daylin, Inc. Sigoloff then proceeded to fire Marcus.

Then Blank, Handy Dan's chief financial officer, walked into the same meeting. He too was fired. Blank left the room and walked down the hall to a large boardroom. Marcus was sitting at the end of the table, looking pale and afraid. Blank sat down and said, "Would you believe this bullshit? This has got to be a joke." Later, they were escorted into their offices, watched while they packed their personal belongings, and then escorted out of the building by guards.

Marcus was one month shy of his 49th birthday. Blank was 35. Both were out of a job. "We got trashed," said Blank. "But it gave us a chance to live our lives over from a business standpoint."

Sigoloff claimed Marcus and Blank helped create a $140,000 cash fund that was used to help decertify a union representing Handy Dan employees in northern California. Sigoloff assumed that the money was used to induce employees to leave the union. "Somebody had to create it," said Sigoloff about the fund. "If you're the chief financial officer and the chief executive officer, it wasn't the guy who did payroll who created it. Once it came to my attention and it was carefully reviewed, the action was taken and it was very swift."

Besides the firing, no action was ever taken against Marcus and Blank, and they disputed the allegations, claiming they knew nothing about the fund. "The company was one of the most successful entities [Daylin] had," said Marcus, who exhibited a paranoid streak later at Home Depot that some attributed to the firing. "But there was a personality conflict." Later, when Blank was confronted by the allegations during the firing, he replied, "What are you talking about? What is this craziness?"

Former Handy Dan employees backed Marcus and Blank. "I worked with them too long," said Rick Mayo, a Handy Dan merchandising manager from 1973 to 1979. "In terms of honesty and integrity, they're impeccable, just impeccable." Clearly, Sigoloff let personal feelings get in the way of Handy Dan's success when he fired Marcus and Blank. That there was never any serious investigation or validation of the charges exonerates Marcus and Blank. Sigoloff never proved that they had been involved. If he had given Marcus and Blank a chance to refute the charges or had simply told them to stop what was going on, whether they knew about it or not, maybe today Handy Dan would be the world's biggest home center retailer— and no one would have ever heard about Home Depot.

The day after the firing, Marcus called former Handy Dan investor Ken Langone, who laughed. "Bernie, you just got hit in the rear with a golden horseshoe and don't even know it," said Langone. "You always told me about this dream of a huge store and great service and low prices. Let's do it." Langone agreed to raise $2 million to start Home Depot. Langone liked the way Marcus and Blank treated their employees and always tried to improve. During the next two decades, he would counsel both men, providing personal and business advice. And he'd also take a keen interest in Home Depot's success, meeting with store employees to hear their complaints.

The firing could have negatively affected Marcus and Blank. Instead, it gave them new careers. Marcus says the experience shaped Home Depot. "We learned how *not* to treat people," says Marcus. "We were so depressed over what he did to us, we vowed we'd never treat anyone like that. A lot of people that run major corporations today lack humility. It was a terrible thing that happened, and it was devastating, and some people don't come back from it."

Indeed, Marcus and Blank are respected today as much more than retailers out to make a buck for themselves and their shareholders. Every year, *Fortune* magazine ranks the most admired companies in the United States. The survey is compiled from more than 12,000 senior executives, outside directors, and Wall Street analysts. For the past four years, Home Depot has been No. 1 when compared to other retailers—and near the top when compared to all companies.

Home Depot's 1998 score in the rankings was 8.07 on a 10-point scale. That put it ahead of Wal-Mart, which scored 7.23. In each of the seven categories comprising the overall score— quality of management, quality of products and services, innovation, investment value, financial soundness, talent, and corporate responsibility—Home Depot ranked ahead of Wal-Mart. Department store chain Nordstorm, widely revered for its customer service, received a rank of 7.11. Home Depot's biggest rival, Lowe's Cos., received a score of 6.10.

Home Depot also fared well against better-known and better-respected companies like General Electric, Microsoft, Coca-Cola, and Walt Disney. Compared to General Electric, Home Depot ranked higher in products, innovation, and corporate responsibility. It was deemed more innovative than Coca-Cola.

It ranked higher than Microsoft in its products, innovation, and corporate responsibility. And Home Depot ranked higher than Walt Disney in every category.

Yet, for the most part, Home Depot is rarely among the corporate titans garnering the ink and attention from the nation's business press and experts. The nuts-and-bolts do-it-yourself retailer based in Atlanta is in the shadow of Coca-Cola even though Home Depot is the largest company in the city, and state, in terms of annual sales. Marcus and Blank's faces have never adorned a *Forbes, Fortune,* or *BusinessWeek* cover—regular treatment for these other companies—despite their overwhelming success.

Marcus and Blank feel fine with that low profile. Their goal all along was to create a company that cared for shareholders—many of whom are also employees—and customers outside of just providing them a rising stock price and good low prices. They've always wanted Home Depot to go beyond just that. The source of their satisfaction has been knowing that they made a difference. "It's about giving back to society," says Marcus. "The customer is very important to us, whether in our environment, our store, or in their own environment, their homes and their communities. We want customers to go away from their experience with the Home Depot believing that we care about them, and not just as a customer."

It's a company refusing to rest on its laurels. Despite its unbelievable success, Home Depot constantly tinkers with its strategy. With reluctance sometimes, it has tried new products, new services, and even new store formats to continue growing. That's why do-it-yourself shoppers today find Home Depot stores in small towns where Marcus didn't think they could be successful, Home Depot stores that sell only remodeling and redecorating items, Home Depot stores that make deliveries to customers, and Home Depot stores that teach preteen children how to make bird houses. "We spend very little time talking about all the things we are doing well," says Blank. "If you attended any of our meetings, you would never believe this company is the size it is or doing as well as it is. We spend 80 to 90 percent of our time focusing on problems, what the competition is doing, what our customers are looking for, what they are not finding, what stores are having problems."

Marcus and Blank are not creative geniuses. They've been successful primarily because they discovered midway through their business careers that the best way to run a company is to give the employees the autonomy and authority to make decisions as to what works best. A ruthless boss taught Marcus and Blank—then employees struggling to develop that autonomy because they saw how it helped morale and boosted sales—that lesson the hard way. Today, a Home Depot employee can make a mistake without it becoming a career killer. Marcus and Blank know the only way Home Depot is going to keep growing is to have its workers look for ways and products that set it apart from competitors.

And because Marcus and Blank actively seek out employees who can think and make decisions, they treat them better than other retailers. "You cannot build a vision if you don't have the people who will accept that vision and carry that vision on," says Marcus. "We wanted to surround ourselves with people who felt as we do, who think as we do, who believed what we believed in. You have to believe in yourself and what the vision is. When you believe in something strongly enough,...then the dream becomes a fact." Enough employees believe in Marcus and Blank and the Home Depot philosophy. Virtually every one of them calls the cofounders by the first names Bernie and Arthur, because they feel they're just as important to Home Depot's success as are the cofounders and leaders. Blank explains it best in speaking of how his partner uses his talents to get others to make Home Depot a great company: "Bernie understands the people side of the equation," says Blank. "People in our company genuinely feel that what they say and do is respected. He gives people the freedom to make decisions and take responsibility for them. I think that creates the commitment."

That commitment at Home Depot, above all else, is taking care of the millions of customers walking into their 700-plus stores every year. "We don't [just] open stores and fill them up with merchandise," says Marcus. "Otherwise, we'd be growing faster than 25 percent a year. It takes qualified people, it takes a different kind of person. Those who shop our stores know our people are different. These are people who are concerned, that do get involved with the customer, that do treat the customer a lot differently [from] other retail environments." It's in such a setting that a store manager can call up Marcus and complain that Home Depot's headquarters is ignoring his request to add another truck to improve delivery times or that a Home Depot lumber buyer can take off his clothes during a budget meeting to make the point that he's stripped off all excess costs in the wood he's selling in the stores. They encourage a competitive nature that leads many Home Depot employees to believe that the only reason they deserve a paycheck is that they have taken care of the customer the right way the first time.

Home Depot has become one of the world's biggest retailers in less than 20 years by focusing on customer service, treating employees like family, and relentlessly pursuing growth.

Building Home Depot is the most ambitious do-it-yourself project ever undertaken. These are the management techniques of an orange-colored giant. This is inside Home Depot.

HOME DEPOT BOOT CAMP

*Where do we find these people? Nowhere. We make them. We tell our
people to make it here because they won't be able to make it at another
organization. They'd be misfits.*

—BERNIE MARCUS

Bernie Marcus walks into a Home Depot training class. He
is dressed in khakis and a plaid, short-sleeved shirt. He
has no notes. There are no charts and no handouts. "I don't
think I have ever kept a note or an outline in my entire life,"
says Marcus. "It's between my ears. But it's very consistent."
He begins talking, telling stories.

Say there's a customer, Marcus explains. He gets in his car
and drives down the street, stopping at lights and intersec-
tions. The do-it-yourselfer gets on the highway. He drives for
several miles and then gets off the highway and enters this
huge Home Depot parking lot. He finds a parking spot—the
store is crowded so the space is not near the door—and gets
out of his car and walks into the store.

The customer walks down the aisles looking for a specific
nut. But when he gets to where he's bought these same nuts
before, there are none there. "You just screwed my customer,"
Marcus tells the class, a group of assistant store managers and
district managers. It could take from 25 to 30 minutes for the
customer to get in front of that peg, but if there's no product
there, the customer is going to leave upset. That, in turn,
upsets Marcus.

Later, Marcus asks an employee in the training class how
to greet a customer. "Hi, how are you doing?" someone
responds. "That's nice and friendly, but it doesn't get you any-

thing," Marcus replies. "You say,`What are you building today?'
Or if you ask,'What are you looking for today?' and the customer says, 'a hacksaw,' you take him to the hacksaw and ask
him what he needs it for."

If the customer is building a window frame, Marcus points
out, what he really needs is another saw. Maybe the customer
thinks the saw he needs is called a "hacksaw," Marcus says.
But if he buys the hacksaw and takes it home and can't do the
job, he's going to be frustrated when he can't finish the project. That do-it-yourselfer will likely blame Home Depot for
not pointing out the right tools and the right way.

Marcus has brought some store signs to the class. One says
"Sink, $69." That's all Marcus needs. "Now look, guys, look at
this sign," he says. "You don't know what sink goes with what
sign. It doesn't say it's porcelain or stainless steel."

Marcus asks questions and prods for answers and then starts
another story. He shows his students—assistant store managers,
store managers, district managers, and others—that they can fix
the problems in their stores. They just need to think like the customer. "Through his constant intercourse with people, and his
incessant desire to talk about the Home Depot, he would then
spend his entire class relating those stories," noted Ned Lenox,
once Home Depot's training director. "Almost always any point
he was making was about the customer."

Such training from Home Depot's top management sets it
apart from competitors. Without it, Home Depot would be like
any other home improvement retailer. "We are in the teaching
process," Marcus says. "We don't hire people to do the teaching; we do it ourselves. There's going to be a class almost every
day of the week in different parts of the country, and the things
we talk about are the culture of the company, how we take care
of the customer, how important it is for the customer who
makes that trip to the store to be able to find what they want
that day and not be disappointed."

Then there's Blank. His training approach is the exact
opposite. He walks in with detailed notes and charts. He looks
as though he's ready to make a presentation to the board of
directors. He knows exactly what he's going to say, how he's

going to say it, and how long it will take. Being an accountant, Blank talks about Home Depot operations from a financial and accounting standpoint. He points out that before he and Marcus started the company, the traditional price markup at home center retailers was about 35 percent, but at Home Depot it has been maintained at approximately 26 percent.

Blank spends hours talking about the importance of lower prices. By selling more products than anybody else, Home Depot can lower prices. More volume means lower overhead. It's a simple, yet classic, tenet of economics Blank is explaining.

But his message is also about giving employees the power to take control. Blank asks management trainees this question: Would it be more valuable for a Home Depot lumber department to hire one person who had six years of experience as a carpenter for $10 an hour or to hire two people for $5 an hour who had once framed a house?

The answer from the store managers and district managers is to hire two people. To Blank, there is no right or wrong answer. It depends on what the store needs. However, if you do hire the person for $10 an hour, Blank says, explain to him or her that you're also hiring two others for $5 an hour and you expect the more experienced worker to teach the others everything about carpentry. "In a very short period of time, I've got three people with eight years of experience," Blank tells his class. He hopes light bulbs are going off inside the heads of his pupils. There is no easy answer to the question. But if you hire the expert, make sure his or her knowledge is passed along to others. That, of course, results in even more training.

"Training is not an event," explains Blank. "Training is a way of life." Especially at Home Depot.

It's Home Depot's secret weapon, and few outsiders have ever seen the company's vaunted training program—what many consider the key ingredient in its success. Home Depot spends millions of dollars annually on training new employees and retraining current employees. As a result, Home Depot's employees provide better customer service and are more knowledgeable about do-it-yourself products than competitors.

For new hires, the training starts with five days of classes ranging from company history to how to greet a customer. After the classes, new employees spend three weeks shadowing a department manager learning how to order, stock, and sell. Once they begin working in a store, they're constantly being trained, either about new products or about how the store is run. Each employee is required to have one hour of training each week. For a company with more than 150,000 employees by the end of 1998, that's 150,000 hours of wages per week used to teach. "It's well spent," says Marcus. "It's the best investment we'll make. How do you make people qualified if you don't train them?"

Marcus and Blank talk about Home Depot's infancy during training, hoping that employees will acquire a sense that they can overcome anything if they believe in themselves.

The first two Home Depots opened on June 22, 1979, in Atlanta. There was one problem. The customers didn't show up. Some who did left without buying anything. Marcus and Bank overestimated the early potential. Home Depot ran four small ads in *The Atlanta Constitution* the day before the stores opened. At the bottom of the ads was the slogan "You've never seen anything like it!" The next day, Home Depot ran a two-page ad in the morning *Constitution* and the afternoon paper, *The Atlanta Journal*. Both ads began with the headline "The Home Depot Comes to Atlanta 11 A.M. Friday" and were stuffed with prices and pictures of what they were selling. There were Chamberlain garage door openers for $87.00, round oak tables for $99.00, Meco grills for $19.00, gallons of Du Pont paint for $7.48, light bulbs at five for $1, and a customer's choice of garden tools for $3.97 each.

Still, Marcus and Blank had no way to teach customers what to expect. That would be something they would rectify. The first Home Depot stores carried nearly 20,000 different items. No competitor operated stores as big as Home Depot— 60,000 square feet. Home Depots looked different from everybody else. Those first ads explained "The Home Depot concept," noting that there were "no fancy fixtures or cute displays" and "no fancy prices." It also said Home Depot was "Atlanta's most complete selection of do-it-yourself products. One trip to The Home Depot does it all."

Pat Farrah, whom Marcus and Blank had hired after seeing his failed attempt at a warehouse-sized hardware store in California called Homeco, designed the stores so that customers, when they entered the front door, would have to first walk down aisles where there were high-profit items in the wallpaper and kitchen departments. The garden center was up front so that the plants would make the store feel full of fresh products. Also up front were furniture and lights. Nails were put in kegs to give the appearance of a bulk volume warehouse—even though it was hard to store nails in such containers. The store was designed to have customers wandering the aisles.

The second day, Marcus and Blank sent their children into the parking lot with wads of $1 bills to give to the first 250 customers—and to ask their reaction to what they had seen. If the customers checked the serial number on the $1 bill against the $1 bills posted on a sign inside the stores and the numbers matched, they could win free hammers and other items. At the end of the day, there was plenty of cash left. "By 5 o'clock, my kids were running around in the parking lot, stopping people and giving them money to come into the store," said Marcus.

Marcus and Blank fixed problems, donning orange aprons and helping customers, asking questions and listening to complaints. "The key became that we worked in the stores, we worked on the floor, we waited on customers during the day," said Marcus. "And we found out by talking to customers what we were doing right, and what we needed to do to make the company better, and things that we were doing wrong. We learned a lesson during those primary years, and that lesson is a lesson that has stayed with us ever since. We listen to customers." While Marcus simplifies how Home Depot righted itself by crediting customers, the duo did spend a lot of time in the stores making changes.

Some items attracted customers in droves. Garage doors hadn't sold well in Georgia in the past. But merchandiser Rick Mayo saw that many new homes being built in suburban Atlanta had garages. He bought a truckload of Genie openers.

In the half of 1979 that Home Depot's stores were opened, they sold 2,300 garage door openers—three times Genie's sales total for the state the year before.

Farrah, Marcus, Blank, Mayo, and others constantly fine-tuned the mix. Furniture, Coca-Cola, and motor oil were dropped. Those products were offered initially because "we needed to develop [customer] traffic," noted Blank. They expanded the garden, electrical, and hardware departments. "Our business has changed constantly," said Marcus. "Our stores don't look the same every year. We're always in the position of having to go back and redo older stores. If you're not moving, you're not changing, you're basically going backwards."

Constantly changing the stores and the product mix was a philosophy developed at Handy Dan and refined at Home Depot that led to its success—and a practice that Marcus and Blank wanted to teach every employee in training classes.

Classes for assistant store managers and district managers are conducted differently from general employee training classes. Marcus and Blank each assume part of the management training. Blank begins the eight-day session, and Marcus ends it. (In between, other executives also hold sessions.) On occasions throughout the year, Marcus and Blank also go into stores across the country—Marcus's trips are called "Bernie's Road Show"—and lead impromptu classes on-site. "Nowhere [else] in any industry, in any company in America, do people running a company our size sit with [employees] and try to impart their philosophy," says Marcus. "Some of these people come from major companies where they've spent 25 or 30 years, and they've never seen the chairman of the board or a president. Here, we spend the whole day with them. It's incredible, and it builds the bond that destroys the bureaucracy because they feel free to pick up a phone and call us any time because they know me as Bernie, and they know Arthur as Arthur."

Experts say there's no other retailer where so much training is done by top executives. "It was more intuitive on their part," said Lenox about Marcus and Blank. "They knew it was very beneficial. By actually spending time themselves, in the training programs, by spending a day with them, the simple fact that they paid attention to these people in any way was a big part of their success. The successful companies are out explaining to their employees at the lowest level what the plan is and how they are going to be successful, investing them in the organization. That was the reason for their success. Both Bernie and Arthur had a way of infusing through stories how people [in the stores] had been successful."

Blank spends one-third of his time annually training employees. That's a task virtually every other CEO at a multi-billion-dollar company designates to subordinates. A Goldman Sachs banker once told Blank that he wouldn't be able to teach training classes once Home Depot grew bigger than $1 billion in sales. He was wrong. "That's one of the strengths of the company," says Blank. "It's a significant part of our jobs to rein-force the culture and keep the training up."

It's not easy. The classes are long, hard, and detailed. The reward for workers who make it through and become good employees: Home Depot employees earn 20 to 25 percent more than their counterparts at rivals like Lowe's, Hechinger, and Builders Square. Store managers can earn as much as $100,000 a year, and employees can buy company stock worth up to 20 percent of their gross salary at a 15 percent discount.

Marcus and Blank have taught well. At an Orlando store, assistant store manager Chris Brumfield tells workers to greet shoppers and then ask, "What project are you working on?" If they ask that simple question, Brumfield knows from what Marcus has taught him, that the employees can go through a shopper's list to see what he or she is looking for. "Remem-ber," says Brumfield, "if they forget something, they'll get frus-trated. More than likely, they'll be mad at us." Brumfield also instructs employees to know about products throughout the store and where they're located. "Never just point to another aisle," he says. "Walk the customer over and find someone to help."

Despite the emphasis on training, Marcus and Blank are never satisfied. They know Home Depot's customer service is far from perfect. Their goal is for Home Depot to get better every single day. Sometimes it does, and sometimes it doesn't.

Sitting in classes given by Marcus and Blank in Atlanta or listening to them as they walk through stores aren't the only ways Home Depot managers are trained, however. They've also got to learn how to rappel down 1,000-foot cliffs, how to raft through rapids, and climb across rope bridges. Sometimes they'll spend four days in the wilderness, living and working together rain or shine.

That's right. Part of Home Depot's training calls for managers to get out into the wild—literally. For more than a decade, Home Depot has sent employees on Outward Bound excursions.

It started with Marjorie Buckley, a Pennsylvania woman who coined the Home Depot name. She was also a founder of the North Carolina Outward Bound School. After the first Home Depot stores opened, she asked Blank to visit the school. He became convinced the school could help Home Depot.

Blank—a New York City native—joined the executive committee of the North Carolina school. Eventually, he led a movement to open an Outward Bound school in metro Atlanta to help at-risk teenagers develop self-esteem and pride in themselves. "He is a role model for all of us," said John Huie, former director of North Carolina Outward Bound. "He exemplifies the role models for Outward Bound in every respect: community service, leadership and physical skills."

Blank saw that Outward Bound could help Home Depot prepare its managers. "I felt it was a good thing in terms of being able to coalesce a group together, to see each other in a different kind of environment where we don't have on coats and ties, to show that we put our pants on the same way," said Blank. "Because we operated in a crisis environment, it is important for our people to test themselves and know that they can do more from an emotional and physical basis."

The Outward Bound program molds Home Depot's future executives. George Collins began his Home Depot career in 1982 as a Florida store manager. But he was afraid of flying, and elevator rides made him nervous. "I got white knuckles when I picked up somebody at the airport," said Collins. In 1983, that changed. Collins and a dozen other employees attended an Outward Bound class in the North Carolina mountains. Everyone flew except Collins, who drove to the site. But once there, he climbed across a rope bridge strung between two trees—60 feet off the ground. Blank told Collins that if he could climb across the bridge, he could fly. After Outward Bound, Home Depot paid for Collins to take a two-week "fear of flying" course from American Airlines. He overcame his fear of flying. Within eight months, Collins was made a regional manager, overseeing eight stores in the Dallas market. In that job, he spent a lot of time flying in airplanes.

Stephen Bebis, a merchandiser, went on an Outward Bound trip in 1985, and when he showed up, he asked where the tents were. He was told they were sleeping on the ground. "Before, I thought that the Holiday Inn was roughing it," he said. Bebis then found himself stuck halfway up a cliff, sweating and hyperventilating. He almost asked for help down, but he was able to pull himself up to the next ledge. He cried. "The experience told me that when you are defeated, you are not," he said. Although he would leave the company, Bebis returned and used those skills as president of Home Depot's fledgling Canada division when it scaled back expansion in 1995 due to economic and hiring problems.

Managers learn teamwork by depending on others to help them survive in the wilderness. A critical component to Home Depot's success is store managers' and merchandisers' relying on each other to make sure they don't sell out of product, hurting their bonuses. "You're not by yourself," says Marcus. "You have to depend on each other. At Home Depot, you have to depend on each other for survival also." Those managers took those lessons of teamwork, leadership, and confidence back to the stores and to Home Depot's headquarters. "When hiking, climbing a mountain or traversing a mountain cross-country, you quickly learn you will travel only as fast as the slowest hiker," noted Don McKenna, Home Depot's vice president of human resources for a decade. "The store is only as good as its least-trained employee. You have to have everybody well trained."

As good as Blank feels about the Outward Bound program, however, Home Depot doesn't force anyone to attend. Going into the woods is voluntary—and not going hasn't impeded anyone. Still, more than 1,000 Home Depot store managers, district managers, and other managers and executives have gone. "The ultimate bottom line is not whether I think it works or not," says Blank. "More importantly, the people who go every year think it works."

And for the company's success, it's what they learn that helps Home Depot to grow. "Typically, we find that when management fails, it is not due to lack of technical knowledge, hard work, or loyalty," says Blank. "It is due to what Outward Bound would term the 'soft skills.' It is in the areas of leadership, team building, group support, personal self-esteem, and confidence that we reap the benefits. Learning how to handle stress in a positive manner is where the Outward Bound courses excel for our management people." Consider the letter written by Dick Hammill, Home Depot's senior vice president of marketing, to Bill Murray, director of professional development at the North Carolina Outward Bound School after a visit in the early fall of 1996. Wrote Hammill: "We all walked away revitalized to be better team players."

It's not just new employees or store managers who are getting trained, however. Marcus and Blank and other executives go through their own training. Marcus got the idea in 1994 from General Electric CEO Jack Welch, who told him about a process called the "360-degree review" through which executives are evaluated by subordinates as well as bosses. Welch told Marcus the reviews provided new insights in helping train leaders. Impressed, Marcus had a similar review developed for Home Depot, with a focus on skills such as taking care of customers, getting the job done, and building relationships.

Blank got reviewed first. The review noted that he's smart and diligent but also a control freak. If you want to schedule a meeting with him, you have to book it weeks in advance and write a memo outlining the topics you want to discuss. "I do this to impose discipline on the meeting," says Blank. "I'm one of the best people I know at time management."

Others got different reactions. Bill Hamlin, executive vice president of merchandising, was reviewed by seven people who report to him, nine peers, and Marcus and Blank. On a scale of 1 to 5, Hamlin was rated a 4 or higher in his reaction to customers' needs, understanding of how customers think, and challenging of employees to provide outstanding customer service. But he scored low on his ability to listen to others with an open mind, on understanding how his actions and decisions impact others, and on creating an environment in which people can say what's on their minds. In the last two areas, Hamlin rated himself higher than his peers did.

Hamlin discussed this with others at Home Depot. "When I have those conversations, what I'm trying to do is understand, from the people who filled this out, their perspective of what all those issues mean," he said. "So I have been listening to try to understand what their perspectives were so that I can work on that particular perception." Hamlin added that he wasn't surprised by the critique of him.

After Marcus and Blank and others went through the process, additional managers underwent 360-degree reviews, including store and district managers. Many found it helpful. "It helps to develop yourself in areas you might be weak in," said Eric Johnson, a regional vice president. "The 360 forces us to work closer together with all of our associates by asking them for feedback that you otherwise might not have had. Knowing how to adjust my management style from individual to individual develops personal growth. If you are open to suggestions, the power of the results is endless."

Still, the 360 reviews caused concern within Home Depot. Some reacted with shock and disbelief at their results. "The concept is wonderful," said Peter Cleaveland, former vice president of logistics. "The failing may be that it tends to be negative because you're forced to use some negative measures and you tend to overanalyze. And I don't think there was enough follow-up." Others got angry at how others felt about their work. What Marcus and Blank tried to teach was that training is a lifelong process involving constant feedback—as in the 360—from coworkers. Indeed, many saw the 360 process as a way to improve on what they were already doing.

One district manager felt the 360 process would help him

become better in his job. "It really opened my eyes and let me see what I really knew all along but just was afraid to admit," said Jim Tullius, a district manager in Pennsylvania. "I appreciated the honesty of everyone who responded, and it has surely opened up my eyes in becoming a more effective leader. My feeling is that this is one of the best things we have ever done in the company."

Others saw the 360 review as a way for all Home Depot managers to treat employees as if they were the same—a criticism leveled against the company in the form of gender discrimination lawsuits at about the same time the 360 reviews were implemented. "People are not all the same, and we have to make sure we come across in a fair and respectful way," said Ramon Alvarez, a manager at a Home Depot store in Visalia, California. "I think the 360 is going to help us in trying to get a grasp on how employees see us. It will be tremendously helpful."

At a Home Depot that opened in 1997 in Garden Grove, California, nearly 6,000 people applied for 150 jobs. In Valdosta, Georgia, about 7,500 applicants sought to fill 132 jobs. In the Bronx, almost 7,000 people filled out applications for 300 jobs at a new store. Home Depot has become a preferred employer because of how they treat workers. "People looking for just a job—we don't want those kind of people here," says Marcus. "People looking for a career—those are the kind of people we want."

Marcus and Blank look for people to mold through training to take care of customers. "We don't want to bring somebody in who doesn't have any tendencies in one area and put them in that position and then tell them,'Well, you have to make it,'" said Blank. "That doesn't do the company any good, and it doesn't do the associates any good, and it doesn't create the kind of environment that's important for us to create in terms of taking care of the customers."

Around the country, more people want to work for Home Depot than there are spots available. And it's not just because of the training. Home Depot employees are paid better wages than their counterparts working at Lowe's or Hechinger or

Builders Square. But that's not all. They have also benefited from Home Depot's rapid stock price increase. Employees can set aside 20 percent of their wages to buy Home Depot stock through a payroll deduction plan. Marcus and Blank also share the company's profits through an employee stock ownership plan. Salaried employees—assistant managers and higher—receive options to buy stock at a fixed price and can exercise those rights for 10 years. And store managers receive bonuses based on sales and profits.

Marcus has never liked paying commissions for sales because he feels that commissions give workers the wrong incentive. Instead, Marcus and Blank train workers to make sure that the customers get the right products for their needs, whether it's a 59-cent nut or a $59 power tool. "The day they lay me out dead with an apple in my mouth is the day we'll pay commissions," says Marcus. "If you pay commissions, you imply that the small customer isn't worth anything."

Their pay system has helped Marcus and Blank create workers whose zeal is unsurpassed. When employees see how much money can be made at Home Depot, many turn into believers of the customer service training. "When you talk about taking care of the customer, it really starts by creating the environment where we show the kind of caring for ourselves, for our own family, as we do for our customers," explains Blank. "We do that by paying people what they are worth. We do that through stock option plans, stock purchase plans."

If those employees had bought—and many early ones did—$1,000 worth of Home Depot stock in 1982, when the company had four stores, their shares would now be worth more than $150,000. Marcus estimates this system has created as many as 1,000 Home Depot millionaires. "A lot of people who have made the most money with us don't have advanced degrees," adds Blank. "But we've given them a chance to earn through hard work a way of life they never imagined they could have."

The money is a reward for hard work. Working at Home Depot is rough and laborious. People like Bruce Berg, the southeast division president who spends half of his time in the stores, admit: "Home Depot is a tough place to work. Your feet hurt. Your back hurts. That's why I want to keep letting my associates know that I feel what they feel. What I want to do is wear out my shoes on the floor of a store."

Some can't handle the long hours and tough standards. "They usually tell us, and that's OK," said Gregg Gerstenberger, a store manager in the Atlanta area, who wears his orange apron six days a week, 12 hours at a time. In the early years, people like Farrah, Marcus, and Blank regularly worked 14- and 16-hour days. Some of the executives experienced burnout. Jim Inglis, after 13 years of workweeks that sometimes totaled nearly 100 hours, took a sabbatical in 1996 and never returned. "Have you ever heard of Pecos Bill, who jumped on a tornado and rode it across the West?" asked Inglis. "Well, I'm like Pecos Bill."

The pay structure has its downfalls, however. Employees get nervous when Home Depot's stock price drops. That's an issue Marcus and Blank constantly battle, and it is one of the reasons they continually look to grow Home Depot's business. If the business grows and profits increase, then the stock price will increase, boosting the income of their employees.

Employees wondered about the stock price in September 1990, when the country was hit by a recession. Sales, particularly at retailers, took another hit due to the Gulf War, where U.S. troops invaded Iraq and forced Saddam Hussein to curtail his military movements. That scared consumers, who cut back on retail purchases. Home Depot, like other retailers such as Wal-Mart and Toys R Us, was hurt on Wall Street even though its sales hadn't slumped. Its stock that year fell 23 percent from $43.62½ on July 16 to $33.75 on September 6. "It had better" rebound, said Lisa Lowery, a Home Depot cashier in Atlanta at the time. "A lot of people are going to get really poor if it doesn't." To alleviate concerns, Marcus and Blank did what they do best. They went to their employees—in their unique fashion—and told them not to worry. They could pull through this together.

A group of Home Depot employees, all wearing orange aprons, are cheering and hooting and clapping. It's as if they're seeing the Rolling Stones in concert—except for the fact that it's 5 A.M. and pitch dark outside. "Good morning, America, from Colma, California," screams Home Depot store manager Buz Smith into the microphone. "Unbelievable crowd here tonight. These people are going absolutely crazy." Marcus and Blank are introduced, and they stroll into huge cheers. Part pep rally, part comedy routine, part training session, this is "Breakfast with Bernie and Arthur," a quarterly Sunday morning telecast to Home Depot stores allowing the cofounders the chance to preach to their disciples. It also gives the converted the opportunity to ask questions to the ministers of orange.

Marcus is wearing khakis and a pink shirt with a white collar and white cuffs. Blank is wearing khakis and a green polo shirt. After the crowd dies down—but not before Blank leads them in a cheer of "Give me an H! Give me a D! You got Home Depot!"—Marcus complains that there's no coffee in the store despite the early hour. The first question, from Roy Brinkly at the Chula Vista, California, store, gets right to the point. Why is the stock price losing ground? Marcus responds. "We have an awful lot of young people in the company, and the Home Depot stock may be the first stock they've ever owned," explains Marcus patiently. "You are concerned about it. We are concerned about it also. We live in very difficult times. There is without a question a recession." He tells employees that the stock has dropped because other retailers are struggling, so Wall Street investors have been selling all retailing stocks.

With that somber introduction, Marcus then works the crowd. "Have you seen a drop-off in people shopping our stores?" he asks. The reply: "No." The crowd brightens up. "If you didn't know there was a recession going on, would you say there's a recession going on?" asks Marcus. This time, the answer is a more resounding "No."

Marcus then talks about how Home Depot is unique and a recession-proof retailer. He's right. While even Wal-Mart's earnings growth has dropped, Home Depot has reported 14 consecutive years of sales and earnings growth. In 1990 during the recession, Home Depot's sales grew 38 percent to $2.75 billion from $2 billion, and net income increased 46 percent to $112 million from $76.8 million. In 1991, when the recession continued, Home Depot's sales rose another 38 percent to $3.8 billion, and net income increased another 46 percent to $163.4 million. Then Marcus explains that there are Wall Street money managers who get nervous about retail stocks as a group when one reports lower profits and sales. They sell all their retail stocks instead of just one or two, Marcus explains, and fail to examine Home Depot separately. "Take your mind off the stock on a day-to-day basis," continues Marcus, "and say to yourself, 'Where is the Home Depot going to be five years from now? Where is the Home Depot going to be 10 years from now?'"

Other questions are asked. An Atlanta store employee wants to know when new telephones will be installed in stores. Another asks whether Marcus and Blank are considering smaller stores. A worker in the Colma, California, store asks if the company will install computers to track special orders and will-call items. Marcus and Blank patiently answer each question, and for a while the crowd forgets about the stock price. Before time is up, however, Marcus brings up the subject again—and masterfully turns it around so that he can use it as a training tool. It's almost as if he's back in the training room, telling assistant managers and district managers stories that illustrate how to provide better customer service.

To keep the recession and slumping retail sales from affecting Home Depot, Marcus tells the crowd, his voice rising ever so slightly, you're going to have to take even better care of the customer than you do today. "You are going to have to treat these customers with the greatest amount of tenderness that you've ever done," says Marcus. "They can never feel unhappy. They can never feel as though they had a bad shopping experience. They have to feel as though they walked out of a place that was their own home."

"This is not a cult group, and we're not cult leaders," adds Marcus. "We're talking about people's ability to earn a good living and to end up with a career. If you bust your butt, if you go out there and take care of that customer on a constant basis, and this company ends up successful, making money, you're going to end up making a hell of a living, and one day you're going to have a nest egg that's worth an awful lot of money."

The message is clear: Training will pull Home Depot through good times and bad. As long as employees practice what he and Blank constantly preach, they will all be just fine. And, foremost on the employees' minds, the stock price will increase as long as they take care of the customer. Because if they take care of the customer, sales and profits will increase.

"There's a certain security that they have in working for the Home Depot that they're not going to get from anybody else," Marcus would say later. "If I had a choice of working for somebody, would I want to go to work for a company that's kind of reached its maturity, or would I want to go with a company where there's just unlimited growth potential?"

There would be many times when Marcus and Blank would return that loyalty to their employees. Little did Marcus and Blank know at this time, however, how much they actually could do for their workers. In the next decade, they would stretch their commitment to a handful of Home Depot employees to the limit. And they would incur the wrath of some of their employees. How they reacted in each case provides key insights into their management style and the Home Depot culture known as "Bleeding Orange."

MANAGEMENT LESSONS

Home Depot's success is based partly on the fact that co-founders Bernie Marcus and Arthur Blank have always believed in having the best-trained workers. When employees are trained, they are taught by the highest-ranking executives at the company and then they are given more training as they continue at Home Depot. Such training makes employees feel like management cares about their work and makes them work harder, helping to build a strong culture.

1. Smart employees help grow Home Depot's sales because if the workers know how to use the products they're selling, they can suggest other items that could be used in the same do-it-yourself projects.

2. Top management at Home Depot train workers, giving employees a sense that executives care about what it's like to work in the stores and handle customers. In many cases, the executives themselves once worked in stores.

3. Teamwork helps Home Depot achieve its goals, because no one employee or executive can do it all. Employees who work together realize that they need to rely on each other to keep store shelves stocked.

4. Management also go through training at Home Depot, because no matter how high up you are in an organization, you can continue to improve to better the entire organization.

5. Training is constant at Home Depot. Employees should always be learning, whether in the store aisles or in the training room, so that they can continue to make the retailer better.

6. Home Depot management talks openly with employees. Such conversations send the signal that executives care about the workers in the stores and want to make their workplace better.

BLEEDING ORANGE CULTURE

Doing the right thing means living our values every day—walking the talk.

—Arthur M. Blank

Any company with strong-willed leaders and employees with the autonomy to make important decisions about the future of the business will have a strong corporate culture. Home Depot is no different. But inside the orange walls of America's largest home improvement chain are two separate and distinct cultures. One is to be admired. The other is to be feared if you should get in its path.

One is couched in principles of doing the right thing no matter the cost. It is a set of beliefs that could be the guiding light for any operation that wants to be known as a societal role model. It is all that is good in the business world.

The other is a go-for-the-jugular, win-at-all-costs attitude found in most leading American corporations. It prides itself on militaristic overtones, rallying troops into battle with doomsday predictions of dire consequences should the soldiers, that is, employees, fail in their mission. It is the part of corporate America most big businesses don't talk about in public. But virtually all of them have some vestige of it.

This is Home Depot's Bleeding Orange culture, part corporate do-gooder and part corporate bully.

Mike Modansky remembers the budget meeting at the old Home Depot headquarters—a renovated A&P grocery store—as if it happened yesterday. In reality, it occurred more than a decade ago. Blank sat at one end of a conference table, and merchandisers like Modansky, Home Depot's lumber buyer, sat at the other end, presenting next year's plans.

In most companies, the budget process is civil, with the boss reviewing the numbers and asking questions about why sales of certain products are expected to increase and others to decrease. The budget is approved, and then the head of the next department comes in and goes through the same process. Not at Home Depot.

Modansky remembers an hour-long shouting match. Blank screamed, "This is not realistic!" and got so mad that Modansky remembers spit coming out of his mouth. Blank, known to schedule his days down to each minute, was likely also upset that the extra time had thrown off his calendar. "You could tell Bernie and Arthur, 'Go fuck yourself,'" said Modansky. "They would say, 'Fine. Fuck you too.'"

But what Modansky remembers best is what happened that night while he was getting ready for bed. The telephone rang, and Modansky picked it up. The person on the other end said, "It's Art."

Modansky replied, "Art who?"

The Home Depot cofounder answered, "Arthur, your boss."

"Oh. Why are you calling me?" asked Modansky.

Blank was also getting ready for bed. "I was brushing my teeth, and I was looking at myself in the mirror and wanted to let you know something," said Blank. "I wanted to find out how strongly you felt about what you were putting in your budget. All the yelling and the shouting was in that direction. I respect you. I didn't want to go to bed without telling you that."

This is the quintessential example of the Bleeding Orange culture—mostly good—that Marcus and Blank developed. It's macho confrontation. It's Blank teaching a manager to defend his strategy. It's screaming and shouting. It's respect for differing opinions. It's strong relationships between two people allowing them to get in each other's face, yelling. And it's got entrepreneurial spirit. "Frankly, from time to time, our relationships will be tested," says Blank. "If we have strong relationships—built on trust, honesty, and integrity—we can work through difficult times together." Said Cleaveland, a former Home Depot executive, about Blank: "He'll get in your face and go toe to toe with you, but when you're done, he'll say, 'Good job.'"

If anyone is pushing Home Depot's culture in recent years, it's Blank as he takes a bigger role as its leader. He's promoting values and culture to store managers, district managers, and other employees through store visits, training sessions, and other meetings. To Blank, the culture keeps customers coming back to Home Depot time and time again. "Bernie and I have always been in absolute agreement about these principles, beliefs, and standards that have driven our company since 1979," says Blank. The Bleeding Orange culture isn't hard to learn or exotic, adds Blank. But it's not easy to define in some pithy mission statement. It means "something only when you live it. By living our values every day, by being a role model for new associates, we will have the same level of success in the future as we've had in the past."

Bleeding Orange means taking care of people. "Taking care of customers is incredibly important—that's where our business starts and ends—but the way you take care of customers in our business is by taking care of the people that take care of the customers," says Blank. And, Marcus adds, it's Home Depot employees that will set the stage for its future success. "All the training programs we give you, all the orientation material we give you, all the films mean nothing in terms of getting that new employee to bleed orange compared to the value of setting the right kind of example, day in and day out, in your store," Marcus told a group of employees once. "That's where that Bleeding Orange comes from." That means allowing a merchandiser to take off all his clothes, as Modansky would one time during a budget meeting, to make a point. It's Marcus and Blank getting up at 4 A.M. to go talk to employees at "Breakfast with Bernie and Arthur" shows where they answer questions.

It's inviting employees to make suggestions on improving the company, as Marcus and Blank do through "Issues and Answers" gatherings. Consider one meeting held in December 1995. An employee wants to know why products sold in Home Depot aren't scanned on their way into the stores as they're scanned at the cash register when sold. The answer: That slows the receiving process. Another store worker wants to know why the company isn't increasing special-order sales of products not typically sold in stores. Answered Blank: "What we do best is sell the product on the floor. Our goal is not to grow the special-order program." But Bleeding Orange respects differing opinions. Blank admits special-order purchases are important to Home Depot because they indicate new products that could be added to stores. Blank promises to gauge how special-order sales fluctuate.

Bleeding Orange means encouraging people to speak up and take risks. That means recognizing and rewarding able performers—such as the employees who won trips to the 1996 Olympics for providing customer service. That means developing employees from entry-level workers into division presidents. It's board members who visit stores unannounced to talk to employees about their concerns. "Everything good starts by taking care of your people, by having the right kind of people, and by allowing people to become the best that they can be," said Blank.

Bleeding Orange means teaching the customers. Many do-it-yourselfers don't know how to use products sold in Home Depot—or how to complete a home improvement project. It's the job of Home Depot employees to provide that knowledge. "If associates don't know about the product, the customer is in trouble and we are in trouble," says Blank. "And, we want to sell the customer the least amount of product to solve their problem and make their dream come true. If we sell them the least, they keep coming back. Then, we'll sell them the most over the long-term relationship."

Bleeding Orange means providing employees the entrepreneurial freedom to make decisions, giving them a say in the company's success. Walk into many Home Depots today, and you'll see signs in the ceiling fan aisle or the electrical aisle that the products being sold in the area are proudly maintained by a specific store employee. "Somebody is taking absolute ownership of either 8 feet or 16 feet of a whole aisle," explained Larry Mercer, Home Depot's executive vice president. "And then they are able to say, 'Look, if it's in stock, I did it. If it's out of stock, that's my problem.' It's the same kind of thing as putting your signature on your own handiwork."

Bleeding Orange means giving employees the chance to make mistakes—as long as they'll learn from errors. "Creating new ideas is a real strength—it has helped us grow—and now we realized, that in addition to creating ideas, we need to become much better at sharing ideas," says Blank. "We as a company need to understand how to put best practices in place—to share the best of our great ideas—within this environment that encourages entrepreneurial spirit."

Bleeding Orange means strong relationships not only with customers and employees but with companies making the products sold in Home Depot stores. It means telling those companies what kind of new products customers are asking for and what products aren't selling and need to be dropped or changed. Bleeding Orange means making sure the vendors ship enough product to the stores so there are never any empty shelves. "We recognize that without capable vendors, we're nothing," says Marcus. "If we don't have product to sell in the stores, what are we? You can advertise all you want or have people trust you all you want, but if you get into a store and you have empty shelves, you're in deep trouble."

Many times, Home Depot's relationship with vendors is strained because the company demands low prices and demands that some vendors sell only to Home Depot. Marcus and Blank don't hesitate to drop a vendor when necessary. In January 1996, Home Depot stopped buying carpet from Shaw Industries, after the nation's largest carpet maker decided it was going to open stores that would compete with Home Depot in many markets. The move has hurt Shaw. It closed nearly 100 stores in late 1997 and early 1998 and sold its remaining locations to another retailer.

Bleeding Orange means providing strong returns to Home Depot investors. "One of the value systems of our company is not only to do right by customers and do right by associates, but it is to do right by the people who are providing the capital for us to grow our business," says Blank. "They have choices they can make every single day. Do they invest in the stock market? Do they invest in the home improvement industry? If they do, which horse do they choose to ride, and how long do they want to stay on that horse?"

Bleeding Orange means doing the right thing—living the Home Depot values every day, or as Blank likes to say, "walking the talk."

"Ten years ago, I believed that we would have to do things differently in order to pass on our culture and prepare the company for future growth, that growing too quickly would dilute the orange-blooded culture in our business," says Blank. "Today I believe that if we do the right thing by our customers and associates, if we make the right choices and make sure the store feels right for the customer, then we will have the same kind of successful company four years from now when we have [more than] 1,000 stores."

Bleeding Orange means giving back to the community, donating millions to causes in towns and cities with Home Depot stores. "We help our communities grow because it's the right thing to do," says Blank. "The magic is that our associates give back because they want to. We don't tell them to. Associates go into communities to help people to help themselves because it's so much part of our culture. It's not something we do to get more customers into the stores, or for recognition. Our associates go out there because they want to make a difference in people's lives."

Then there is the other Bleeding Orange culture, the side customers don't see, the side kept out of the public's eye altogether. Home Depot often throws its weight around to get its way or to intimidate rivals.

Home Depot has been for most of its history a brash and macho company where store managers and their bosses would gather for retreats and drink late into the night—an attitude that would later lead to gender discrimination charges. "A group of animals, hard-drinking, hell-raising cowboys," said Cleaveland, a reserved former vice president of logistics who nonetheless got caught up in the atmosphere. "On one side it was a culture shock," said Cleaveland. "On the other side it was a lot of fun." Others, however, remember locking themselves in hotel rooms during manager retreats so they wouldn't be a part of the revelry.

That party atmosphere had been encouraged in Home Depot's early days by Farrah, who started his hardware career at California-based National Lumber and Supply, Inc., in 1963. Farrah's Homeco, discount store—what many consider the first home improvement warehouse—in Long Beach attracted Marcus and Blank, who were impressed with Farrah's ideas, including the vast assortment of goods stacked on pallets, the low prices, and the do-it-yourself experts hired to provide customer service. "It looked like a Home Depot at a very early stage," said friend Robert McNulty. But Farrah was a dreamer, not an operator. Interested in buying Homeco, Marcus and Blank asked to see Farrah's financial records in 1978. Farrah reached under his desk and pulled out a cardboard box full of bills and receipts. Homeco went bankrupt and was liquidated. "What Pat needed was guys like Bernie and Arthur," said McNulty.

Farrah became intoxicated with Home Depot and was one of the reasons for its early success. But his hard work and lifestyle took its toll. "I wasn't real good at moderation," said Farrah. "I worked more than I should have. I drank more than I should have. I did everything to the extreme." While the company needed gung-ho executives to fuel its growth, such an attitude eventually took its toll. Others downplayed Farrah's drinking, noting he didn't drink on the job and only drank during after-hours catalog or merchandise meetings to get in a creative mood. By 1985, however, Farrah, needing a break, quit the company. Others also burned out.

To some extent, the hard-partying, hard-drinking ways of Home Depot have died down as some longtime managers and executives left in the mid-1990s. They, to a certain degree, gave way to a new breed of manager and executive patterned after Blank—disciplined both inside and outside the office. A few renegades, particularly Bruce Berg, remain.

It's also a culture that churns through employees, particularly at the store level, because of the conditions. "Those that remain are hard-working and driven," said Inglis. For those that can make it through, it's a badge of honor to wear the orange apron. "There's an esprit de corps," added Inglis. "There's a zealotness. The Home Depot is an all-consuming task. That's what the Home Depot environment requires."

Bleeding Orange is also a culture where executives and managers who worked in the stores are more valued than others who join as managers from other companies. "If you're from the store, you know what you're talking about," added Inglis. "If you're not from the stores, you're a bureaucrat, and that's an indictment." Many managers and executives have left Home Depot because they were not able to overcome that perception—even though they had something to offer the company.

Bleeding Orange is militaristic and wants to destroy anything in its path. At sales meetings in the late eighties and early nineties, managers cheered cartoons of Homer, the company's handyman mascot, visiting competitors in hospital beds and unplugging life-support systems. This is the Home Depot culture Marcus and Blank don't discuss with people from outside the company. Take their response when arch-enemy Lowe's expanded into Atlanta—Home Depot's home turf—in 1997.

Home Depot's Atlanta employees—the troops, if you will—gathered for a pep rally. They were told the gravity of the situation. The report was melodramatic, exaggerating how much business might be lost to Lowe's. Home Depot, after all, had an estimated 52 percent of the area's home improvement sales. It wasn't as if Lowe's was going to force Home Depot to close stores. In fact, Home Depot has never closed a store because of a competitor.

Still, this is what employees heard: "These people are in your back door," said Eric Johnson, a southern division vice president, wearing battle-gear camouflage. Johnson, who has glasses and a mustache, is considered to be one of the more rabid Bleeding Orange disciples. "They're taking food from your family's mouth," he continued. "They are taking what is rightly yours, your futures, your stars that you wanted to go out there and reach for. They're hindering that to a degree. Are you going to allow it?" The crowd responded with a loud "No!!" Johnson then denigrated Lowe's, saying, "They've copied us...and they're fine-tuning themselves to really put a hurtin' on us. We can't allow it. We need to blow them off the face of this earth." The last comment received a standing ovation and cheers.

Marcus appeared at the pep rally. In stores and in interviews, Marcus is typically calm and smooth, able to win over the most cynical with his charm. This was not that Marcus. This was Marcus with anger, disgust, and paranoia in his voice. "How do these guys have the nerve to open up in our face," snarled Marcus. "You want to talk about somebody that's arrogant, you're talking about those folks out there in blue." (The facade of Lowe's stores are primarily blue.) Marcus wasn't through. "I can't even say their name 'cause it gets me nauseous," he said, drawing out the last two syllables of the last word for effect.

It got more defensive. *Home Depot Television*, the in-house department designed to beam Marcus and Blank's gospel to the masses, developed a "newscast" for the southeastern stores. The "news" show breaks away to present a special report on "The War in Atlanta."

"Special anchor" Al Dale begins, "HD TV is just receiving word from its highest levels that the Home Depot has officially declared war against chief competitor Lowe's." Dale cuts to supposed "live" reports from the battlefield. The reports are actually taped scenes staged to make the Home Depot-Lowe's competition look like real war with guns and bombs. Johnson, wearing a camouflage shirt and dark sunglasses, is standing across the street from a Lowe's in Cartersville, Georgia, about an hour north of Atlanta. Johnson notes "the enemy has launched an all-out attack against the men and women of Home Depot." Then the sound of guns and cannons are heard, and Johnson ducks. "Whoa," he says as he stands back up. "Did you hear that?"

Then the "war" coverage cuts to Tony Brown, another southern division vice president. Brown, also wearing camouflage, stands on the site of a future Lowe's in Woodstock, a northern Atlanta suburb. "Al, as you can see, I'm in a very dangerous location," says Brown. "It's going to be a very ugly scene around here." Brown goes on to say, "This very dirt that I'm standing on today could be the very dirt we bury Lowe's in."

Then Berg, the southern division president and Marcus confidant, appears dressed in a full camouflage outfit including a hat with two stars and army boots. His imitation of a general preparing his troops to go into war and possibly die for the better good of the country—that is, Home Depot—is convincing. His goateed face does not crack a smile, and his eyes are piercingly serious. "The enemy previously encamped in North and South Carolina has begun to open bases in a southwesterly direction approaching our home territory," said Berg. "Looking at the state of Georgia, we see that across from all of our customer service bases, the enemy is setting up offensive stations to attempt to take our customers away. The customer will decide who wins this battle, and we are determined to win through customer service. Use the weapons available, and kick these cooters back to Booger Holler where they belong."

This is not the only time Home Depot has used military-like examples in developing its culture. Managers have been taught by a training company how to prepare and carry out the company's business like fighter pilots. In 1996, Afterburner Seminars taught 1,800 Home Depot managers, dividing them into 12 squadrons, to defeat an enemy—Lowesnia. Home Depot says it uses such seminars to instill teamwork and reinforce competitive spirit. Some former managers say the strong macho and military overtones quickly wore out and upset others.

To be sure, the good parts of Bleeding Orange outweigh the bad and are gaining strength as the company undergoes changes. But Home Depot today retains many macho and military-like values present since the first stores opened. Blank and Marcus downplay the importance of this side of the culture. But they do realize how vital Bleeding Orange as a whole is to the company's success. "If we had to bring [Home Depot] to a sum zero of no growth to maintain the culture in our company, I would do that," says Blank.

Others, particularly the board, are convinced the culture needs to be maintained. "The minute we allow anyone to compromise our values because of potential economic benefit, we haven't got any values," says Ken Langone. "There must be a link between every single thing we do and the customer—as part of our corporate culture and values. And what are our values? They are quality, decency, kindness. Indeed, our values are not inconsistent with profits and sales. We need to continuously create the human condition that reflects our values and our culture. That is why if you apply them to the customer,...you will own the world." What Langone ignores is that decency and kindness are somewhat contradicted by the militaristic, win-at-all-costs form that Bleeding Orange sometimes takes.

Still, Bleeding Orange executes itself in so many ways, from developing employees into the next generation of Bleeding Orange leaders to providing customer service, teaching the customer, giving back to the community, taking care of employees trying to win a spot on the Olympic team, and responding to how towns and cities react to Home Depot.

If Bleeding Orange is anything, it's an employee's ability to do what he or she wants—even if it may seem outlandish—to improve the company. Take Modansky, the former lumber buyer whose argument over his budget showed him how Blank would go to great lengths to make his point. Modansky, who at one time bought all the lumber for Home Depot's stores east of Texas, would show just how far some at Home Depot could go to make their point to Marcus and Blank.

His family started and operated Ajayem Lumber in Walden, New York, and after a stint in Vietnam, Modansky entered the lumber business himself, rising to vice president of Erb Lumber in Michigan. "I was born with sawdust in my blood," says Modansky proudly. He could look at a piece of wood and tell what country it was from. Blank, as Modansky discovered, was also interested in the lumber business. Wood brought in hundreds of customers who might pick up an electrical cord or a box of nails along their way to the lumber department. Modansky learned the Home Depot way, maintaining prices low enough on lumber to keep customers coming through the doors. Blank still wasn't satisfied. By 1989, Blank playfully admonished Modansky that lumber prices could be lower. Each month at the sales meeting, he would tell Modansky,

"Get naked, get naked. Your sales are driving the rest of the company."

"He wanted me to cut my prices," remembered Modansky. "It was a company slogan every time we got together." In November of that year, the merchandising department heads presented their budgets for the next year to senior Home Depot executives in the board room, which contained a fancy wood table and swivel chairs with high backs. The budget meeting started, and Blank sat at the end of the table. Around him were Berg, Inglis, and other executives. Modansky walked in to present his budget and sat down in a chair.

He took off his shirt, exposing his hairy chest. Then he took off his pants. Then he took off his socks. And finally his underwear. Modansky sat back down in his chair. Many around the table were laughing so hard they had tears in their eyes. Modansky remained calm and opened his budget presentation. And he looked at Blank and said, "You said for me to get naked, so I got naked."

Modansky made his point. He cut lumber prices in the next year's budget. And by disrobing, he showed he was willing to take a risk—even if it meant becoming the subject of laughter. "That's part of the renegade in the company," said Modansky. "The personality of the company was such that you could take off your clothes to make your point and keep your job."

There were other nonconformists. Terry Kinskey started as a lot worker and rose to regional manager through his brash style of standing up in group meetings in front of Blank and Marcus and telling whoever was speaking that he or she was wrong about what was going on in the stores. "I just love what I'm doing," explained Kinskey back in 1990. "It's a religious experience to me, and I practice it intensely." "Terry runs on pure emotion," said Rich Herter, who worked in Home Depot's human resources department. "Terry is a very emotional person who bleeds orange more than any other person I've met in my life."

One time Kinskey blew up at a meeting in San Francisco, complaining about district manager workloads in front of the top Home Depot executives. At most companies, that would have ended Kinskey's career. The next morning, logistics vice president Cleaveland went running with Blank. Quickly, the conversation turned to Kinskey's tirade. "Wasn't that beautiful?" said Blank, noting how Kinskey had the courage to stand up and say what he felt was wrong at Home Depot.

"Yeah, it was," Cleaveland responded.

"Of course, I don't expect you to do that," Blank replied. "But it shows us what we need to be looking at."

And for employees who don't have the gumption to stand up in front of Marcus or Blank and tell them what's wrong at Home Depot, the cofounders have other ways of learning. Langone goes into stores and talks to the employees. One time, he found rats in a store. It wasn't the rats that bothered Langone. That the rats had been a problem in the store for three months was more troublesome. At the next board meeting, Langone mentioned the rats. "The problem is getting rid of the bureaucracy," said Langone, who was able to make one call and get rid of the rats by the next afternoon even though the store manager couldn't in three months. "That tells me volumes about how bad bureaucracy can be," said Langone. "And bureaucracy is like weeding a garden. Just when you're done, you'd better go back and start again."

Marcus and Blank decided that all board members should visit 12 stores each quarter to find out what was happening and, more importantly, what were the concerns of the workers. "You don't have to worry about being fired for opening your mouth," says Marcus. "This company is very unique and unusual. We have an open-door policy that's really meaningful in this company. And these young people, or older people as they may be, are not fearful of it, and in fact do bring up subjects to our members of the board."

Langone once heard complaints from a saleswoman about how baby-sitting problems made her late for work and hurt her review. Langone made suggestions, but when the employee continued complaining, he brought her concerns before the board. "The more they beat up on me, the better it is for the company, because it shows that we're not pulling ranks," said Langone.

Added Alan Schwartz, a former Home Depot board member, "You would go into the stores and walk around and ask questions and they didn't know who you were. Then, you'd go back and tell them you were a board member and wanted to know if there were any issues. One thing that stood out was when you talked to an employee or manager in a Home Depot store, you were dealing with somebody who felt like an owner, who felt involved. They cared very much about their company and their store and the customers. It also sent a good message, that the people on the board were interested."

These employees talking to board members may very well end up running the company during the next 10 to 20 years.

Bryant Scott started working at Home Depot in 1980 at the third store on Jonesboro Road in south Atlanta. "I was going to school and needed a job," he said. "I happened to look in the paper." He saw an ad from Home Depot, asking for workers to load lumber into people's cars and trucks. It was a thankless job, working outside in the rain and the cold, lifting and loading heavy items. Turnover was high. "The lot job is probably not one of the most desirable jobs in the store," said Don Singletary, Home Depot's vice president of human resources. "That is not a real pleasant task."

Scott survived and was promoted to a sales manager. Then he became a department manager. "The thing that was always great about it was they made you feel like part of the business," he said. "They would give me an aisle and say, 'This is your aisle.'" And when Home Depot opened stores in south Florida, Scott went there and became an assistant store manager. Then Scott moved west, helping Home Depot expand into Arizona and then San Diego. "To watch someone like him grow over the years gives me a tremendous amount of satisfaction," says Marcus. "We have hundreds, maybe thousands, of stories like that all over Home Depot. When you hear those stories, it's hard not to be driven every day."

In San Diego Scott faced a critical make-or-break career decision. He had just opened a store, and he had some of his employees sign training sheets stating they had gotten the company-mandated training when they hadn't. Scott realized this was wrong. At a meeting in Atlanta, Scott stood up and told Marcus what he had done. "He was smart enough to realize that he was putting himself on the line," said Lenox, the training director at the time. The move showed Marcus and Blank that Scott was trying to do what was best and that he realized he had made a mistake. "Bryant is successful I think because of his people skills," said Herter, former director of personnel. "Bryant loves people. He is probably one of the happiest people I have ever met. He's always smiling. He's always laughing, yet he's always listening."

Despite his mistake, Scott was promoted again to vice president of merchandising for the southeast division. And in 1995, Scott became the president of Home Depot's Expo Division. He now oversees one of the company's expansion efforts. "I'm not a rocket scientist or a brain surgeon by any stretch of the imagination," said Scott, whose straight blond hair and laid-back demeanor make it seem as though he's spent his life on the beach, not working in Home Depot stores. "I work hard and I try to treat people nicely, treat people as I want to be treated."

Scott is one example Marcus and Blank use to show what can happen to an employee when he or she believes in the Bleeding Orange culture. Scott worked his way up through persistence and attention to customer service. "We cannot be involved with every decision in the company," explains Marcus. "The answer was to develop some people who could be making the decisions. If we had to make every decision in this company, this company would go backwards. What happens as you get bigger is our—Blank and myself—ability to communicate is diluted. We have a lot of division presidents and other people out there taking the message out and keeping the message alive."

There are others, of course, who began at the lowest levels of Home Depot now helping spread its gospel. Larry Mercer started as an assistant store manager at one of the first stores. He rose through the ranks, becoming president of the northeast division, and is now executive vice president of operations. In 1988, Mercer appeared on the cover of Home Depot's annual report—the image of the ideal company employee. Wearing a green sweater and an orange apron, he pointed to a chart showing the company's sales growth during its first decade.

Mercer is now considered a possible replacement for Marcus and Blank when one retires. "I remember hiring him," said Marcus in 1992. "Blank, and myself and Pat Farrah interviewed him. I guess it's got to be 12 or 13 years ago. Just a hungry guy, whom we hired as an assistant manager." Today, Mercer is considered a father figure to a lot of Home Depot employees, helping them and coaching them.

Lynn Martineau also started at one of the first stores, working in the paint department. He too grew with the company, holding a number of jobs, including vice president of operations and vice president of merchandising for the southeast division. In 1996, he became president of the western division. "I'm proud of the fact that I look around and I see kids that worked for me 10, 11, 12, 13 years ago, without college educations, who really had no career," said Marcus. "If you looked at what their possibilities were in the economic world, they were limited, and today these people are very wealthy."

It's opportunities and careers like that—and a commitment to the company—that Marcus and Blank tell new employees still exist at Home Depot today. "These are people who have made it up the ladder who demonstrate all the things that we talk about," says Marcus. "They didn't have the schooling. They didn't come out of Harvard Business School. Bryant Scott made it because he had the heart, he had the brains, he understood the culture, the culture of the company, which is total dedication to both the employees and to our customers. There are those who make it. There are those who don't make it. Some are smarter than others. Some are more highly motivated than others. Some have more heart than others. Some have more courage than others."

Scott agreed that it's the culture that makes the difference. "The culture has remained consistent," said Scott. "We want people to take an ownership position. And the opportunities are still consistent. We've got another 400 stores to open up in the next couple of years."

Outside of the conference room next to Blank's office is a framed poster with a lion and a gazelle. Below the picture is a saying: "Every morning in Africa, a gazelle wakes up. It knows it must run faster than the fastest lion or it will be killed. Every morning a lion wakes up. It knows it must outrun the slowest gazelle, or it will starve to death. It doesn't matter whether you are a lion or a gazelle: When the sun comes up, you'd better be running."

Bleeding Orange means running all the time. "We understand that at times we look like lions and at times we look like gazelles," explains Blank. Home Depot's secret is that its Bleeding Orange culture means that everyone runs constantly and is always looking over his or her shoulder.

"We're always looking for somebody to crawl down our back," explains Marcus. "And we're not willing to accept anybody catching up to us, so we run faster." And they run faster by providing better customer service than any other home improvement retailer—and arguably any retailer—in the world. That running analogy would prove apt for a handful of Home Depot employees who were shown first-hand how far Marcus and Blank would go to help their workers.

Management Lessons

Every successful company should have a strong culture, and Home Depot is no different. Home Depot believes that it should continually seek ways to help the customer, and that it should give employees the freedom to make decisions that will improve customer service. Home Depot's competition is also very competitive, and it fights hard to maintain leadership in its field.

1. A strong company culture is important to Home Depot's success because it provides the belief that employees should place the interests of the customer first.

2. Home Depot helps communities by giving do-it-yourself supplies to charities, which fosters a spirit in towns and cities that the retailer cares about them.

3. Home Depot employees are allowed to speak up and take risks. Quite often, that's the only way to get management attention and to make the changes necessary keep the company growing.

4. Home Depot's culture protects it against competitors, providing a win-at-all costs mentality that has made it a winner in most of the markets where it has stores.

5. Store employees have been able to rise through Home Depot to management positions, becoming role models for current store employees and sending a message that executives value their role.

GOING FOR
THE GOLD

The core belief that we have [is] that if our associates don't feel like we care for them, that they're not going to care for the customers in our stores.

—ARTHUR M. BLANK

It is 6:30 A.M. on a Sunday morning in August 1992. No Home Depot stores are open. The thousands of do-it-yourselfers—weekend gardeners, plumbers, electricians, and painters—who will visit a Home Depot store this day have not even begun thinking about their projects.

But Marcus and Blank are working the crowd in a tent set up in the parking lot of a Home Depot in Atlanta. The gathering is mainly Home Depot employees. Some have orange paint on their faces. Some are shaking orange pompons. All are wearing orange aprons.

It's *Breakfast with Bernie and Arthur,* the television show Marcus and Blank use to talk to employees, building morale and keeping workers informed about what's going on at the company. But this telecast is different from most others. Marcus and Blank are about to explain how they're going the extra mile for some employees who helped Home Depot become the world's biggest home improvement retailer.

The duo walk in, wearing matching print polo shirts, khakis, and, of course, orange aprons with their names in the upper left-hand corner. The crowd cheers. Blank kisses Marcus on the cheek, and the crowd cheers some more. "The last time I heard screaming like this was at the Braves' championship game," says Blank. "Arthur, we've got to be careful here," replies Marcus. "We've got people from California, people from Texas." After nearly 20 years in business together, Marcus and

Blank have honed their shtick well, raising the spirits of their workers.

Marcus and Blank begin by telling poignant stories of other employees. A mentally retarded worker at a California store cleans bathrooms and sweeps floors. "He's just a great asset to us," says his store manager. "He doesn't shy back from anything." A Jacksonville, Florida, employee has developed a Home Depot coloring book for children. And a Home Depot employee who fell out of a tree and broke his neck, partially paralyzing himself, is recovering. "We are waiting diligently for you to get back," says Marcus to the employee, Chris Owens, who is in the tent. "We love you, and you're one of our family." He then turns to the crowd and says, "You work for this company and you know you've got tremendous support." These examples show that while Marcus and Blank are about to go out of their way to help a handful of special employees, they are also assisting and praising other workers.

Marcus and Blank are now ready to show how far they will go for their employees. "These stories very much remind me of the Olympics," says Blank to the crowd. "There's a lot of similarities between the spirit of the Olympics and our employees." Adds Marcus: "It's a lot like what Home Depot is doing. We're going to continue the best service. We've got to be dedicated in the same way. We have to reach our goals." And one of the ways Home Depot has reached its goals in the past—and plans to reach its lofty targets in the future—is by treating employees as though they were family.

Marcus and Blank made Home Depot a sponsor of the 1996 Olympics in Atlanta. Much like Marcus and Blank when they started their company, the city faced long odds when unknown real estate lawyer Billy Payne decided in 1987 he wanted it to host the 1996 Summer Games. Most thought Athens, Greece, would host those games, given that it would be the 100th birthday of the modern Olympics held in the Greek city. In 1990, Payne pulled off the impossible. Atlanta would host the Olympics in six years. Payne needed to get busy.

He called on Atlanta's biggest corporations to provide financial support. Payne based his Olympics bid on the projection that the cost of the entire event, nearly $1.7 billion, would be privately funded. To do that, however, he had to sell a half-billion dollars in sponsorships. Some, like Coca-Cola, which had been involved with the Olympics since 1928, were a given. But they could only do so much. Payne needed more. One company he soon visited was Home Depot, and the offices of Bernie Marcus and Arthur Blank.

In 1992 Home Depot was certainly not as large as Coca-Cola. The retailer would finish the year with $5.1 billion in sales and $249 million in net income. Its profit for the year would be what Coca-Cola and its bottlers would spend on Olympic marketing alone four years later. Still, Marcus and Blank were intrigued by the idea, and they felt that becoming an Olympic sponsor would give something back to Atlanta, the city where they started Home Depot.

Payne sold them a top Olympic sponsorship, which cost Home Depot an eye-popping $40 million, enough to build and open three new Home Depot stores. To sign on at that level, though, Marcus and Blank wanted concessions. For one, they wanted Home Depot's sponsorship spread to its key vendors, allowing the home center retailer to sell what amounted to minisponsorships to suppliers and dubbing them "The Home Depot Olympic Family." The move would help a growing Home Depot pawn off the cost to its vendors. "I don't see how their suppliers had much of a choice, given [Home Depot's] buying power," said David D'Alessandro, president and chief operating officer of insurer John Hancock, another Olympic sponsor. "I can't imagine 3M saying they don't want to do the sponsorship and potentially losing the Home Depot business." Home Depot also wanted the rights to distribute order forms for Olympic tickets. That would bring customers into its stores.

Payne, in need of money to start building sports arenas, dorms, and other projects required for the Olympics, agreed. "I've seen what the Olympic spirit can do for Barcelona," said Payne during the August 1992 announcement of Home Depot's sponsorship. "Now I can see what The Home Depot spirit can do for the Olympic movement." But Home Depot's sponsorship concerned executives at the U.S. Olympic Committee. They didn't want Home Depot vendors like Stanley tools and Casablanca fans using the Olympic rings in ads, making it seem as if they were sponsors. That could hurt attempts to convince other corporations to become sponsors.

A compromise was struck, according to those in the negotiations. Vendors would be allowed to advertise their Olympic relationship only through in-store ads and television commercials clearly naming Home Depot as the sponsor. "That essentially restricted those smaller vendors from prostituting or cannibalizing that whole effort," noted John Bevilaqua, an Olympics marketing consultant who talked to Home Depot about their effort. He thought Home Depot's strategy of siphoning most of its sponsorship cost to vendors was brilliant, allowing the company to have the sponsorship prestige without most of the expense. "It was somewhat unique, but it fit," said Bill McCahan, chief marketing officer for the Atlanta Committee for the Olympic Games. "These [vendor] companies were not given any Olympic rights on their own." A similar strategy has been used by the U.S. Postal Service, an Olympic sponsor from 1988 to 1992 that signed foreign postal services to agreements resembling those Home Depot reached with some of its vendors. Still, such a tactic chafed other companies taking on the full sponsorship cost and U.S. Olympic Committee officials.

There were other problems for the first-time Olympics sponsor. Coca-Cola executives learned that Home Depot had bought the rights to distribute ticket order forms. They complained to the Atlanta Committee for the Olympic Games, the organization overseeing the planning for the 1996 Olympics, noting that only the world's largest soft drink company, selling soft drinks in thousands of grocery stores, convenience stores, and other outlets, could provide the needed distribution. Coca-Cola got its way, distributing most of the 36.5 million brochures through Kroger grocery stores, although Home Depot got brochures in its locations too. "The reason for the change was that we realized we needed broader ticket distribution than we otherwise would have gotten," said A. D. Frazier, the Olympic committee's chief executive officer. "We added another 15,000 distribution outlets through Coca-Cola servicing outlets throughout the country." Home Depot, with slightly more than 350 stores in 1995, couldn't provide such a broad reach. The new kid on the Olympic sponsorship block had been pushed around by the old pro.

Home Depot also convinced Payne and Frazier to let it market engraved bricks to pave the plazas and walkways of Centennial Olympic Park, a downtown attraction being built for the Games. When the program was unveiled in November 1994, Dick Hammill, Home Depot's senior vice president of marketing and advertising, predicted the $35 bricks would be hot holiday gift items and estimated 2 million would be sold in a year. ACOG, as the Olympic committee was known, needed that money to pay for the park. With the bricks came a certificate signed by Marcus and Payne recognizing the buyer's contribution to the Olympic movement.

Hammill's projections were too optimistic, however. Although Home Depot's advertising agency, the Dallas-based Richards Group, developed commercials and print ads for the bricks, Hammill didn't believe such marketing was necessary. Displays inside Home Depot stores, which would be passed by tens of thousands of customers each week, could easily sell the bricks, he thought. Customers could also order bricks by phone.

By the end of the holiday selling season, only 60,000 bricks were sold. Payne started to worry. When less than 100,000 bricks had been sold by spring, Payne had two lieutenants take over the brick selling program from Home Depot with a $2.5 million advertising and public relations campaign. Home Depot, new to sponsoring global sporting events, had failed. One of the problems was that its store displays often were nothing more than a table and a form pad. But a bigger issue was that Home Depot thought the bricks would sell themselves, much like the do-it-yourself products that flew off their shelves. But roof shingles and windows were necessities. A $35 engraved brick was a luxury many Home Depot shoppers saw as contradictory to the retailer's strategy of saving them money by offering the lowest prices on home improvement items. Even with ACOG's involvement and better store displays, Home Depot—which filled brick orders after the committee took over the marketing—was able to sell about 500,000 bricks by the end of the Olympics. The park had been designed to hold more than 1 million. Hammill clearly had egg on his face. When asked at Home Depot's 1995 annual meeting about the brick sales, the executive said he was through making predictions.

There was one part of Home Depot's Olympic involvement, however, that became a rousing success and typified the company's commitment to helping others. Marcus and Blank decided to help Home Depot employees who had an Olympic dream— and find jobs at Home Depot for other athletes with similar aspirations. For the next four years, Home Depot stores would be filled with athletes training to make the Summer Games. That would cost Home Depot millions as it paid benefits to part-time workers. But Marcus and Blank felt the benefits would outweigh the costs. They thought the athlete program would boost morale inside stores, giving employees a daily reminder that Home Depot would go further than any other employer for their workers.

The Olympic Job Opportunities Program was developed in 1977 by former U.S. Olympic Committee treasurer Howard Miller. The program was designed to resolve the conflict many athletes face, at one point or another, in choosing between Olympic goals and a business career. The U.S. Olympic Committee felt that if they helped athletes overcome their financial hurdles, they could concentrate on training and produce better results during competition.

The Olympic Committee acts as a broker between athletes and companies. Before Home Depot got involved, retailer J.C. Penney was the biggest employer of athletes training for the Olympics, hiring 80 in the first 20 years of the program. Marcus and Blank quickly lapped the field. Home Depot began hiring athletes in training in 1993, and by the time the 1996 Olympics began, they had employed more than 100. No other employer had ever hired so many athletes in the program's history, let alone for one Olympics. In their typical way, Marcus and Blank had thrown themselves into a project and made sure Home Depot was the best. Said Patty Sabo, manager of the

U.S. Olympic Committee's athlete support department: "Home Depot's sheer number has been phenomenal."

Home Depot shelled out more than $1 million a year to subsidize salaries and benefits for the athletes. (The athletes work an average of 20 hours a week, allowing them time to train and compete, but they are paid for 40 hours of work.) The payoff: A stock of future employees and role models for its current workforce. "It's not a charitable thing," said Lora Castellanos, Home Depot's Olympic marketing director. "They contribute every minute they're on the clock. They bring that work ethic to the floor. Those athletes are out there and they need jobs."

Ed Kaminski was one of those athletes. Before joining Home Depot, Kaminski worked 60 hours a week for a Kansas City mortgage company and used his "spare time" to train for the Olympics. After he found a job at Home Depot, he worked 20 hours per week in the building materials department at a Home Depot in Jonesboro, a south Atlanta suburb, giving him time to practice javelin throwing. One result: At the U.S. Olympic Festival in July 1995, Kaminski won a gold medal. "This makes things so much nicer," said Kaminski. "It's been very flexible, allowing me time to travel and to train."

Indeed, Home Depot filled a big need for many athletes by simply offering them jobs. Sabo often had trouble finding work for athletes through other employees. "There just aren't a lot of jobs," she explained. "We have to ask for too much." Home Depot helped alleviate that problem with flexible work schedules and locations across the country, providing options for any athlete. The major problem for the U.S. Olympic Committee was fitting an athlete's training and competition schedule into a work schedule and convincing employers to pay benefits and salary. Longtime sponsor Coca-Cola, for example, wants to expand its role in the program but most of its jobs require full-time attention. Coca-Cola may have been better at handling ticket order forms, but it took a back seat to Home Depot with hiring Olympic athletes. Home Depot didn't find this to be a problem, allowing athletes to set their schedules. Marcus and Blank deduced that the athletes would work more than the minimum 20-hour-per-week requirement because they were already overachievers in one field and would want to do the same on the job. In most cases, they were right.

To help them find jobs, Sabo's department queries athletes about education, previous work experience, and preferences for locations. Many athletes, she said, will move to take a job. Again, that wasn't a problem for Home Depot, which had stores in more than 30 states the year before the 1996 Olympics. Now it has stores in more than 40 states and is adding its first stores in Alaska and Hawaii, providing even more options for athletes. "We really seek to find career-oriented jobs," explained Sabo. "None of the athletes with Home Depot had considered a job with the company. Now, many of them want to make it a career."

Despite the fewer hours and flexible schedules, Home Depot doesn't coddle athletes. At Home Depot, the athlete's only advantage over other applicants is a guaranteed interview. The company screens athletes as it does other potential employees, requiring a drug test and interviews with district and store managers. Once hired, the athletes are expected to be as knowledgeable as other employees about home improvement products. "If there were a violation of company policy, the punishment would be the same," said Castellanos. "But we don't have to create jobs for these athletes. We're looking for people. If they don't make the Wheaties box, we have an opportunity for them. They bring that work ethic to the floor."

The athletes performed the same tasks as regular workers—stocking shelves, cutting wood, and working the cash registers. They preferred it that way. Athletes didn't show up in any Home Depot advertisements. But some stores stocked pictures for the athletes to sign. And at the company's annual meeting in May 1995, athletes dressed in U.S. team warm-ups and collected shareholder proxies and sold bricks for Centennial Olympic Park. Even though that was special duty, the athletes spread goodwill for Home Depot.

The next year, diver Kent Ferguson, who worked at a south Florida Home Depot, spoke at the annual meeting, taking the podium—and the spotlight at what is often a love-fest for Marcus and Blank—away from the cofounders. His story showed many why Home Depot got involved in the Olympic Job Opportunities Program.

In April 1994, Ferguson faced a critical decision. He was working 50 hours a week at a real estate job and trying to dive. But he struggled with a reduced training schedule and thought about retiring from competition. "I felt locked into a field that would not allow me my dream," said Ferguson. "Deep in my heart, I didn't want to end my diving career on this note, but I had no choice."

Then Ferguson called a friend, Tracy Benson, a Home Depot assistant manager. She made phone calls and helped Ferguson get an interview, which led to a job in a store's electrical department. "Once I started working with the Home Depot, I realized that working out there in 'the dreaded real world' wasn't all that bad," said Ferguson. "It really wasn't different from working as a team toward one common goal of attaining that Olympic gold." Ferguson credited his improved diving to working at Home Depot. Standing next to Marcus and Blank, he received a standing ovation at the annual meeting.

Because of the success of athletes like Ferguson, Home Depot expanded the program to Canada, where it blazed a trail with a similar deal through the Canadian Olympic Association. Before Home Depot's involvement, Canada didn't have a program for athletes. Afterward, a dozen Canadian athletes worked for Home Depot. Once again, Marcus and Blank helped others in need.

Home Depot expanded its involvement to the Paralympics. Consultant Bevilaqua was on the executive committee of the Paralympics, to be held in Atlanta after the Olympics. Bevilaqua thought Home Depot would sponsor the Paralympics, given Marcus's fund-raising for the Shepherd Center, an Atlanta hospital that specializes in spinal injuries. Bevilaqua made a Paralympics presentation to Hammill in 1993. At the end of the meeting, Hammill excused himself and returned with a carousel of slides. Hammill then made a presentation about Home Depot's growth plans for the next five years—adding nearly 500 stores. The point was that Home Depot had enough to worry about without sports sponsorships. Hammill told Bevilaqua,

"We just don't need to do this stuff. We're doing it because it's the right thing to do and it's here in Atlanta."

Home Depot became a Paralympic sponsor, and it hired athletes too. One was weightlifter Bill Strickland, who worked in a Home Depot in Birmingham, Alabama. There, he fielded calls and questions from customers through its telephone sales center. Strickland had been injured in a 1980 car accident, leaving him without the full use of his legs. But that didn't keep him from a weightlifting career, graduating from the University of Alabama, and a Home Depot job. "When I started, I didn't know what to expect," said Strickland. "It has been crazy around here, and those phones never stop working. But all the other associates have been a tremendous help. Working at the Home Depot is definitely helping me. "

Such feelings were shared by Marcus and Blank. "All of the athletes that will compete in the Games here share the drive and the determination and the enthusiasm that every single one of our associates has today," said Blank before the 1996 Olympics. "The challenge to be the very best is the heart and spirit of the Olympics, and it's the heart and spirit of our company." Marcus and Blank learned in developing their own careers that if they were given the opportunity to succeed, they would thrive. Now, they were doing the same for others who needed a chance.

Home Depot also hoped to develop store managers and district managers from the Olympic job program. One candidate was Bill Shanahan. The judo athlete fell out of the qualifications for the Olympic job program when his national ranking fell a year before the Atlanta Games. The U.S. Olympic Committee notified Home Depot that he was being dropped from the program. But Shanahan wanted to keep working at a store in Albany, New York, and his manager agreed to give him a paint department job. "I enjoy the work, and I enjoy the people I work with," said Shanahan.

The story of another athlete who works at Home Depot vividly depicts how the company, and the employee, got what each wanted out of the program.

In 1994, athlete Kevin Braunskill took advantage of Marcus

and Blank's reaching out to help employees. How he mixed his Home Depot schedule and his training regimen is the perfect example of what Home Depot intended when it began the program—find overachieving people who are athletes and give them a career.

Braunskill is one of the world's fastest humans—at one time he was ranked No. 3 in the 200-meter dash. But when he dons his orange apron, he wants to be treated as one of the 150 employees at the Home Depot store where he works. Sometimes, that has meant running a 200-meter dash in work boots.

Fearing that he will get hurt, managers have asked him to get off ladders and stop running through the aisles. Fellow employees rib him about his diet when he buys Snickers out of the snack machine. "I could walk around here and trip and my career could be over," acknowledges Braunskill, trying to contend for the U.S. Olympic team following an injury layoff. "You never know. There's no guarantee. Home Depot has been my guarantee. But I want to be treated like everyone else."

As part of the job program, Braunskill was required to work at least 20 hours a week at his Home Depot, located in southeast Atlanta. Because of his injury—he tore the tendon connecting the hamstring with his knee in an accident suffered on the track, not on the job—Braunskill isn't competing as often in track meets. He is able to work more than 30 hours per week, a schedule he kept even during the summer before the Olympics. He normally works from 8 A.M. to 2 P.M. during the week and sometimes on weekends. "I kind of like it here," says Braunskill. "It's laid back. Time flies by." In return, he is paid for 40 hours of work, and he receives insurance benefits, and time to train. "At Home Depot, being a team player is vital," said Bea Swanson, manager of the store where Braunskill works. "Kevin is a team player. Olympics or not, it's always good to find someone with such a work ethic and determination. We're thrilled to have him. He's a hard-working and dedicated individual. Customers love him, and he's very friendly."

Still, juggling his job and training at a nearby track can be hectic for Braunskill. On workdays while training, Braunskill must get out of bed at 6:15 A.M. Although his nutritionist wants him to eat eggs, toast, and grits, the New York native prefers Fruit Loops.

Braunskill drops his grandmother at a nearby train station and is at his Home Depot store by 7:45 A.M., wearing blue jeans, a blue shirt, Mizuno track shoes, and knee pads. A tape measure is stuck on his pants near his right pocket. He is wearing an orange Home Depot hat and an orange apron. His first task: Check for out-of-stock items in the tile and floor department. "That's the first thing I do," he explains. "It's easier to do when no one else is around."

Braunskill began working for the store east of downtown Atlanta in November 1994. By the following summer, he easily handled customer questions. He attended training classes on everything from ceiling tiles to grout, and he also went to classes Home Depot offered shoppers. "I was worried how I was going to fit in," said Braunskill. "I didn't want to feel lost." Despite concentrating on his training, Braunskill took time to learn how to assist customers.

His outgoing personality has helped. Braunskill enjoys talking to shoppers. "Excuse me, do you have one of these already assembled?" asks a woman, pointing to a bookcase. They don't. But Braunskill gives pointers on how to assemble it and loads one in her cart. "It's self-explanatory," he reassures her. "Everything's in there." Braunskill explains: "That's just my personality. I want to be treated just like [the customer wants] to be treated. I can see the confusion on their face. I was worried how I was going to fit in. That's never come up. I feel like Home Depot is doing me a favor. I'm going to bend over backwards. Patty Sabo tells me not to feel that way, but how can I not?"

Braunskill normally skips lunch. At 2 P.M. he changes in the bathroom into Spandex shorts and a T-shirt. By 2:15 P.M., he's whipped his 1995 Ford Mustang into a nearby track's parking lot.

While he's outgoing at work, Braunskill becomes quiet and serious on the track. "If I let the job get to me, if I feel that's deterring from practice, it will," he explains. "But it doesn't. I was on my feet more when I was in college. I've always got to keep moving. And Home Depot is a place where I can vent some energy."

During his two-hour workout, he runs sideways, jumps down the track on each leg, highsteps, and runs timed sprints. Three days a week, he lifts weights. He trains during the workday, hoping that will help pay off during the Olympics. After a quick bite, he heads home to be with his wife. Like many in the Olympic job program, Braunskill dreams of a job with Home Depot after his track career ends. "I want to stay with the company that has supported me," he says. "It's an ideal situation."

Braunskill did not make the U.S. Olympic team for the 1996 Games. But Braunskill remains a Home Depot employee at the same store in suburban Atlanta. He has learned more about the products and about how the store operates. "The thing that drew me to Home Depot was the overall attitude," says Braunskill, a North Carolina State graduate in business who would eventually like a management job at Home Depot. "It's an opportunity, not just for me but for other athletes, to get some exposure. In Home Depot, you're always talking to people."

In all, 26 Home Depot employees—25 percent of the Olympic job program athletes employed by the company—qualified for their Olympic teams in 1996, and they worked in stores ranging from Edmonton, Canada, to Casselberry, Florida. Marcus and Blank's experiment paid off.

During the Atlanta Olympics, Home Depot's athletes brought home three silver and three bronze medals. Two Canadian employees, synchronized swimmer Janice Bremner and rower Brian Peaker, won silver medals. U.S. rowers Dave Collins and Bill Carlucci, who worked at stores in Augusta, Georgia, and Philadelphia, respectively, won bronze medals. Employee Townsend Saunders, who wrestles, won a silver medal, and Antonio Tarver, who worked in the Casselberry store, won a bronze medal in boxing. Kent Ferguson did not make the U.S. diving team. But he still came to Atlanta and was involved in Home Depot's events during the Games. Bill Strickland made the U.S. Paralympic team as a weightlifter.

Another Paralympic athlete who worked for Home Depot, Gabriel Diaz DeLeon, won a bronze medal in the discus.

Hiring and helping athletes meet their goals garnered attention and good publicity for Home Depot. But it was only part of how Marcus and Blank used the Olympics to show how much they cared about their employees.

Most big Olympic sponsors use the Games to hold parties for their biggest customers and suppliers. Their employees rarely get to see such glitz. Coca-Cola computer information systems experts filled vending machines at a downtown Atlanta hotel where company guests were staying for the Olympics and being treated to lavish parties and front-row tickets.

But Marcus and Blank used the 1996 Olympics as a chance to reward employees—the people they considered their VIPs—who went above and beyond the norm in customer service, leadership, and job performance. Before the Olympics began, Home Depot store managers gave Olympic Spirit Awards to employees. Their names were put into a hat, and the company drew 600 winners to send to the Games. The awards, like Marcus and Blank intended, boosted employee morale and made Home Depot's workers improve their customer service. Once again, they thought about the employees and about what they could do to make them feel wanted despite the fact that they work for a huge corporation. Sometimes companies their size ignore their workers, Marcus and Blank realized. They wanted to make sure that didn't happen at Home Depot, remembering how Sigoloff treated them as employees who could be discarded at whim.

The awards led employees to provide better customer service. Jane Zienkowicz, a cashier in a Home Depot in Ontario who won a spirit award, said she was "just doing her job. If I see an opportunity, I go for it and I give 100 percent," she says. "I try to lead by example, and I don't expect any more from people than I would expect to give." She says she greets customers with a smile: "[I try] to develop a relationship with our regular customers. I see the customer as paying my salary. The customer leaving happy is everything—it means he or she will return." Another employee who won the award, Larry Larkin from the Home Depot in Orland Park, Illinois, agrees. "The customers are what make this business go," he says. "I treat them as I want to be treated. This is really important to me because I believe in 100 percent customer satisfaction."

When the winners got to Atlanta that summer, they were given tickets to Dream Team basketball games and treated to dinners with famous athletes like boxer George Foreman—who even donned an orange apron. "This wasn't a party for VIPs," said Hammill. "It was a way of recognizing the performance of our associates. Most companies would do this externally. We do this internally."

For Marcus, honoring the employees who made Home Depot so successful in the city where the company had started humbly just 17 years earlier was a fitting tribute. "You have to remember, if it weren't for the people in Atlanta, if it weren't for those good folks who are going to be in our stores today, none of us would be here," he said. "And certainly, we wouldn't be the great company that we are today." And then in what is his inimitable style he turned the tables, noting that he and Blank and the other Home Depot employees celebrating the Olympics couldn't stop providing customer service. "We've got to be the ones that win in 1996 and thereafter," said Marcus. "How are we doing to do it? We're going to do it by taking care of those customers, starting today, better than we have ever before, because we are champions."

After the 1996 Olympics, athletes like Braunskill showed their commitment to the company by continuing to work at Home Depot. The next year, Marcus and Blank reciprocated. Home Depot signed up once again to be an Olympic sponsor, this time through the 2004 Games. (Home Depot has become large enough to pay the entire fee by now, and it doesn't need to add its top vendors to the deal.) And they have hired athletes training for the Winter Games, including Stacy Blumer, a freestyle skier working in a Home Depot in Norwalk, Connecticut. "The Home Depot and the [Olympic job program] have been the catalyst to my Olympic pursuits," said Blumer. "It's been an ideal situation—the program provides the flexibility I need to train and travel while allowing me to work and earn a steady income."

Once again, Marcus and Blank decided that Home Depot's Olympic involvement wouldn't be just for athletes. Home Depot began a Coaching Spirit Award to recognize the "coaching" employees give customers and fellow employees. Marcus and Blank emphasized that employees who are good providers of customer service would be rewarded.

The winners of the awards were flown to Salt Lake City, the city of the 2002 Winter Games and a growing Home Depot market, during the 1998 Winter Games in Nagano, Japan. There, they were given tours of future Olympic sites and attended parties at night where they watched the Nagano Games with past Olympians. Marcus and Blank saw the awards as a chance once again to reinforce customer service, but to have some fun in the process.

Marcus and Blank caught the Olympic spirit because it so closely matched their feelings for competing, helping others achieve their goals, and giving back to the community—all vital parts of the Bleeding Orange culture they instill in their workers. They saw the good they could achieve simply by offering a struggling athlete a job and a chance to compete in his or her sport. Despite the initial controversy and problems with Home Depot's Olympic sponsorship, Marcus and Blank saw that goodwill helped boost the Home Depot name in the eyes of its shoppers.

Indeed, during the 1998 Winter Games in Nagano, Home Depot ran a television commercial on CBS-TV showing a 6-year-old Japanese girl walking through a village, becoming entranced by an Olympic banner. Suddenly, the banner's calligraphy comes to life, as Japanese kanji characters morph into a downhill skier. There is no mention of Home Depot's do-it-yourself supplies in the ad, only a voice that states: "The magic has returned, and we're proud to be a part of it all." Home Depot's headquarters was flooded with telephone calls and e-mails from customers, thanking the retailer for recognizing the magic and spirit of the Games. Their ads for the 1996 Games showed store employees helping customers and used the line,

"As America's home improvement coaches, the people of Home Depot believe in building dreams." Ditching the sales pitch during the Olympics was winning over customers.

While Marcus and Blank were helping these athletes achieve their goals and rewarding others for being good workers, however, a larger group of employees began complaining that their goals and aspirations were being ignored. It would lead to a battle threatening the core beliefs of the Home Depot culture, and it would publicly call into question for the first time the manner in which employees were treated at the retailer.

Management Lessons

The best thing a company can do to connect with its employees is to do something for those workers. In Home Depot's case, the retailer has provided jobs and support for more than 100 employees who have had the dream of becoming an Olympic athlete. In addition, the retailer has used the Olympics to recognize hundreds of other employees for their hard work in providing customer service. Every business should pay attention to their employees' wants and needs, because that provides loyal workers.

1. Home Depot helps employees achieve their personal goals, because the company knows that such workers will pay it back by working harder on the job.

2. Corporate involvement in the Olympics brought positive attention to Home Depot as it has expanded across the country, giving it name recognition in new markets.

3. Home Depot rewarded employees for providing excellent customer service by giving them free trips to the Olympics, making them more loyal to the company and re-enforcing the idea that customer service is paramount.

BLEEDING ORANGE ATTACKED

*We don't care who you are, whether you're black, white, woman, man,
whether you're older or younger, you're going to have an opportunity at
The Home Depot.*

—BERNIE MARCUS

When Vicki Butler applied for a job at a Home Depot in
Sacramento, California, in 1992, she had more experience in the do-it-yourself world than other female applicants.
She'd been an Air Force mechanic, a greenhouse manager, and
a carpenter who had done home repairs. But Butler claimed she
was forced to work behind a cash register because that's the job
given most women at Home Depot. Later, she was promoted to
a sales job. Even then, though, she worked at a register more
than male workers. When Butler complained, she was fired.

More than 2,000 miles away in Louisiana, Carol Lee Griffin
had been hired as a designer and salesperson at a Home Depot
in New Orleans in 1991. "I always felt as though I was fighting
a battle," said Griffin, 53 when she was hired. When she asked
the store manager why he never spoke to her about work-related
matters, he replied, "I think of you as my mother." As part of
her job, she tracked design trends and sales promotions at
competitors who were also selling wallpaper, blinds, and other
items. One day, she was reviewing such material in the break
room when a manager asked if she was on a break or clocked
in to work. Griffin gathered her materials and returned to her
department. At the end of her shift, Griffin was asked to come
into the manager's office, where she was fired.

Two different cases separated by thousands of miles and
hundreds of Home Depot stores. Yet Butler and Griffin weren't

alone. By the early 1990s, other female employees began complaining about unfair treatment at Home Depot. By 1994, they filed lawsuits against Home Depot, claiming they were being denied opportunities given male counterparts.

Marcus and Blank faced the biggest test to Home Depot's culture at a time when the company was struggling with a slowing stock price and deciding how to grow in the next decade. From January 1992 until November 1995, Home Depot's stock traded between $40 and $50. It was not a time to be distracted. Yet these women threatened to change how Home Depot had done business, growing by leaps and bounds in its first 15 years to become one of the world's biggest retailers, if they won. Marcus and Blank's management style exposed them to these lawsuits. How they handled these allegations would determine Home Depot's future.

Home Depot stores were a male-dominated workplace from the time that the first locations opened in 1979. "We do more business with the professional customer [in the building trades], who on balance tends to be more in the male gender," said Blank after the gender discrimination lawsuits were filed. But he also noted that "when you talk to a couple about remodeling a kitchen, remodeling a bathroom, the kind of window and wall treatment you might have in a room, the kind of lighting that might be in a room, often in our garden departments, in our nurseries, it's the female shopper that is driving the decision more than the male shopper."

According to the U.S. Labor Department, in 1986, only 2 percent of construction trade workers were women. A decade later, that figure budged slightly upward to 2.5 percent. "It's a business that never had women in it," explained Marcus. "Twenty years ago, the world, our world as we know it, was populated by hardware stores, electrical stores, lumber stores, paint stores...women just didn't shop these stores," recalled Marcus. "I remember about 20 years ago my wife went into a lumberyard. She could not get waited on, and she was angry about it. Nobody would pay attention to her. Well, it's changed now, and when we open our [stores], we look for women because, in fact, we noticed that there were a lot of women shopping our stores. They were shopping our stores because they had a lot to do with the decision making in the house—whether or not it's painted—…what color it was painted, what kind of faucets would be put in the bathroom." Yet, the low number of females shopping and working in construction-related retailers had nothing to do with the allegations against Home Depot, and Marcus's comment about his wife avoided the issue.

Still, Marcus and Blank encouraged women to join Home Depot. By 1994, women had held many positions in the company, including those of district managers.

One was Ann Marie Johnson, who started at a California store in the late 1980s. She rose through the ranks and became a store manager. Said her boss, Lynn Martineau, back in 1990 before the lawsuit: "Ann being young and Ann being female isn't anything that she has as a barrier. She goes out on her own ability and her own strengths and her will and desire to succeed." Johnson learned she could succeed at Home Depot through hard work. You've got to "work your ass off every day," said Johnson. "You've got to stay focused. It's so hard, because we're running so fast all the time. It's real easy to get sidetracked and distracted. You've got to come in every day with a plan. The secret is you've got to treat people the way you'd want to be treated."

Marcus and Blank had placed more women in jobs at the decision-making level of operations. In 1996, Home Depot named its first female division president, and the company had two female board members—former Spelman College president Johnnetta Cole and Bank of America executive vice president Faye Wilson. The female division president and Cole joined Home Depot after the discrimination lawsuits were filed, however, raising eyebrows. Marcus denied that the moves were based on an ulterior motive. "If the women are knowledgeable, we want them," said Marcus. "We need them. We're doubling in size."

But there were problems for female Home Depot employees in the aisles. Because of prior floor and tile sales experience, Cheryl Williams was one of the few female salespersons hired in Corona, California. After six months, she was asked by her manager to train two men. "Within several weeks—and without any notice—I was called into the manager's office and told my job had been eliminated," she said. "I was given an envelope with my wages in cash and told to leave. The men I had trained took over my job duties. It was humiliating and unfair. I don't want it to happen to anybody else."

Felicia Funderburk was a cashier in Pittsburg, California, for more than two years and had asked about promotions. "First, I was told I did not have enough experience with the company," she said. "Then, I was told Home Depot did not want women in certain departments. Then, I was told women can't be department heads because they 'bitch and whine too much.'"

In late December 1994, eight California women filed suit against Home Depot, claiming that the company had denied them higher-paying jobs, training, promotions, and equal pay. They claimed women were primarily hired for lower-paying cashier and clerical positions and provided little opportunity for promotions, while men were more often hired into or promoted to sales positions, allowing them to move quickly into managerial jobs.

The lawsuit contained racier events. Susan Ellis, a kitchen and cabinet designer in Fairfield, California, claimed a photo of several assistant store managers and a nude woman was placed in a store conference room. Four months later, a store manager asked her, "How are you today?" Ellis replied, "I have a sinus infection. I don't feel good." The manager, a male, replied, "Thank God you don't have a yeast infection." Another employee, Jacqueline Genero, said she received sexually suggestive telephone calls at home from coworkers. Home Depot denied the assertions.

The California case sought class-action status, meaning if a judge agreed, the lawsuit would cover tens of thousands of current and former female Home Depot employees, as well as applicants, on the West Coast. Marcus and Blank were not named as defendants. But since they were symbols of what Home Depot stood for, the charges hit them hard. Never before had the company—the operation they had built from scratch by sheer will—been accused of such wrongdoing.

Other cases soon followed. Griffin filed a lawsuit in January 1995 in New Orleans that asked to be given class-action status covering female employees and applicants east of the Mississippi River. Another was filed in New Jersey that asked to cover female Home Depot employees and job applicants in the Northeast.

Marcus and Blank were in the legal fight of their lives. Their being fired by Sigoloff over union tampering allegations had placed Marcus and Blank in a legal hotseat once before. These new cases threatened much more—the very Home Depot culture they had nurtured, developed, and credited with much of the company's success. The allegations ran counter to everything the duo had vowed to uphold at Home Depot. Because of how they had been fired by Sigoloff, they had vowed that their employees would be treated with respect and dignity.

Still, some Home Depot stores had a macho atmosphere that made some women feel uncomfortable. But in the years before the lawsuits were filed, Home Depot had taken some major steps in diversity. In 1990, Marcus and Blank approved a diversity management program designed to provide all employees equal opportunities. All company managers, from Marcus and Blank to store supervisors, participated.

The same year, Marcus and Blank started an associate manager program to train women and other minorities to become assistant store managers. Three years later, Marcus and Blank began a "Respect Program" to deal with on-the-job harassment, particularly sexual harassment. Everyone at the company was required to attend workshops. Such moves had been noticed. In 1992, the YWCA of Greater Atlanta presented the company with its Prowess Award. The award recognizes Atlanta-based companies with programs and practices "which empower women to participate more equally in the workplace." The company had also been recognized by *Fortune* as the country's most-admired retailer. Part of that recognition was based on how they treated employees.

More females had moved into management positions. In

1992, Home Depot had 9 female store managers. By late 1994, it had 20. In 1992, 101 assistant store managers were female. By late 1994, that figure had more than doubled to 210. In 1992, there were no female district managers. By the end of 1994, there were 2. To the lawyers representing the women, however, it wasn't enough. Their claims, if true, would refute the culture Marcus and Blank said they had achieved at Home Depot. The women threatened to tarnish the image of Home Depot as a place that cared for its workers.

If Marcus and Blank were to lose these cases, they might have been forced to change how they treat workers. They would have lost that sense of closeness many employees feel with the top executives, calling them "Bernie" and "Arthur." They would have had to change to a more rigid employment structure where workers simply did their jobs and went home at the end of the day, sheltered from executives too constricted with following employment guidelines. They would have lost that esprit de corps in the stores, where employees felt like Home Depot's owners. Worse, they would have been told how to hire workers. Marcus and Blank feared if they lost control over what they considered their most important asset—the hiring and training of their workers—that would surely decimate everything they had accomplished.

They vowed to fight. Spearheading Home Depot's defense was Marcus's nephew Larry Smith, vice president of its legal department. Smith had joined Home Depot in 1983 as its first lawyer and was a graduate of the University of Bridgeport and Brooklyn Law School. In the early years, Smith spent his time on real estate matters as the company bought land in new markets. Smith was a tall, lean, and bald man who typified the hard-working but employee-friendly Home Depot culture. Most days, he eschewed the typical attorney garb of suit and tie for blue jeans and polo shirts.

After the California case was filed, Smith discussed the pitfalls of defending such a lawsuit with Home Depot's board. There was bound to be bad publicity. Attorneys might bring up Blank's divorce and marriage to a younger Home Depot employee. And no company had gone to court to defend itself against such charges after a 1991 change in federal law that allowed larger damage awards. Smith was not optimistic about Home Depot's chances, even though he made public statements vowing to win.

The board wanted to go to trial. "I felt terribly wounded by this," said Ken Langone, who had helped Marcus and Blank raise the money to start Home Depot. "We were absolutely all totally in favor of fighting this issue." As Smith gave the board regular updates, "they became more and more firm in their beliefs," said the attorney. "Home Depot is going to be the one company to stand up. We're going to go on the offensive, and let our people do the talking. We're not pursuing the trial to be legal pioneers, we're doing it because it's right for this company. We're not claiming we're perfect. But when something happens, we take immediate action."

Marian Exall was also part of the legal team. A graduate of the University of London and the Emory University Law School, Exall had joined the company in 1994 from an Atlanta law firm and helped lead the fight. As a woman, Exall's calm arguments against the allegations gained credence when she spoke about the case. "This is such an absurd situation with a few individuals with a few disputed claims purporting to represent a large class," said Exall.

Smith and Exall, however, were battling some of the country's most powerful lawyers. The California women were represented by Saperstein, Goldstein, Demchak & Baller, an Oakland law firm known for getting huge monetary settlements from big corporations. The firm handles more employee discrimination class-action suits and recovers more money for workers in those cases than any other firm in the United States. It had won $250 million from State Farm in a March 1992 settlement of a case accusing the insurer of denying women positions as insurance agents. The firm was also about to settle a $81.5 million case against Publix Super Markets, Inc., which it had accused of putting women in low-paying, dead-end jobs. *BusinessWeek* once called the law firm "the SWAT team of bias litigation."

The battle did not go well. A California judge granted class-action status on the West Coast, meaning that the lawsuit covered all women who worked for Home Depot in the area and those who had applied for a job. (The northeast and southeast cases had not been allowed class-action status, and therefore they lagged behind the California action.) Home Depot appealed the decision to the U.S. Supreme Court. But in March 1997, the court turned down its request, clearing the path for a trial to begin that fall.

Home Depot argued that the trial would put it at a handicap. The company would have to defend itself in two stages. First, a trial would determine if the company discriminated against the women. If that was proved, a second hearing would focus on how much Home Depot would pay each woman. That's an incredibly lengthy and expensive process that could last decades. If found guilty, Home Depot would have to defend itself against an estimated 217,000 women, each eligible to receive as much as $300,000 in damages. That would make Home Depot liable for as much as $65 billion in payments—nearly twice as much as the entire company was worth in 1997. That wasn't likely to happen, however, although the number was used by Home Depot to make its point, albeit poorly. No company had ever paid out more than $300 million in a discrimination case.

That's because no company had gone to trial, preferring to settle the allegations outside of court. It wasn't much consola-tion for Marcus and Blank, who wanted to defend themselves. Smith and Exall hoped the case wouldn't get to the second hear-ing. Their strategy was to have female employees testify that there was no way Home Depot discriminated against women.

They also raised questions about some of the women in a hardball, put-the-victim-on-trial strategy that could have back-fired if a jury felt that Home Depot was picking on them. Butler had once choked a coworker, a Home Depot filing noted. Another woman, Genero, had been fired for embezzling at her most recent employer, Macy's. Another woman involved in the lawsuit, Sheryle Jones, was complaining that managers wouldn't teach her how to drive a forklift. But the same man-agers accommodated her drunken-driving conviction by rear-ranging schedules so that she could work as part of a prison furlough program. (Jones claimed that when she asked about a sales job in lumber, she was told, "There is no way Home Depot would put a female in lumber.") Griffin's salary was higher than that of some supervisors when she was fired.

Smith hired Los Angeles attorneys, and they designed a computerized trial management system. They took more than 200 videotaped depositions, retained seven outside experts in labor economics and management, and conducted three mock jury trials. "We spared no expense," said Smith. "It was the biggest case we ever had. Nothing here [in Atlanta] was as important as what was happening in California."

Home Depot hadn't counted on the Equal Employment Opportunity Commission (EEOC) entering the picture. In early March, Home Depot's law department received a telephone call from the federal agency. When Smith and Exall returned the call, they couldn't get through. They also responded with a letter. What they wanted was a chance to talk to the EEOC before it made any moves.

They didn't get that opportunity. The next week, the agency filed a request to intervene in the Griffin case in New Orleans. The EEOC's general counsel, Gregory Stewart, said: "Home Depot's glass ceiling began with a glass basement. This case, which challenges Home Depot's steering of women into jobs with little opportunity for promotion, should serve to tell employers that such steering is unlawful." Smith, for one, was livid. "Their obligation is to avoid litigation," he noted shortly afterward. "We're going to show that the EEOC has not followed its own procedures, which is to allow us a chance to talk to them [to] broker a settlement."

The EEOC itself was under criticism about whether the agency should get involved in discrimination cases where the plaintiffs had already been granted class-action status or the help of experienced labor attorneys. The previous year, it backed off from pursuing discriminatory hiring charges against Hooters, the restaurant chain with scantily clad waitresses. Shortly after the agency filed its motion to intervene in the Home Depot case, the congressman chairing the House subcommittee overseeing the EEOC wrote a letter to EEOC Chairman Gilbert Casellas, questioning its strategy. "While I do not question EEOC's interest in these cases nor do I have an opinion on the merit of the underlying lawsuits," wrote Rep. Harris Fawell (R-Illinois), "I do have a concern whether or not it is the most efficient use of the commission's scarce resources to allocate time and budget to pursue discrimination charges which are already being litigated by the private bar."

The day the EEOC held its New York news conference to announce its involvement in the Home Depot case, however, television stations across the country ran the news that Home Depot had a "glass basement." Yet, a New York station showed two Home Depot cashiers in Flushing. "I chose to work as a cashier," said Germaine Gedeon. "No one put me there." The other, Jelemia Cox, said, "I don't see women being held back in any shape or form." The next morning, newspapers picked up the story and told readers that the Home Depot where they shopped for plants and ceiling fans might be discriminating against employees.

The bad publicity was a turning point. Employees talked more about the allegations. Some, particularly long-time employees, were bitter about how the company was treated. A former female employee, Cathy Iles Davenport, wrote an E-mail to Marcus and Blank, and said, "I disagree wholeheartedly and would stand up for Home Depot in court if you need someone. Let me know if I can be of any help." Others, particularly some female employees, were secretly hoping the cases would change the company. They had called reporters writing stories about the cases, looking for the phone numbers of the attorneys representing the women suing Home Depot.

None, however, was more upset than Marcus, the cofounder who for years had been Home Depot's leading spokesperson. Now, he would have to defend his creation, possibly before a jury in a hostile courtroom.

It's a pretty spring day in April in Atlanta. The birds are chirping and the wind is lightly blowing. It's one of those days that can put a smile on even the most sour face.

But not Marcus's, at least not this day. Marcus is mad enough to drill nails with his bare hand. While he is known to show his temper in private, this is a rare display in front of a reporter. This is the Marcus well known to his competitors. The topic, of course, is the gender discrimination lawsuits. The reporter, sitting in Marcus's office with Exall and senior public relations manager Jerry Shields, can barely get in a question.

Marcus says he once was a "great believer" in the Equal Employment Opportunity Commission. But he's changed his mind after the federal agency took on his company. "We're right and they're wrong," he said. "This is a case of something being really wrong. Why they're in this case, I have no clue. It's easy to fold your tent and settle. But I think that's wrong. People capitulate because they don't want to fight the government. It is highly implausible that they could ever intervene without talking to us and giving us an opportunity to respond. This is our government as well."

Marcus is just getting started. He rants against the attorneys representing the women. "They don't look at the consequences of what they're doing," he adds. "It's like the great rip-off of America. This is their business; they create class-action lawsuits. They are the worst kind of ambulance chasers." He says he recently visited Home Depot stores in northern California, and two female employees told him they had been called by attorneys. He rails against the letter the lawyers representing the women sent out months before the Butler case was filed in which the law firm brags about its "track record" of huge settlements and states the attorneys are now "investigating several companies including Home Depot." Recipients of the letter were asked to call a toll-free telephone number if they felt they had been discriminated against by Home Depot.

Marcus also talks about the letters he's received from people around the world, including one from a Paris man who wrote: "I send you my most heartfelt wishes for your success in defending your company against [this] ridiculous and unwarranted action."

Then Marcus defends the company he has built in the last two decades. "It's a business that never had women in it," he says. "The difference between us and everyone else is our people. We all carry the same Black & Decker drills and the same

Stanley tools. What we look for are qualified people. We've allowed women to learn. We've broken down barriers. For us to be attacked is moronic. To say that we discriminate against anybody, you've only listened to one side of the story."

The reporter, after about 30 minutes of nonstop ranting by Marcus, asks if Home Depot might settle the case. That sets Marcus off again. "I don't care if it takes the rest of my life," says Marcus. "There will be no settlements. They are guilty, not us. They are guilty of the misuse of power. We're not going to go to any kind of quotas. We're just not going to do it." Will Marcus testify during the trial? "I'll be there. I'm looking forward to it. Wait till they start with me."

Marcus says he's never thought about people's gender or color when hiring them, only whether they could do the job. "Knowledge was key to our success," he says. "It's what made Home Depot No. 1 in the world today, not numbers. Anybody who is willing to learn and come up the hard way, going to classes and learning to communicate and work with people, he or she has got a job at Home Depot."

The conversation, if it can be called that, finally ends. But as the reporter stands up, Marcus grabs him by the shirt and again states his adamant belief that Home Depot has done nothing wrong. Marcus's jovial, back-slapping persona has disappeared. His tirade shows how strongly he believes in what his company has done to develop a good work environment for tens of thousands of employees.

Whether he would keep his promise never to settle, however, was still in question. The California case was scheduled to start in five months, and a lot can happen in that time. If the case started, Home Depot would be the first major U.S. corporation to defend itself against such accusations before a jury. And success for the lawyers wearing the orange aprons was, at best, an outside shot.

Shortly after the EEOC filed to intervene in the Griffin case, Marcus and Larry Mercer, the company's executive vice president for operations, went before a live studio audience at Home Depot's headquarters—the show was also beamed to the stores—

and answered questions about the allegations. During the taping, Marcus addressed some of the specific charges, noting that Griffin had complained about being thought of as a mother by her store manager. Said Marcus: "I loved my mother, and I respected my mother. Because people look at me as a father figure, can I go to the EEOC? This is what we have come to." Marcus's comparison of his status within the company to Griffin's is slightly absurd and avoided the real issue. Few at Home Depot looked at Griffin as a mother figure. And her other claims were far more serious.

Still, it was Marcus at his calmest—in comparison to his earlier ranting. To be sure, he still had choice words for the attorneys representing the women, calling them "barracudas" and saying "It's all very suspicious; we think it smells a little bit." But his voice was reassuring, and he told employees that Home Depot had been successful because of the special way it had hired and trained its employees. If that changed, said Marcus, then Home Depot would no longer be different from its competitors. He asked Home Depot employees to write their elected officials and tell them what was happening to their company.

"The lawyers would like us to operate our business one way," said Marcus. "Everybody out there, you have a job today for one reason. Because the customers love to shop our stores. They come into our stores the way they don't come into any of our competitors' stores. They come in because they know they're going to come in and find somebody on the floor that's going to take care of them." The message was simple. If Home Depot was forced to put unqualified people in certain jobs just to fill quotas, then the company would lose sales, lose its customer service focus, lose its culture.

Marcus—and Blank—were not about to let that happen. Shortly thereafter, Marcus told Home Depot shareholders at the company's annual meeting, "I don't intend to back away from this battle, and I won't let anyone sully our reputation." His statement drew cheers from the crowd. They, of course, didn't want to see the stock price fall.

Marcus and Blank were fighting what appeared to everyone else to be a losing battle. The judge in the California case was

Susan Illston, a Clinton appointee and former plaintiffs' lawyer. She had already rejected Home Depot's motion to bar four expert witnesses for the plaintiffs, including William Bielby, head of the sociology department at the University of California at Santa Barbara. Bielby had examined Home Depot stores in California and their hiring practices. Bielby noted that 70 percent of the workers in sales were men, while 70 percent of the employees in operations jobs such as cashier were women. Bielby also noted that in Home Depot's western division, 94 percent of store managers, 90 percent of assistant managers, and nearly 90 percent of department supervisors in sales were men. The statistical probability that a distribution like that could have happened in a system in which men and women were treated equally, said Bielby, is less than 1 in a trillion.

Illston had also denied Home Depot's request for 260 hours to present its case at the trial. Smith and Exall wanted to call dozens of female Home Depot employees who had been promoted and given raises. The judge limited the time for both sides to 80 hours, hurting Home Depot's strategy.

On top of that, two-thirds of the people involved in the mock trials that Home Depot held indicated in questionnaires that they believed that companies, in general, systematically discriminate against women. "We knew we were right," said Smith. "But the question was, were we willing to risk a huge judgment just to satisfy our own emotions." Smith began thinking about a settlement. In fact, the attorneys representing the women had secretly made a settlement offer to Home Depot in April 1997. It was turned down because it was considered so outlandish. And Marcus and Blank were still adamant about fighting the case.

Three weeks before the trial began, Judge Illston ordered the two sides to try to mediate a settlement. A Home Depot team including Smith, Mercer, and Singletary, vice president of employee relations, met three days later with the attorneys for the women. A mediator, Atlanta lawyer Hunter Hughes, told the Home Depot folks: "If the Home Depot culture can be maintained or enhanced through a settlement, then you should settle. But if the culture is going to be hurt, then you should go to trial." Said Smith: "He was right on. He picked up on our concerns right away."

Facing the hammer, Smith persuaded Marcus and Blank to strike a deal. For the next two weeks, attorneys for both sides met virtually every day, with Hughes as an umpire. Smith told Marcus and Blank during late night telephone calls that the judge's rulings would cripple the company at a trial. Slowly, Marcus and Blank came around to settling the cases—as long as they were able to use the settlement to maintain the company culture. "Frankly, we didn't want to do it," said Marcus. "But we found out we weren't that far apart. It maintains what we have always done, and that's that the right people are in the right jobs. That part of the culture of the company is not changing."

Both sides realized they weren't far apart on a settlement. A few months before, Home Depot had begun designing a computerized job application system and objective tests for promotions.

Home Depot didn't want an outsider supervising its hiring practices. (In a race discrimination case against retailer Circuit City, a judge installed someone to oversee the retailer's hiring, training, and promotion practices.) The two sides agreed to have Home Depot board member Cole, a black female, supervise its employment strategy. Cole, now an Emory University professor, was known as someone who wouldn't let someone's rights be trampled. "We weren't going to have a stranger overseeing us," said Marcus. "We're in control over our own destiny."

Home Depot agreed to install computers and telephone systems in its stores where its employees could apply for other jobs at the company. The system, called the "Job Preference Process," steers more women into sales and management jobs.

In addition, Home Depot agreed to give cashiers training about products sold in the stores, to formalize a complaint procedure and train employees in how to investigate discrimination complaints, and to develop job-related qualifications for sales, supervisor, and manager positions so that promotions aren't arbitrary. For example, sales associates would be required to pass a test assessing how they handle customer questions and complaints. One question would ask what a salesperson would do if he or she were helping a customer and another came up and asked for assistance. They also agreed to name a company manager to monitor Home Depot's compliance with the settlement. Before the settlement, Home Depot had in place a network of human resource managers spread across the country to investigate discriminations, as well as a toll-free telephone number where employees could lodge complaints confidentially.

It wasn't until the very end that the two sides discussed money. Marcus and Blank approved paying $65 million to the women on the West Coast and another $22.5 million to their attorneys. Another $17 million went to settle the northeast and southeast lawsuits and to make changes in the employment programs. Shortly before the settlement was announced, Blank noted the total—$104.5 million—was two weeks' pretax profit for Home Depot.

Three days before the trial was scheduled to begin, the agreement was announced. Marcus, Blank, and Smith sat in a conference room next to Marcus's office and discussed the settlement an hour before it was officially announced. All of them looked relieved. "We're just happy this is finished," said Marcus. "It's like a sigh of relief. It eliminates the cloud over us." Marcus and Blank had stared down a major threat to their Bleeding Orange culture and won—at a price they were willing to pay.

Yes, they had backed down somewhat from their macho stand—a company attitude that likely led to the lawsuit in the first place—of battling the allegations to the very end. Still, existing female employees note that many of the discrimination claims occurred in the western division when it was run by Bill Hamlin, now a rising star at Home Depot. That, they say, sends a chilling message to female workers.

And Marcus and Blank's posturing of fighting the allegations until the bitter end showed the weakness in their management style: Because they were so involved in maintaining the culture, sometimes they didn't know how Home Depot's culture was hurting some employees. But the case taught them a valuable lesson. They could keep intact everything they had worked to build by finding a middle ground. "The workplace programs really help formalize and cement our culture, which is the key to our success," said Blank, rationalizing the decision to settle rather than fight it out during a lengthy trial, although the full ramifications of the settlement have yet to be felt. "And the bottom line is that we would never have agreed to settlements that would jeopardize our culture. With these lawsuits ended, now is the time to focus on our opportunities and on doing what we do best: serving our customers, providing outstanding returns to stockholders, and growing our business."

It's something you can't see, touch, or smell. Yet Marcus and Blank put their company's future on the line to save what they saw as the most important aspect of their operation—the culture. Said Blank the day the settlement was announced: "If we can't maintain the culture, we wouldn't be able to make money in the future."

Rarely has an equally successful company put such faith in an intangible. But Marcus and Blank had seen the magic in the past. They wanted to make sure it would survive for the future. They had fought back to ensure that it would happen.

MANAGEMENT LESSONS

The Home Depot culture has long been dominated by males, but the retailer has been making an honest attempt to attract more female employees into its stores. That wasn't enough for some women workers, who sued the retailer because they felt like they weren't getting the pay and promotions they deserved. The retailer was able to overcome that criticism by believing in its culture and compromising so that its culture could continue. Any business can be faced with the same issue, and how they deal with and solve the problem could determine their future success.

1. Home Depot has been willing to help women expand their role in the company (even as it fought allegations of gender discrimination) because it saw that more women were shopping its stores.

2. Home Depot has always believed in its rights and defends itself vigorously, a trait which has helped it overcome criticism of its practices.

3. Company executives put their faith in the company culture when it was at risk, feeling that the strong culture would pull it through the tough times.

4. Any company should provide programs and policies that will prevent discrimination and harassment. Home Depot had such policies, and has expanded them to ensure it will be able to attract the workers it needs to keep growing.

5. Don't be afraid to compromise if it maintains your culture. Home Depot settled discrimination allegations when it saw that it could do so while keeping the culture that made the company so successful.

CUSTOMER SERVICE IS JOB NO. 1

They can never feel unhappy. They can never feel as though they had a bad shopping experience. They have to feel as though they walked out of a place that was their own home.

—BERNIE MARCUS

In the Home Depot store in Baton Rouge, Louisiana, an employee learned sign language so that he could help deaf customers. Slowly, the stream of deaf shoppers—the Louisiana School for the Deaf is nearby—into the store grew and grew, forcing the worker to teach his fellow Bleeding Orange counterparts how to talk with their hands.

A Home Depot store on Long Island ran out of Black & Decker snake lights. So a store employee found another Home Depot nearby with plenty, drove there and bought them with his credit card, and then went back to his store and returned them at the return desk. When he was done, he called customers who wanted a light and told them the store now had them.

A woman in a wheelchair came into another Home Depot in the northeast and told a worker in the lumber department, "I have $25, and I want to build a ramp to my house so I can get my wheelchair off the porch." The Home Depot employee asked for the dimensions and said, "Ma'am, you can't build anything for $25." She replied, "That's all I have, and this is the first time I've been off my porch in three months. I can't get out of my house; there's no accessibility." The worker told his store manager, who visited her house. On weekends, employees built—on their own time—a ramp at the store. Then they installed it—and painted her house.

In 1994, Home Depot's customer service in North Carolina

was tested against competing stores for Lowe's, Home Quarters, and Builders Square. It was no contest.

At each store, employees were asked to find a 5½- by ½-inch wedge concrete anchor bolt used to fasten wood to masonry. At Home Depot, it took a minute. After searching for nine minutes, a Lowe's clerk gave up and suggested a 5-inch lag screw instead. At the Builders Square, the employee gave up after six minutes and called a local hardware store.

Each store was also given a kitchen remodeling job—with a budget of no more than $1,000. The Home Depot kitchen designer suggested priming and painting the cabinets antique white, adding new hardware, painting the walls, and designing and stenciling a border above the backsplash. Total cost: $260. The Lowe's clerks suggested buying a do-it-yourself kitchen design book. The Home Quarters designer suggested replacing the countertop—assuming the shopper had carpentry skills and access to a circular saw. The Builders Square clerk suggested replacing the flooring and countertop, putting up wallpaper and a border, and painting the appliances for about $400. The other suggestions cost more and took more expertise than what was actually needed.

This is Home Depot customer service, and these are just a few examples of how the retailer does more for customers than its competitors and arguably, any retailer. Since the first day Marcus and Blank opened Home Depot's doors in 1979, their goal was to provide the best customer service possible. Sure, all retailers say customer service is important. But walk into most of their stores and you're ignored or you do locate a clerk but he or she doesn't know where to find what you're looking for. And most retailers think they're smarter than the consumer.

That's not likely to happen at Home Depot. Marcus and Blank see customers—and their needs and wants—as the only reason for their success. That's why they send employees from Home Depot's headquarters into the stores to work. "Every function in our company, every single function whether it be advertising, whether it be merchandising, accounting, financial, just about every area, everybody has to understand that their entire goal is to create an environment where our employees have the ability to take care of our customers," explains Marcus. "Every one of them has to answer this question: 'What have you done to help the customer in our stores?'"

It's a tough standard, but even Marcus and Blank live up to it. Marcus and Blank regularly don orange aprons and walk the stores asking questions: What do you think of this place? What's good? What's bad? What do we need? What don't we need? What aren't we doing that we need to do? Despite their stature as multimillionaires who no longer need to work, Marcus and Blank remain committed to improving Home Depot's customer service. "I love it when people say you and Arthur must be geniuses—you are so bright," says Marcus. "The truth is we are not that bright. But we have an ability to listen, and we listen very carefully. I can walk through a store and remember when this idea came up. I remember who brought it to us—a customer or an associate. Isn't it funny that lots of retailers don't do that any more? We have not gotten away from it because we are not bright. We go directly into the stores. That's where we find out what is happening. That is what keeps this company alive."

Blank notes how customer service trickles down and affects what products Home Depot sells. "A very important part of our philosophy...is letting the customers provide the yellow brick road to our success," says Blank. "As long as we respond to the customer, we will continue to improve the stores and add merchandise assortments and change merchandise assortments that they think is important. A retailer gets in trouble when they begin to believe they know what the customer wants. We have always felt that if we listen, they'll give us the answer that we need."

Sometimes it's hard to convince every employee that customer service is vital. That's the biggest obstacle Marcus and Blank must overcome. "Of course, there's cynicism," says Marcus. "When people first hear us talk about this, if they've worked somewhere else in the past, their first reaction is that they've heard it all before, and it's just talk. You've also got to walk the walk. You've got to back it up in action."

Some new employees test that commitment to customer service. "The first time they might help a guy who has come into the store looking for a faucet for $150; they tell him that all he really needs is a washer for a few cents," said Marcus. "They half expect to be reprimanded, but when we congratulate them on it, they begin to believe. They test you again, and then when they find out you're serious about this stuff, they lose their cynicism, they become part of the family."

Sherry Voorhies, an employee at the Home Depot in Bothell, Washington, believes in customer service. "When a customer walks out of the store with a frown, most likely that customer won't be back," she says. "Unfortunately, negative stories spread rapidly. If just one employee in a store has a bad attitude or is rude to a customer, the whole store suffers. We are never so busy that we can ignore a customer or refuse a request for service of some kind. Nothing should be considered too much trouble."

Marcus and Blank have spent countless hours—in training sessions and in their walks through stores—emphasizing customer service. Greet each customer with a smile and a positive attitude, they tell their workers. Don't ask, "May I help you?" Ask, "What project are you working on, and what do you need for it?" Don't ask close-ended questions because the customer may feel intimidated by the project they want to tackle and will answer no. Listen to the customer and explain each product completely. Don't force the customer to buy a product. If a customer is upset or angry, empathize and correct the problem.

This is the customer satisfaction they want: "Whenever you ask people at Home Depot anything, they always know the answer," said shopper Rose Pavona of Tom's River, New Jersey. "And if they don't, they find out for you. And they take you to it."

Once the Bleeding Orange recruits have been converted, they then believe how important it is to greet every customer with a "Good morning, what can I help you look for today?" or to offer advice on which kind of paint to use on concrete, or simply to mention that they may need hinges, screws, and stain to complete installing that new door.

What if a customer is building a deck? If the Home Depot employee asks what kind of deck and the customer replies, "Pressure-treated," the employee takes him or her to the lumber department. Or if a shopper needs help in designing a sprinkler system, the employee knows he or she can get help in the plumbing department and takes the customer there.

For professional contractors who demand more service than a do-it-yourselfer, employees called "Homers" do nothing but help pull products for orders and deliveries. Other employees called "Bernie's Buddies"—retired contractors or home builders who have expertise in do-it-yourself projects—spend time handling customers on the floor. There is "Arthur's Army," a cadre of electricians, plumbers, and painters who also help with customer service. "Our customers can shop at any of the competitors and buy the same products at close to the same price," says Kipp Rix, who works in a Home Depot in El Paso as a plumbing expert. "The service they receive from us is what will bring them back to Home Depot."

It's this almost blinding devotion to customer service, experts argue, that keeps customers coming back to Home Depot stores in record numbers and buying more and more each time. "Home Depot's service is legendary," says Kurt Barnard, a well-known retail consultant and publisher of *Barnard's Retail Trend Report*. "That has helped make Home Depot the company it is." And others too. Companies like gasoline giant Mobil Corp., one of the largest U.S. companies with more than $70 billion in annual sales, sought out Home Depot for advice on how to improve customer service at its revamped gas stations.

"Customers paid for my kids' education, my house, my car, everything I have," says Marcus. "I owe my life to our customers. They're like part of my family." He asks Home Depot employees to have the same attitude. "When you put it in those kind of terms, it's a different kind of ball game. The most critical thing is to have people around who really care about you as a customer. And [at] most companies,…customers are like a pain in the ass. In most cases, they resent the customer." Marcus and Blank try to make sure that never happens at Home Depot.

Before Home Depot opened its doors, Marcus, Blank, and Farrah considered customer service the focal point of their strategy. They wanted each store to produce annual sales of $8 million—double the industry average. To do that, they wanted every conceivable home improvement product, from hammers to garage door openers, in their stores. With so many different products, they wanted the lowest prices, and they figured that would happen if they bought products in bulk direct from the makers. Low prices, they reasoned, would mean more customers and more sales. "One of the key things we decided on was to buy directly from the manufacturer and avoid warehouse distribution that adds cost," said Marcus. That was an important strategic decision that would help Home Depot succeed. Buying directly from manufacturers allowed the company to offer products at lower prices than competitors. It was more difficult to run a retailer that way because Home Depot had to deal with thousands of manufacturers. But they were committed to offering customers the lowest prices.

It's common sense. But when Home Depot started, no other home center retailer had such low margins, passing along the savings to customers. We were "looking at margins at one-third less than normal margins," said Marcus. "We're talking volumes that were at three times the volume of stores that were in existence in those days. People bought into that, bought into a fairy tale, because nobody could believe it could happen."

By the end of 1983, Home Depot had more than a quarter-billion in sales and $10 million in profits, double from the year before. That growth meant Home Depot needed more hardware experts to handle the customers. Dixieline Lumber executive Jim Inglis knew Farrah and became interested in joining Home Depot. Inglis called vendors selling merchandise to Marcus and Blank. Although Home Depot had become profitable, Inglis got a less-than-glowing report. "I was basically told they were doing it with smoke and mirrors," he said. "Their stores were too big." Still, Inglis flew to Orlando and looked for himself. Marcus took him to the stores, and Inglis spent time with Langone. Both gave Inglis a hard sell, telling him Home Depot's success could be replicated countrywide. They wanted to move west into Arizona and California. "The store was exciting in terms of a merchandise standpoint, the amount of product available," said Inglis. "There was also the excitement of the employees, the zeal they had of going into these markets and becoming the market leader overnight. The store itself was fun to walk through. I decided to take a gamble." Inglis accepted Home Depot's offer and became a key player in its customer service culture and growth.

Using its customer service strategy of low prices and wide selection that others seemed incapable of copying to its fullest, Home Depot fought many competitors and won. In the 1980s, Home Depot stores on the West Coast began opening at 7:30 A.M. to attract contractors and began holding special "Contractor Nights" to acquaint professional customers with the store and products. At first Marcus and Blank didn't want to attract contractors because they weren't sure such customers could be profitable. "They were very nervous about it," said Inglis, who convinced them the idea would work. When the California stores showed big sales increases at profit levels at or near target, Marcus and Blank relented. The contractor program—a customer service—spread to other Home Depot stores.

Through such moves, Home Depot distanced itself even further from the field. Yet in the 1990s, the company became a victim of its success. On busy days, crowds were so big and lines so long that shoppers would give up and leave without buying anything. Some employees simply pointed shoppers in the direction of items rather than taking them there, contrary to company policy. And despite hours of training, employees sometimes weren't versed in the products from other departments. That bothered Marcus and Blank. They realized Home Depot had to stay ahead of the competition and attacked the problems as if they were fighting for survival. Their ideas would yet again radically change the home center business.

To alleviate crowds and long lines, Marcus and Blank intentionally opened new stores close to existing sites, essentially "cannibalizing" sales from older locations. While the move cut Home Depot's sales growth in many locations, it increased its overall sales and made customers happy. "By opening new stores not far from old ones, we are able to keep our existing stores from becoming choked with customers," said Tony Brown, then a Home Depot regional manager. "Second, if you properly locate that new store on the periphery of two trade areas—one served by the older store and the other not served conveniently by any store—you not only relieve customer traffic at the older location, you also develop a new base of customers who are attracted to the more convenient location."

There were other ways to improve service. In the early 1990s, Home Depot overhauled its stores. The company hired Deloitte & Touche to evaluate what worked and what didn't inside a Home Depot. The result: Lumber departments were moved from the back of stores to the side, and separate cash registers were set up for lumber purchases to reduce the log-jam of lumber carts in other parts of the store. Aisles were widened to help shoppers get by others, and higher shelves were installed to hold more products.

In stores from West Springfield, Massachusetts, to Escondi-do, California, the wider aisles were lit by skylights, and the higher shelves allowed for merchandise to be taken out of the aisles. The kitchen, wallpaper, and bathroom departments were put in the back of the stores, giving shoppers some relative quiet to consider purchases. Cleaveland, who joined Home Depot as vice president of logistics when the store changes were being made, was awestruck by the moves. "Here was one of the most successful retailers in the world, and they were tearing it apart even though it wasn't broken," he said. "It sent a strong message through the company that nothing was sacred."

In the 1990s, employees began restocking shelves at night so they could wait on customers during the day. "When you have a store doing $55 or $60 million, just getting the product in the back door and getting it up on the shelves is a major task," explained Marcus. "When you have everybody in the store trying to keep up with that kind of volume, you find that after a while they're so busy putting away merchandise that they have no time for customers. That's not the name of the game. The name of the game is to have time for the customers." Despite Home Depot's success, Marcus and Blank knew they needed to keep emphasizing customer service to remain a leader.

Marcus and Blank got creative. They added wedding reg-istries to stores. Home Depot didn't start selling Wedgewood china. But the registries were a symbol of the practical nineties when newlyweds were picking lawnmowers over silver tea sets. Some of the first to use the service signed up for wheelbarrows, garden hoses, and shovels. Again, they provided a customer service.

Marcus and Blank have taken care of millions of do-it-yourselfers, contractors, homemakers, and others. More importantly, Marcus and Blank often know when to correct problems with Home Depot's customer service and when to back away from a service when it's not being provided at the high levels they demand.

The two men realize, however, that Home Depot is not going to please everyone. They know customers with a complaint about Home Depot's customer service will either keep quiet, go to a competitor, or call the company.

Marcus and Blank hope they call and talk to Ben Hill, perhaps Home Depot's most valuable customer service employee. Ben Hill is the fictitious name given employees who answer phones and handle complaints. The name was taken from a sign on a road near Atlanta's Hartsfield International Airport that Marcus and Blank pass on their way out of town on business trips.

Early in Home Depot's history, Marcus and Blank knew they needed to address customer complaints and questions. Because they desperately wanted feedback on what they were doing right and wrong, the partners set up a phone line and advertised the number in their stores with signs of "Ben Hill"—an orange-aproned man with a Home Depot baseball cap drawn as a likeness of cofounder Pat Farrah, the merchandising expert, who in the early days was the one who most often raised the spirits of employees with his upbeat attitude.

Ben Hill gives customers a name and a voice to associate with the company—making Home Depot more personal. Sure, other companies have phone lines to handle customer complaints. But Marcus and Blank went to the extreme. Home Depot often manned the phones with home improvement experts who could also answer questions about do-it-yourself projects.

One was Bill Sanders, a long-time do-it-yourselfer who had worked for Marcus and Blank at Handy Dan and had even built his own house. Want to build an arbor to produce some artificial shade? Sanders's observation: "They are easy to build, long-lasting, and a practical-sized arbor (8 by 12 feet) can be constructed by a home handyman in one weekend." The lumber is standard size, eliminating the need for cutting. Sanders recommends using pressure-treated lumber, but he adds that you can also use cedar or redwood.

If only all the calls to Ben Hill were that easy. Most are from complaining customers. The register lines are too long. The stores are too big and confusing. It takes too much time to get in and out of the stores. A customer can't find an item advertised in the newspaper or on television. There's not enough help in the stores, particularly on the weekends. A special-ordered item hasn't arrived yet. Despite Home Depot's vaunted home improvement expertise, there were still areas for improvement. A July 1995 study by Wall Street firm Merrill Lynch & Co. noted that 65 percent of Home Depot's customers in Winston-Salem, North Carolina, and Livonia, Michigan, would like to see customer service improved even more—even though both stores were ranked ahead of nearby Lowe's and Home Quarters in terms of provided customer service. Twelve percent in Winston-Salem and 8 percent in Livonia wanted better project advice.

Marcus and Blank know they can keep improving Home Depot's customer service. When customers complain about crowded parking lots and long lines at local Home Depot stores, Marcus and Blank open a new Home Depot nearby to divert some of those customers. When shoppers get frustrated that there aren't enough employees to help them, Home Depot tests a computerized scheduling system matching the number of workers needed in a department to the number of items sold from that area. (Still, the lack of enough workers to take care of customers and the company's intense cost control that often focuses on employee work hours is seen as a possible chink in Home Depot's armor as it faces new competition.) When a Home Depot store runs out of a product, other stores transfer the product until the supply can be replenished. Or in some cases, Home Depot will buy the item from a competitor to sell in its stores. Marcus emphasizes in training classes that everything possible must be done to get the product to the customer.

"Instead of being embarrassed your store received a complaint, you should be proud that your customers have confidence in your ability to fix anything," says Larry Mercer, executive vice president, to employees who receive Ben Hill complaints. "You should take the opportunity they have given you and rise to the occasion. When the consumer is satisfied, you can be proud that you won back a lost customer."

This customer service also serves as market research. This on-the-job feedback keeps employees alert to helping the next customer by learning from the problems and successes of the last one. "The difference between ourselves and most retailers is that we really live for the customer," explains Marcus. "From a value standpoint, from a quality standpoint, from a pricing standpoint, from a feeling like someone is treating them like human beings standpoint—that's really our goal. If we continue to do that, I don't see any limit to where The Home Depot can go."

By 1996, Home Depot was responding to 800,000 response cards, 30,000 letters and phone calls, and 5,000 electronic messages such as facsimile or e-mail. Each Home Depot region now has a staff of Ben Hills to answer questions and field complaints. The feedback is explored to find the causes of complaints and the solutions to problems.

Take a look at a common scenario at a Home Depot, particularly on spring weekends when do-it-yourselfers crowd the stores, buying plants or fertilizer or grass seed for a quick outdoor project. Quite often, the lines are long on the weekends. Why were the lines long? Maybe there weren't enough registers open. And why weren't there enough registers open? Maybe it was because the store had two fewer cashiers than it needed. Why were there not enough cashiers? Maybe it was because two were sick. Well then, why weren't more store workers trained to fill in and run the registers? The training may have been scheduled, but the store needed immediate help in the lawn and garden department because it's that area's biggest selling season. That's how Marcus and Blank want their employees to look at such situations.

By addressing the Ben Hill calls and seeing what caused the complaint, Marcus and Blank tell employees, they can then be prepared the next time they're faced with that situation. "There is nothing more difficult than listening to criticism," says Mercer. "By listening to the customer's criticism, however, we can learn from our mistakes."

Here's one result: When shoppers visited a Home Depot in Clifton, New Jersey, during the winter, they often had trouble getting in and out of the parking lot—much less getting to the store—during the harsh winter weather. That's not Home Depot's fault, but it caused complaints. When customers recently showed up at the store during particularly harsh weather, they were greeted with 17 tons of salt, or 20 free pounds per customer, to help them thaw the ice. "Hurrah for Home Depot," said one shopper. "This is better than coffee and doughnuts."

Perhaps the most important service Home Depot has provided its shoppers, however, is knowing when to correct a problem hurting customer service.

When it comes to Home Depot customer service, shoppers get more than salt to melt the ice in their driveways. They're also getting other requests listened to. Two things customers began asking for in the 1980s was a way for the stores to install more of the products like kitchen cabinets and carpeting and to have purchases delivered to their homes.

True, the number of do-it-yourselfers who had gained the confidence to complete home improvement projects had grown because of Home Depot. But there were many others out there who simply didn't have the time to learn or didn't want to learn.

As Home Depot entered the competitive California market in the mid-1980s, it needed to provide services to shoppers that would set itself apart from HomeClub and others. Marcus and Blank noticed that department store chain Sears Roebuck successfully installed products sold at its stores. Sears' installation business had $1.5 billion in sales at the time. The only product Home Depot installed at that time was garage door openers. So the company explored other products tough for do-it-yourselfers to install themselves. "We're doing this not because we want to, but because customers want it," said Marcus.

In the Home Depot in Chula Vista, California, the company first tested installing water heaters, doors, and windows, placing them on the other side of the registers, separating them from other items in the store. "It was very successful," said Inglis. "We started selling a lot of products." In fact, Home Depot sold too much. More and more products that could be installed were added to the other side of the store. It became too unwieldy, so the installed products were moved back into the rest of the store and employees were trained to promote the installation service. Home Depot still had not found the best way to sell installed products.

Installation spread to the rest of the San Diego market, and in the next few years to most of Home Depot's West Coast stores. By the end of 1992, with the program in 122 stores in 10 states, Marcus and Blank approved expanding installation to the rest of the stores. They wanted it done slowly because it was hard to find contractors who would follow the company's stringent standards. The installers were not company employees but workers hired by the retailer to perform the jobs. "We are not in the business to try to sell labor," noted Inglis back in 1993. "What we're in the business of is trying to sell products. We're trying to find another way to expand our penetration into the market, through selling more home improvement products through installed sales. Our customers trust us in two areas. One is for total satisfaction. And the other is for incredible value. And the combination is going to make for a great installed sales program."

Still, Home Depot went into installed sales with the same gusto Marcus and Blank displayed with the company's expansion. Tom Kessling, director of installed sales, talked about passing Sears as the largest installer. While customers in many markets liked and demanded the installation service, it grew too fast and became a problem. With a rapid expansion, the service suffered.

For one, Home Depot tried to install hundreds of items sold

in its stores, at one time offering nearly 750 different items for installation ranging from ceiling fans and faucets to carpet, tubs, and showers. That made the service unwieldy.

Another issue was the contractors themselves. Many completed the jobs professionally and on time. Orlando contractor John Twilley began installing carpet for six local Home Depots in February 1992. Because of the work, he was able to go from a three-person operation to nine crews of installers, increasing his revenue by 180 percent in the first two years. Twilley said he enjoyed being part of a team focused on "total customer service."

But others didn't have the same customer service focus. Because they weren't Home Depot employees, there wasn't much control. There were problems with installations. Contractors would scratch floors and walls. Or they wouldn't connect the electrical wiring for a ceiling fan. Customers complained with increasing regularity.

Marcus and Blank wanted so badly to give the customers what they wanted from Home Depot that the service suffered. They admitted their mistake and made changes. "Installers are not under our control," said Marcus. "These are all outside people. They don't look like us. They don't act like us. They don't conduct business like us. This is an opportunity to find out who can. We have to identify these people and work with them."

Marcus and Blank reduced the installed products to a handful, including kitchen cabinets, heaters, carpeting, and garage door openers. Those had been the products customers asked for the most. And the contractors installing these offerings were easier to control because these products were easy to install. "We rolled it out too far," said Marcus. "We just did too many things, and none of it effectively. So now we've gotten it down to a workable level where we think it can work. We are not going to expand it until we can handle what we have."

Marcus and Blank learned a valuable customer service lesson with the installed sales. They learned that even though customers may ask for a service, Home Depot may not be able to provide it at its normally high level of satisfaction. Despite their goal of providing do-it-yourselfers with the best customer service, there are some things Home Depot can't offer.

Knowing when to back off from installed sales when the program wasn't working may have been the best way of all to maintain a high level of customer service. Marcus emphasizes to new employees that Home Depot will always be a place where mistakes can be made, as long as they are corrected and people learn from them. With the installation program, Home Depot was smart enough to know when it made a mistake.

Today, as household income levels increase and do-it-yourselfers grow older, more customers want someone to complete their home improvement projects. Because of that, Home Depot is now studying ways to better serve customers who want products installed as that group of shoppers becomes a larger portion of its consumers.

There were other services customers were asking for beside helping them install garage doors. Some shoppers, particularly professional contractors, wanted a better delivery service, especially for stacks of roof shingles, wood, and sheet rock to the locations where they were building or remodeling.

Virtually since the doors opened, Home Depot has provided delivery service for large orders. But it hasn't always been a smooth operation. The deliveries have been handled by stores already stretched to the limit in many cases. Early on, many stores had only one truck to make deliveries. When orders were piled up, the truck would get behind in making shipments. And with larger deliveries, sometimes product had to be culled from three or four stores to fill the order. That often took days, upsetting the customer and frustrating the store manager taking the irate calls.

In 1990, Home Depot looked at the delivery service and realized changes needed to be made. The company bought more trucks, including some with forklifts on the back. And they gave more trucks to stores receiving a lot of delivery orders. A scheduling system for the deliveries was also developed.

All of those improvements "certainly helped, but it didn't solve the problem," noted Cleaveland, then vice president of logistics. "We were increasing costs in the system. We didn't hire the right number of drivers to keep the trucks busy all the time. So we started looking at it again." A survey revealed that the customers didn't think the delivery service was professionally run. "We realized we needed to wipe the slate clean and start over," said Cleaveland.

By 1993, Blank wanted to change how Home Depot's customers looked at the delivery service. So the company hired retail consulting firm Kurt Salmon Associates to make suggestions. Cleaveland and the consulting firm concluded that the delivery service would be more efficient if it were operated separately from the stores. They picked Dallas to test a delivery warehouse, but at the last minute, Blank told them to move the test to Atlanta. Home Depot's test of its upscale Expo store had just opened in Atlanta at the same time, and its closeness to Home Depot's headquarters helped Marcus, Blank, and others track its performance. By testing the new warehouse near the headquarters, they could do the same with the delivery service.

Cleaveland developed the warehouse, which was located in a northeast Atlanta suburb within a couple of miles of a Home Depot store. After going through delivery records for the preceding year to see which items were orderered most often, the company picked 500 items—basic building materials like studs, sheet rock, kitchen cabinets, plywood, and pressure-treated wood—and placed them inside the warehouse. With those items, they could fill more than half of the delivery orders without going to the stores. And they promised that if an order was placed by 3 P.M., the shipment would be delivered the next day. They also started giving customers a specific time frame—between 1 and 3 P.M., for example—when the order would arrive. Previously, customers were just told what day the order would arrive. In addition, the trucks were sent out according to a new grid format, going to locations in a specific area. Previously, deliveries overlapped or were too far apart.

The new delivery system improved the quickness of shipments and decreased complaints to store managers, who also rid themselves of having to worry about department of transportation records, finding qualified drivers, and liability concerns about truck accidents. "The stores were very strongly in support of it," said Cleaveland. "Store managers would come up to me and say, 'I haven't had a delivery complaint in six months, and I used to get five a day.'"

The biggest problem, noted Cleaveland, was that the delivery service still relied on stores to pull merchandise the warehouse wasn't stocking. And to expand the delivery program to other markets, he also had to fight Home Depot's financial experts, who felt the cost of a warehouse delivery service was too high. Even though the new delivery warehouse improved the service, it cost more to deliver the products than what Home Depot was charging. Marcus and Blank wanted to offer the best service they could, but they weren't prepared to provide the service if it meant losing money. "If we end up rolling this thing out,...sooner or later those costs have to be reflected in the cost of our product," said Marcus to employees in August 1995.

Despite the delivery service's apparent success in one crucial area—improving the service to a key segment of Home Depot's customer base—it has yet to roll out across the country because the company has yet to find a way to cut its costs. Such a conservative and slow approach to expansion of the delivery service was also prevalent in other Home Depot tests at the time, most noticeably rural stores, upscale Expo stores, and international expansion. Despite a common perception that Home Depot aggressively and quickly expands into new ventures, they are actually methodical in making sure such moves will be successful before expanding, and that caution is a key to Home Depot's steady growth.

And while Marcus and Blank have always emphasized customer service when they talk to their employees, they also realize that there is a limit to those marching orders. "Taking care of the customer is the key to our success," says Marcus. "As we add more products and services, we must continue to give the best customer service, day in, day out." And while the delivery service has yet to prove itself, it hasn't impeded Home Depot employees from providing the best customer service they can. Indeed, by getting the delivery service out of the stores, at least the two dozen stores in the Atlanta market, Home Depot has improved customer service by allowing employees in those locales to focus on the customers actually in the stores.

Home Depot still hasn't figured out a way to make its delivery service efficient in most markets. But as the company continues to find better ways to take care of its customers, improving the delivery program is high on Marcus and Blank's priority list.

MANAGEMENT LESSONS

Home Depot's singular focus is on providing the best customer service it can to the millions of shoppers who visit its stores each year. Because of that, the retailer is constantly looking for ways to improve its customer service and provide new services that will make shoppers happy. Every business, no matter what industry they're in, should pay as much attention to customers.

1. Excellent customer service keeps shoppers coming back to Home Depot because they know that their questions will be answered and that they'll be given the right advice.

2. Top management at Home Depot constantly emphasizes service because it knows that's how the retailer can distinguish itself from competitors selling the same products.

3. The goal at Home Depot is to constantly improve customer service because shoppers who are treated properly will expect even-better service the next time they're in one of their stores.

4. Home Depot listens to customer complaints and correct the problems because it knows that if a dissatisfied customer sees it trying to improve, that customer will likely return to buy something.

5. Home Depot is constantly extending its customer services through new ways that allow it to grow sales and meet the changing needs of shoppers.

TEACH THE CUSTOMER

When people come into our store, they expect that somebody is there that has knowledge, that has the experience to give them the proper kind of information so that they can do what they have to do, whether it's fix something or design something or repair something.

—BERNIE MARCUS

There are thousands of people like Kurt Schulz working for Home Depots across the country. A certified kitchen designer, Schulz works in a Home Depot on Highway 78 in Lilburn, an Atlanta suburb. He dresses like a typical Home Depot employee, wearing blue jeans, a flannel shirt, and tennis shoes. His glasses give him the appearance of your favorite uncle, who always knew the right answer to any problem.

On this January night, however, Schulz should be wearing a professor's cap and gown. That's because he is teaching how to install kitchen cabinets. It's 7 o'clock, and the crowd has died down. The Home Depot is filled with contractors buying supplies for tomorrow's job, and a handful of homeowners. Some are simply getting ideas for their next project.

In the kitchen department near the rear of the store, Schulz talks to his lone student, a thirty-something man whose mother-in-law wants to replace her kitchen cabinets. He explains in a low-key, fatherly tone that there are two types of cabinets—one where the door covers the entire cabinet and the other where the door just covers the box. "They're installed basically the same," says Schulz.

Schulz explains how cabinets are all 34½ inches tall, but before you begin marking the height on your wall, you need to find the high spot in the kitchen floor. That ensures that the counter top will be level once it's installed on top of the counters. Then you install the cabinets from the corners in. Be sure to locate the studs in the wall to anchor the cabinets. And don't forget to connect the cabinets together. "Secure them together and install them with the doors off so you don't nick them," advises Schulz. "Never, ever nail a cabinet in place. You need to be able to adjust the cabinets."

If the wall isn't flat, you may need to shim the wall to get it even, he adds. That will help when installing the counter top. For the top cabinets, you need to make sure they're securely fastened to the wall before you fill them with dishes and glasses, he adds. "You don't want them falling off the wall and have those heirloom dishes crashing down," he says with a hint of knowledge. He shows a box of 10 by 3 cabinet screws that look like they could hold together two buildings.

"They look like they're overkill," he says. But it's better to be safe than sorry. A recent customer didn't attach his cabinets properly, and they fell. As for the counter top, Schulz has some simple advice: "You need to make sure your corners are square. This has to be very precise. You have to be careful you're not reading on a high spot or a hole in the wall." If the counter top fits closely enough, small cracks can be caulked, he adds.

The counter is then attached to the floor cabinets, but not to the wall, he explains. "Counter tops are very heavy," he said. "You don't need to overkill. It's not going to fall off and hurt somebody."

In an hour, Schulz is done. He has explained molding, drilling pilot holes for screws, overhangs, toe fronts, and getting measurements for the kitchen. He then walks over to a computer and shows how the measurements are put into a software program to design the cabinets and kitchen. Be patient, says Schulz. Plan ahead. "If it's going to take you an hour, it will probably take you two hours," he adds. "You have to teach yourself what to do. You're going to get frustrated. You might have to take some down and start over."

Truer words were never spoken. There is no other retailer in the world of this size teaching its customers how to shop its store and use the products stacked on its shelves the way Home Depot does.

Sure, many grocery stores offer cooking classes. But does Wal-Mart teach its shoppers how to find the right dress or pair of pants? Does Toys R Us have toy experts roaming the aisles, making sure Mom and Dad have picked out the right size batteries for that Tickle Me Elmo doll or are buying a bike that's the right size for junior? The comparison sounds simplistic, yet it makes the point that Home Depot helps its shoppers more than any other retailer.

Home Depot teaches and directs customers to the right products for their projects and makes sure they have the right tools—and so much more. There are classes on wallpapering, painting, installing a garage door, laying tile, or building a storage shed. There's a class on wiring a light switch, or installing a garbage disposal. There's a class on laying ceramic tile or installing ceiling fans or a security system. There's a class on organizing your closet or installing a water heater. Want to tune up your mower? There's a class. Install chain-link fencing? Come to the Home Depot class. "Most of us aren't plumbers," explained Leonard Berry, director of Texas A&M University's Retailing Studies Center. "Home Depot helps you through the mystery of home upkeep." To Marcus and Blank, that's one of Home Depot's competitive advantages. They've developed the expertise to teach customers how to attack do-it-yourself projects.

Want to know the tools to install a new window? Just ask a Home Depot employee. Need advice on the best color scheme for your living room? Talk to a Home Depot worker. Don't understand the difference between two saws? A Home Depot expert can explain. By passing along such knowledge, "We take someone whom I would term a light do-it-yourselfer and turn him into a serious do-it-yourselfer," said Blank.

There's been a far-reaching societal by-product as a result. Home Depot has been at the forefront of a shift in how consumers care for their homes. Today, more people feel confident in doing home repairs and projects than ever before because of the tutoring from Home Depot experts and the classes they offer almost nightly at its stores.

That will be one of Bernie Marcus and Arthur Blank's greatest legacies, as the tinkerers of the 1940s and 1950s gave way to baby-boomers who grew up with the disposable income to go out and replace what was broken. Many baby boomers, unlike their fathers, hadn't learned how to fix leaky plumbing or faulty electrical wiring when growing up. They eventually were taught by Home Depot's experts.

If they had gone into any Home Depot in the 1980s, economists and sociologists could have predicted the impending end to the freewheeling "spend-now" ways of consumers. They would have noted millions of Home Depot shoppers undertaking home repair and remodeling projects—and learning how to do the job. And economic forecasts show that trend will continue well into the twenty-first century as homes get older and more homes are built. Home Depot, primarily through smart planning by Marcus and Blank, are at the forefront of this societal shift.

In the 1990s, Marcus and Blank recognized this trend was building. So they spread the Home Depot name in ways the company would have never considered a decade earlier. In 1995, the company began a one-hour television show on the Discovery Channel called *HouseSmart*. The show features experts finishing home improvement projects that aren't as complicated as they look. The same year, the company published *Home Improvement 1-2-3*, a 480-page book covering the most frequent problems people face when tackling home projects. And it introduced a Home Depot magazine called *Weekend* and a CD-ROM offering do-it-yourself advice.

And in 1997, the world's largest home improvement retail chain began offering "Home Depot Kids' Workshop" in its stores. The classes are aimed at getting more 6- to 12-year-olds into its stores. The idea, which sprang from some of Home Depot's West Coast and northeast stores, teach Boy Scout-like skills such as building a birdhouse and tool safety. It's aimed at building Home Depot brand loyalty with kids and getting them to stores at an early age. Plus, parents, who make the home improvement purchases, must accompany the children.

To Marcus and Blank, the ultimate goal is to make Home Depot customers as knowledgeable as their employees. But their success in teaching shoppers comes from finding the right people. "We wanted to have on the floor of the stores the most knowledgeable people that you could possibly find, so that anybody that came into the store, whether it was a consumer or professional, could walk into the electrical department or the hardware department or the plumbing department or the lumber department, and he or she would be able to find somebody on the floor that would help them," said Marcus. "They would understand technicalities, talk about how you use it, what tools you need, what all the related items are. In order to do that, we reached out to people who are plumbers, who are carpenters, who are electricians, people who worked in hardware stores."

Marcus and Blank had tinkered with classes at Handy Dan. But those didn't attract big crowds and weren't successful because they were often taught by manufacturer representatives who thought the sessions were a waste of time. Others were for simple projects like finishing furniture and decoupage. Marcus and Blank wanted more. To achieve that, they would have to hire and train the best experts to work in the stores.

"I hear over and over again, 'Where did you find the people who work in your stores?'" says Marcus. "'They are so different. They have such personalities. They have such great knowledge.'" What Marcus and Blank did was attract experts by paying more than others. And then they got those experts to teach their knowledge to everyone else in the store.

Home Depot's customers "aren't browsers," adds Marcus. "These aren't people walking through shopping centers. They walk in here to buy something. They come in here because they have a problem; there's a problem with their plumbing or their electrical. They want the advice of the people that we have here." Home Depot employees are "in a position to help people with a problem, and every one of them wants to hear a solution to that problem. We're here to show them how to do what they want to do." That's a critical component to the strategy that Marcus and Blank felt was important to their success.

In the beginning, they advertised the clinics in the catalogs mailed to homes near the first stores in Atlanta. It was mainly a marketing ploy. "It accentuated the fact that we had knowledgeable people that could make you knowledgeable," explained Mayo, one of the original merchandisers hired to help develop that hardware expertise in Home Depot stores. Mayo had been the Handy Dan merchandising manager in Texas and was convinced by Blank and Farrah to join the new company. "I was one of the few people in the world that could look at Bernie, Arthur, and Pat and how well they complemented each other and how doable and credible this concept was," said Mayo. "Pat was merchandising at the next level, and I aspired to that. Pat had an ability to create excitement, energy. He was a spark plug." Mayo, who had a similar energy and creative ideas, joined the team. "We were going to enlighten the customer," he said. "Maybe we'd start with paint and wallpaper." That customer goes home and tries that project, and if he's successful, comes back. "He becomes the next best customer to take on low-voltage lighting outside or that leaky faucet."

Teaching customers is hitting the nail on the head. During his first trip to Home Depot in 1991, customer Pete Flanagan was overwhelmed. He stood in the bathroom aisle, looking at toilet seats, sinks, and mirrors, confused by the number of choices. "I was thinking, 'Forget the whole thing,'" said Flanagan. Then an orange-aproned employee appeared by his side. They discussed fixing a leaky tub. The employee suggested caulking products and offered how-to advice. Flanagan fixed the tub and became bolstered by his success. He then tackled fixing the siding of his Huntington, New York, home. "Normally, I wouldn't consider myself handy," said Flanagan. "But the Home Depot guys make it easy. They have the items. They have the people to tell you what to do. Projects that I used to have someone else do, I now do myself."

Or consider Stan Lambert. When the Atlanta resident remodeled the kitchen in his 70-year-old cottage, he asked for Home Depot's help. "Before, I always bought tools and supplies," he said. "But now I knew that I needed design help as well as cabinets. I knew what cabinets I liked, but I wanted professional assistance because there are things you never think of." He got the help of Lisa Holden, a certified kitchen designer who received training through the National Kitchen and Bath Association. Holden designed a new kitchen free of charge.

Other Home Depot employees across the country go through the same teaching process each day. "I ask [the customer] a lot of questions," said Drew Hecht, a certified kitchen designer in a Home Depot in Corona, California. "Such as, how many people in your family cook? How do you cook? How many kids do you have? Do you entertain a lot? Are you neat when you cook? The purpose of my questions is not to be nosy, but to really get an idea of how people use their kitchen, and how I can best design to accommodate their needs."

Another Home Depot certified kitchen designer, Meredith Rell of the Home Depot in Danbury, Connecticut, asks questions about kitchen remodeling issues. "I'll ask how high they want the cabinets to go. Do they want a soffit? If they have a cathedral ceiling, do they want the top of the cabinets to be proportional to the height of the ceiling? Are you left- or right-handed? This tells me whether the dishwasher should be to the left or the right of the sink." That's the level of expertise Marcus and Blank and, more importantly, Home Depot shoppers, expect when they enter the stores.

But it's not just through experts' giving classes or one-on-one instructions to shoppers that Home Depot teaches do-it-yourselfers. Walk into any Home Depot store today and you'll find handy instructions next to the products on the shelves. For example, next to the display for Pergo laminated flooring—a product that makes floors look like real wood—is a stack of one-page sheets that have a 15-step explanation of how to install the pieces.

Other stores offered different advice. Home Depot's Canada stores handed out tip sheets in the winter from their in-store experts on how to prevent freezing pipes and how to operate sump pumps in basements. In the spring, the Canada stores in locations like Markham, Scarborough, and Whitby gave away planting soil and offered gardening advice.

Marcus and Blank taught their employees to think of every possible way to teach customers. But there would be even more ways outside a Home Depot store that they could help do-it-yourselfers learn.

Despite the classes and help provided do-it-yourselfers in the stores, there were still many home improvement wannabes who needed questions answered or suggestions for their projects and weren't tapping into Home Depot. Marcus and Blank soon found ways to make sure they were also taught. That strategy became an important piece in the company's growth, which in turn helped boost the company's stock price that so many employees were relying on to fund their kids' college education or their own retirement.

How could Home Depot take this knowledge base about home improvement projects and make it available to the masses? One way was to put that expertise in a book offering tips and suggestions on everything from insulating and weatherproofing to wallpapering. Marcus and Blank gave Dick Hammill, the senior vice president of marketing, the task of overseeing the project. It became a nearly two-year process involving more than 2,000 Home Depot department managers and experts across the country. First, they were asked what questions they most commonly received from customers and what projects homeowners most actively pursued.

Then, Home Depot and Better Homes and Gardens, which collaborated with the company on producing the book, talked to customers. This time, they asked, "What do homeowners need to know to get the job done right?" Two sample books were designed—each based on the research—using different layouts and designs. The books were then shown to focus groups of homeowners and Home Depot customers. The response: Give us information that's clearly illustrated and easy to understand, with advice for each project. The goal was to keep the text under 250 words in each instance.

Home Depot and the publisher then compiled the actual pages, sending sections to Home Depot experts for review. The advice and suggestions were subjected to another round of expert review—the most experienced Home Depot do-it-yourself experts known as "Homers." They made more than

700 changes to the text. "The book was actually born out of the experiences in Home Depot stores," said Hammill. "We haven't found a book on the market that was conceived from a store's aisles."

The result became *Home Improvement 1-2-3*, a 480-page compilation that was introduced in Home Depot stores and bookstores in 1995 for $34.95. The book became an instant hit. Within the first year, Home Depot sold more than 100,000 copies inside its stores, and book retailers sold another 150,000 copies in traditional bookstores.

The book contains everything from picking the correct paintbrush to buying the right ladder, as well as pictures showing the right way to complete simple, and hard, home repairs and remodeling jobs. For projects, the book gauges electrical and mechanical skills needed to complete the task and lists the necessary tools. (For removing and replacing a sink, a do-it-yourselfer would need a basic tool kit, a basin wrench, silicone caulk, a bucket, plumber's putty, and possibly new supply tubes and shutoff valves.) It also gives the do-it-yourselfer an estimate of how long the job will take. For the sink, it would take an experienced do-it-yourselfer about two hours. A beginner would need about five hours.

The book also contains helpful hints like common mistakes and tips called "Homer's Hindsight." For example, in unclogging a toilet bowl, the Homers noted: "It began as a simple clog and ended up as a heap of broken china! That toilet may look big and strong, but don't use the closet snake like a battering ram. You can crack or even break the bowl, especially on inexpensive toilets. And there is no way to repair a cracked toilet—you'll have to replace the whole thing."

The *Home Improvement 1-2-3* book was so successful that Marcus and Blank extended its format and helpful hints to another book called *Outdoor Projects 1-2-3*. Again done in conjunction with Better Homes and Gardens, the 1998 book again culled the expertise from store employees like Leonard Chambers in Baton Rouge, Louisiana, and Renee Andreuzzi in Canton, Michigan, to teach do-it-yourselfers projects such as how to build fences and gates, construct outdoor sheds, and even build decks. It also contains the same helpful hints, including a reminder that such projects normally require government permits.

Marcus and Blank weren't done exploring multimedia possibilities for teaching customers. *Home Improvement 1-2-3* and *Outdoor Projects 1-2-3* were joined by a do-it-yourself magazine called *Weekend*. Again done in conjunction with the Better Homes and Gardens publishers, *Weekend* became another offering making Home Depot's expertise available to a wider audience. Using a group of 30 Home Depot advisors, the magazine offers tips and guidance on everything from replacing a window to repairing a driveway. An edition published just before the holiday season details poinsettia care. And the magazine even asks readers for their tips. Some readers have responded with suggestions on how to keep mortar from drying during a project or how to clean hard-to-reach corners.

Marcus and Blank also gave the go-ahead to put the Home Depot name on a do-it-yourself television show, again overseen by Hammill, a bespectacled man with a roundish face. They reasoned that the show would help build awareness of the company's name, products, and services as it expanded across the country. A cross between *This Old House* and *Tool Time*, the fake TV show featured in the sitcom *Home Improvement*, Home Depot's *HouseSmart* show is lively, with short segments, many done before a live studio audience. The host, Lynette Jennings, already had a show on the Discovery Channel for six seasons before she teamed with Home Depot. "It's one thing to have a TV show that exposes wonderful home designs," said Jennings, explaining the show's strategy. "But if you can't teach, you really have done your viewer an injustice."

To be sure, Home Depot had explored the potential of television, hawking doorbells and hammers in a four-times-a-year experiment on the shopping channel QVC. But *HouseSmart* broadcasts handy tips and suggestions and expertise available to 63 million homes each morning on the Discovery Channel, although nowhere near that number actually watch the show. Television gave Home Depot a much bigger audience, and more exposure. Jennings and her helpers on the show don't wear the trademark orange Home Depot aprons. And the show doesn't look like an infomercial. Yet, Home Depot's involvement was apparent. Its sponsorship is mentioned as the show cuts to commercial breaks, and the company is a heavy advertiser.

Jennings doles out practical advice. One show begins with an 8-month-old baby girl named Madeline playing on the floor of a room. Dressed in blue jean overalls and a white shirt, Madeline turns around and pulls on a half-dozen electrical cords plugged into an outlet. "That's exactly what we don't want to do," warns Jennings as she walks into the room and scoops little Madeline away from danger. "Although we've exaggerated the condition, this is something I've seen people do in their houses. And Madeline came along, and sure enough, went for the fires." How to solve this problem? Jennings suggests a cord mate, a plastic tube where electrical cords can be inserted and then snapped shut so children and others won't pull on them. The cord mate can then be attached to the wall and even painted the same color as the room so it blends with the design, notes Jennings.

The show then moves on to how to take care of African violets. The flowers, notes guest Mildred Pinnell of the Atlanta Botanical Gardens, don't like to be watered from above with cold water. She suggests watering directly on the soil with lukewarm water, or immersing the pot in a kitchen sink filled with a couple of inches of water for two hours.

Later in the episode, Home Depot employee Doug Cantrell demonstrates how a stool can be made by using one board 12 feet long and 4 feet wide. (Another Home Depot employee, Dave White, also appears regularly on the show. In one segment, he explains how to make plumbing repairs "and be darn proud of yourself in the process.") And then Jennings comes back at the end of the show and explains how she painted the walls in her daughter's bedroom to look like a rainbow and a sunset.

The show moves quickly, keeping the viewers' attention. Wearing a denim smock, Jennings begins one show cutting up plastic bags. The bags, dipped in peach latex paint and wiped on a wall, give an antique finish. The explanation and demonstration take no more than five minutes. After a commercial break, Jennings discusses adding columns around a front door and showing how to build a raised garden bed and picking color schemes for a room. (Her suggestion: Pick colors from a favorite tie or shirt.)

The television show is Marcus and Blank, with the help of people like Jennings, getting Home Depot's expertise available at stores into homes around the country. It's an indirect way of showing that Home Depot experts can help you with any project—although even Jennings and her helpers don't mention Home Depot by name, referring you to your local hardware store or home center. Yet Home Depot's many commercials remind watchers of its involvement.

For sure, putting Home Depot's name on do-it-yourself books, magazines, and television shows gives the company name recognition as it expands across the country into new markets. But the more prevalent theme behind these projects is to make customers more confident in taking on, and completing, repair and remodeling jobs around the house. With better do-it-yourself skills, Marcus and Blank reason, they will be buying more from their local Home Depot. That, in turn, will help the company sustain its 20-plus percent growth rate.

The line begins forming outside the break room in the back of the Home Depot store long before class is scheduled to begin. But these students aren't waiting to learn how to install a door or put up drywall in their basement. These are children as young as 3 years old hoping to make some noise with hammers and sandpaper and screwdrivers.

This is a Home Depot Kids' Workshop, and in 1997 it became the latest tool used by Marcus and Blank to teach customers—albeit very small shoppers—how to do their own tasks. They believe it helps develop the next generation of do-it-yourselfers, building self-esteem by working with tools, and encourages a work ethic. "A child who builds a birdhouse, for example, then watches a family of sparrows set up housekeeping in it, will remember that project forever," explains Suzanne Apple, Home Depot's director of community affairs. "We've seen this happen over and over with our customers. Any time they are able to do some project themselves, it makes them feel great, as though they've really accomplished something. This do-it-yourself phenomenon goes to the very heart of Home Depot's success."

Through the years, Home Depot stores have been holding kids' programs. A store in Mesa, Arizona, sponsored events called "Kids' Club," while stores in Connecticut were hosting the "Children's Building Center." A store in South Attleboro, Massachusetts, even helped build and design two Soap Box Derby racers for the local Boys and Girls Club. Other stores wanted to help kids coming into their stores but didn't know where to begin. So Home Depot set up a roundtable for experts to design a uniform kids' class that could be done across the country. Signs were placed near exits and outside stores to publicize the classes and to give kids a place to register.

The result: On Saturday mornings around the country, kids as young as 3 and well into their teen years attend these classes and build bird cages, racks for books or videos, and tool boxes. Some stores have had as many as 200 children show up in one day.

At a Home Depot in Decatur, an Atlanta suburb, boys and girls start showing up 15 minutes before the class starts. They peer into the room, looking to see what they're going to build this time. Outside it's raining, making this the perfect day to go to a Home Depot and make something. When the time comes, they jostle for position and line up just inside the door, where they tell a Home Depot employee their names. She writes their names in black ink on special Kids' Workshop orange aprons and ties them on the children.

The kids are accompanied by parents and quickly take a seat around a large table. Kits to make videotape racks or birdhouse money banks have already been placed in front of each chair along with a hammer, some sandpaper, and a screwdriver. "Don't stick your hands on those nails—they're sharp," says one of the store employees in the room to help the kids.

The room fills up with about two dozen children ranging in age from 3 to 12. It doesn't matter that some of them have no idea what they're doing. Most of them are just proud to wear the orange apron they see on employees. Another employee gets some of the kids excited, calling them "future carpenters of America" and tells one in particular, "Looks like we're going to have some fun."

Soon, most kids rip the plastic wrap off the kits and begin sanding the edges of the wood. Some are skilled enough to insert the nails in the holes and connecting pieces. Some need the help of their parents. "Most of the time, the parents are needed to hold the project while the child completes it," says Apple. "Their little hands just aren't big enough to, say, hold a birdhouse and put on the roof at the same time. It's also a great way for parents to spend more quality time with their children."

Others want the help of a Home Depot worker because they know that the people in the orange aprons know what they're doing. An employee named Robert Maddox walks through the room, helping some kids. He finally reaches the end of the table where 5-year-old Andrew is attending his first Kids' Workshop and is trying to build the birdhouse. Patiently, Maddox shows Andrew how the birdhouse is put together and even screws the base together while Andrew sandpapers the sides. Andrew's father stands in the background and video-tapes Maddox helping Andrew. The noise in the room rises as two dozen kids hammer away.

By the end of the project, Andrew has hammered the roof by himself. It doesn't matter that there are gaps between the pieces. What's important is that Andrew has built something. At the end of the class, which took no more than 45 minutes, Andrew—still wearing his orange apron—and the other kids are ready to leave. Employees hand them a certificate of achievement, signed by Homer D. Poe—a moniker given to mimic the store's name.

Andrew's experience isn't unique. Take this letter written to Jeff Kiley, the store manager of the Home Depot in City of Industry, California, from shopper Chris Cabrera and his children—Ian and Molly—of Rowland Heights, California: "My two kids and I recently started joining the Kids' Clinics you offer on Saturday mornings. We had to write to let you know how much we enjoy it. So far, we've made a birdhouse, a pumpkin sign, and a 101 Dalmatians figure, among other things. It's great to use the tools and work with our hands to create projects together, and we very much appreciate your providing this service to families in the area." The Cabreras go on to laud the class instructor for being patient with restless kids. And they finish the letter by saying the class is "a great asset to the community, and I'm sure helps generate more business for you. Personally, in the past I've bought additional materials we needed to enhance the projects we've made, and of course, when I have other home repair needs, I automatically come to your place."

Home Depot executives say they never intended the Kids' Workshops to drum up more business for the stores. That may be hard to believe, given the company's singular focus in virtually every area to drum up new business. But to its credit, Home Depot realized such classes make a good impression in the community. That was welcome public relations at a time when Home Depot was working to settle the allegations that it discriminated against some of its female employees. "These kids are our next generation of consumers," said Apple. "We want to help them learn early in life the value and the outright savings of being able to do many things for yourself around the house."

The success of the Kids' Workshops naturally led Home Depot to develop in 1998 an animated television show called *Homer's Workshop* for children. That was another way for Marcus and Blank to nurture their future customers. They understood that the best-known consumer product names like Atlanta neighbor Coca-Cola began cultivating brand-name awareness at an early age. Having former Coca-Cola president Donald Keough on Home Depot's board helped them think about attracting customers in ways, and at ages, they had not previously imagined. The 30-minute show features Homer, the Home Depot character logo, who springs alive and with the help of animated tools and materials takes viewers through do-it-yourself projects such as creating a home garden or designing holiday decorations. The show, which debuted in September 1998, also has a web site where children can ask Homer questions and get project directions.

As the years have gone by, Marcus and Blank have found and developed many unique ways to teach customers both young and old how to start and complete do-it-yourself projects. They first began by offering the expertise in the stores. But as they expanded, they found new ways to provide the vast knowledge collected through the many experiences of shoppers and workers, helping expand the do-it-yourself market in ways they never imagined when they started at Handy Dan in the 1970s. As Home Depot expanded into more markets, such knowledge served as an easy entree that helped attract new customers.

That success would make other home center retailers envious and lead to increased competition from rivals. Home Depot would also find itself opposed by an unusual foe: Some of the very customers it was trying to serve.

MANAGEMENT LESSONS

No other retailer in the world teaches its shoppers how to use the products it sells the way Home Depot does. Such expertise, freely given to customers, allows Home Depot to build its reputation as a place to learn do-it-yourself projects and builds good will, loyalty and name recognition with shoppers. Few businesses teach their customers how to be better shoppers, but they would likely see better sales if they did.

1. Trained employees that teach customers how-to projects is one of Home Depot's biggest assets. These training classes increase sales and further the image of Home Depot as the place to get do-it-yourself advice.

2. Teaching customers brings shoppers into Home Depot stores because shoppers know that they'll be given the expertise to complete their projects. That also gives customers the confidence to tackle harder projects because they know that Home Depot will help them.

3. Providing ways for shoppers to learn outside the stores can also improve sales and promote good will. Home Depot extended its do-it-yourself expertise through books and television, showing customers that they don't need to shop its stores to gain its knowledge.

4. Extending teaching to children helps build consumer loyalty, and Home Depot began workshops teaching projects like building a bird house and a children's television show to increase its visbility and name recognition.

5. Shoppers will rely on your company's expertise if you promote it. Because Home Depot has been at the forefront of the do-it-yourself revolution, its growth has been aided by its teaching capabilities, allowing it to expand even faster.

HOME DEPOT'S FOES

The amount of restraint against these openings is about what it was years ago. It's just that we're opening more stores.

—BERNIE MARCUS

Marcus and Blank faced competition from the moment they opened in Atlanta in 1979. Handy City. Payless Cashways. Builders Square. Lowe's. Dozens and dozens of small independent hardware stores. More than 5,500 Ace Hardware locations spread across the country.

All have tried to fight off Home Depot's aggressive expansion plans down the road from their stores. Known as "Agent Orange" to competitors, Home Depot counters with an in-your-face attitude. It opens stores next door to its competitors. "Head to head, we want to be where the competition is," says Home Depot executive Lynn Martineau. It designed T-shirts decorated with tombstones with the words, "Home Depot buries the competition." Other times, it sent black wreaths and miniature coffins to retailers. Said Berg, the southeast division president: "There's a very aggressive nature that most of Home Depot's management sort of have, a pugnacious attitude. It's not cockiness, but an aggressiveness and a competitiveness."

That reputation is deserved. In 1987, Builders Square came to Atlanta and opened four stores. Marcus and Blank had already clashed with the retailer in New Orleans and Texas. But Atlanta was where they had founded and nurtured Home Depot. There was no love between Builders Square founder Frank Denny and Marcus and Blank. When they were fired by Sigoloff, Denny remained behind and ran the company.

Denny struck first by marketing the "fight" itself. In a smoke-filled boxing ring, a bell signals the match. An announcer introduces the opponents—Builders Square and Home Depot. "You never know how good you are until you come up against the competition," a voice says as punches are thrown. It was only a television commercial. But the slugfest was down and dirty. Builders Square offered local customers $10 in "Square Bucks" coupons for quoting a competitor's lower prices on identical products. And it paid customers $10 for trading in Home Depot discount cards. Marcus and Blank responded with full-page newspaper ads and direct mail to "loyal customers." They also discontinued the discount cards that gave customers 5 percent off the price of a product if they found the same item for a lower price elsewhere.

Marcus and Blank pushed stores to improve customer service to higher levels. It slowly became apparent that Builders Square couldn't overcome Home Depot in Atlanta. Four years later, Denny's stores closed. "They concentrated on us. We concentrated on the customer," boasted Marcus. "That was the difference." By that time, Marcus and Blank had added more stores into the market and had 13 total in the Atlanta area. Other rivals also failed to make a dent in Atlanta—and elsewhere. Lowe's exited the Atlanta area in the 1980s, although it would later return. And 84 Lumber closed its two stores there in 1989. Local player Williams Bros. abandoned the do-it-yourself market to focus on contractors. Handy City, which ran big newspaper ads when Home Depot opened its first stores, closed its six Atlanta locations in 1987.

Indeed, Home Depot's entry into towns and cities has a widespread effect. Home Depot stores affect sales—both up and down—of other retailers, where rivals decide to build stores, how roads are expanded due to increased traffic, and how and where neighborhoods grow or lose value and force residents to seek other homes. That's not exactly the impact Marcus and Blank have intended, although they like the competition. "There are going to be some very interesting local skirmishes coming up in the near future," Marcus told some Home Depot vendors in 1993. "We think there will be some very bloody battles."

Home Depot often tells a town's economic development leaders about the sales and jobs it will add to the community.

Marcus points out how Home Depot increased do-it-yourself sales in markets where it added stores. And to be sure, the domestic do-it-yourself market has expanded from $60 billion in annual sales to nearly $150 billion today. Some of those sales can be credited to Home Depot, which had $30 billion in sales in 1998, spurring millions more in spending from do-it-yourselfers.

But in some cases, sales and jobs are taken away from area businesses when Home Depot comes to town. And that is why Home Depot faces opposition to its expansion. That's a part of Home Depot's strategy Marcus and Blank don't often talk about. How they reacted in some communities showed their aggressiveness in growing Home Depot—and in some cases, their caring for towns and cities.

When Home Depot opened a 173,000-square-foot store in Elmont, a town on Long Island, in January 1991, the effect on nearby hardware stores and lumberyards was swift and unmerciful. Progressive Lumber, NTS Supply, Dave's Lumber, Island Park Lumber, Long Island Building Co., Katz Hardware, and J&B Ceramic Tile shuttered their doors in the next two years. Some, for sure, succumbed to a declining northeast economy in the early 1990s. Others were mediocre operators pushed out of the market. But some just couldn't withstand Home Depot's clout. "It wasn't worth the investment to fight Home Depot," said Ed Ufier, Jr., who owned NTS with his father. In a good year, the tool supply store had 13 employees and $2.5 million in sales. By the end of 1991, sales were down to $1 million, and 8 workers had been lopped off the payroll. At the end of the year, they shut down.

When Marcus and Blank opened two stores in Queens— one in Ozone Park and another in Flushing near where Blank grew up—competitors suffered. "Within one month, sales had dropped by 60 percent," said Morris Hoberman, president of the local hardware store chain Lumber Headquarters, which closed nine outlets. "It was like a horse kicking you in the head. I never thought Home Depot's impact would be so severe." Marcus and Blank had built a retailer noticed by its customers and its foes.

Lumber Headquarters wasn't alone. Pisnoy Lumber on Atlantic Avenue and 84th Street, All Seasons Lumber on Metropolitan Avenue and Fresh Pond Road, and Park Hardware on Rockaway Boulevard and 118th Street all closed. Others were scraping by. "I've run this business for close to 35 years, and I've always made a good living," said Bill Lennox of B.P.H. Hardware & Paint in South Ozone Park. "But now, after paying taxes and bills, there's not much left." Home Depot's opponents had argued before the New York stores opened that Marcus and Blank gained political favor by each donating $6,500—the maximum allowed—to New York Mayor Rudolph Giuliani. (The donations were personal contributions and not on behalf of the company, responded Home Depot.) Still, Marcus and Blank made themselves known.

Such moves occurred elsewhere. In 1993, Builders Emporium closed its 97 stores, including 6 locations in and around San Diego. For years, Builders Emporium chief executive Michael Hecht had opposed Home Depot's plans to build a store in nearby Encinitas, sending a 17-page protest letter to the city. Hecht likely was worried about the impact on his stores from the addition of another Home Depot in his market. Furrow Building Materials, unable to compete with Agent Orange, closed 9 stores in the Houston area in 1997. Ernst Home Center, Inc., a 103-year-old company, closed more than 90 stores in Washington, Oregon, Idaho, Montana, Utah, and Wyoming in early 1997. Home Depot had added stores into those northwest markets a couple of years earlier.

Others fought back. In August 1997, a Home Depot catalog in Chicago attacked competitor Menard, Inc. The mailing told customers to avoid buying "knock-off" products and those of "an inferior quality." The catalog implied those "inferior" products could be found at local Menard stores because Menard wasn't selling Husky tools and lights from Lithonia Lighting. Responded John Menard: "I don't think taking a big swipe at your competition is the proper thing to do. It seems a bit ungentlemanly. There's plenty of room for both of us to prosper as we pursue different courses, and we'd both be well advised to quit taking pot shots at each other." A Home Depot spokesman noted the catalog was in response to Menard ads. In February 1998, however, Menard filed a complaint with the National Advertising Division of the Council of Better Business Bureaus Inc., challenging Home Depot's claims. The council sided with Menard in September 1998, and Home Depot agreed to change its advertising policies.

Home Depot's success caused changes—some good and some bad. There have been dramatic changes in how consumers shop for hardware goods, a decreasing number of mom-and-pop hardware stores, and a rethinking of where a neighborhood ends and a business district with warehouse-sized retail stores begins. To be sure, these are the same complaints heard against other big retailers like Wal-Mart as they have tried to enter new towns and cities with warehouse-sized stores. Marcus disputes the assertion. "The mom-and-pop hardware stores run by the proprietor are going to be there forever," says the Home Depot cofounder. "They are basically convenience stores. What we've tried to do is take a 100,000-square-foot store and create the same type of ambiance." Yet now Home Depot is threatening the existence of those hardware stores with plans to test a smaller, similar store in the northeast in 1999. Marcus and Blank want to be all things to all people, and they aren't afraid of rolling over others to get there.

But Home Depot has also helped revitalize downtrodden urban districts, like downtown Tulsa or Queens, by opening stores where no one else would go. And there's no arguing that Home Depot has been at the forefront of a home improvement boom. It expanded into markets where its products had never been sold before, giving thousands of do-it-yourselfers the ability to do more home repairs than they had ever done before.

In the 1990s, though, Home Depot's rapid growth met increasing resistance in many markets from an unlikely source—the customers it was trying to serve. As Marcus and Blank reached out to shoppers, some resisted the home improvement retailer in ways they never imagined. None of those fights was more hotly contested than one that broke out in North Carolina in 1993. It would be a battle where Home Depot received a black eye from the community.

Greensboro is in the middle of North Carolina's tobacco country—and an hour's drive down Interstate 40 from Lowe's headquarters in North Wilkesboro. Its early settlers were Quakers of Welsh and English descent and Germans who came from the northern colonies before the Revolutionary War. In 1781, the area was the site of a pivotal battle when General Nathanael Greene made a stand against the British troops of General Cornwallis. The Americans lost the Battle of Guilford Courthouse. But the encounter weakened the British troops, who later surrendered at Yorktown. By the 1990s, Greensboro had a population of nearly 200,000 residents and the state's only Ferrari dealership, where basketball demigod Michael Jordan once bought a sleek sportscar.

The area, however, had not seen its worst battle until Home Depot came to town. Hechinger was already operating a Home Quarters store in Greensboro when Lowe's announced in January 1993 it would build a warehouse-sized store there. Less than a month later, Home Depot said it would add a store next to the Lowe's.

Then the battle began. Home Depot applied to the Guilford County planning board for a 163,000-square-foot store site in northwest Greensboro. There was one problem: The location was close to a quiet, upscale neighborhood whose residents didn't want a Home Depot adding noisy traffic to the area. The people fought back with a competitiveness typically displayed by Home Depot. This fight was different from others Marcus and Blank had experienced in other regions where homeowners didn't want a store in their backyard. These neighbors lived in $200,000-plus homes and drove BMW and Lexus automobiles. These were customers Marcus and Blank wanted to attract.

The neighbors collected more than 800 signatures on a petition opposing the store. They attended planning board meetings and objected vociferously. Home Depot's "presence would contribute negatively to an already congested and overdeveloped area," complained James Nearing, who lived down the street from the store site.

They wrote letters to the local newspaper, the *Greensboro News & Record*. One tugged at the heartstrings. "My name is

Jessica Morton and I live in The Oaks of Brassfield," started one published July 28, 1993. "I am 9 years old, and I have lived here for two years. I do not like the idea of making a Home Depot so close to where I live. I have moved several times, and I love my neighborhood. I feel that my friends and I should have a place to play and ride our bikes. Because we do not have any sidewalks, I feel that it is already fairly dangerous now. I have just met a friend who lives in Normandy Hills, and the only way I can get to her house is on Brassfield Road." The Home Depot was scheduled to be built at the intersection of Battleground and Brassfield avenues, meaning that Jessica would encounter more traffic on the way to her friend's house after the store opened.

Marcus and Blank watched the battle unfold. Marcus visited Greensboro in the summer of 1993 and was spotted walking through the Lowe's store. An observant Lowe's manager got on the public address system and welcomed the Home Depot chairman to Lowe's "store of the future." A Home Depot spokesman later quipped that Marcus "was looking to buy something...but they were out of stock." The response was pure Home Depot propaganda. Still, Lowe's watched Marcus and Blank carefully.

At the Home Depot store site, in fact, there was a 54-acre buffer between the store and the houses of the most vocal opponents. The store was slated to face apartments and an existing shopping center—not the houses. The four families whose houses were near the site had their properties purchased by the developer at double the tax value. Marcus and Blank made sure the store posed no problems—from their point of view. The problem was the developer originally promised to build a retirement home, not a retail store. When he teamed up with Home Depot, the residents felt as though the developer had lied to them. Still, in late August, the Guilford Board of Commissioners approved the rezoning that paved the way for the store in an 8-to-2 vote.

Less than two months later, however, the nearby residents struck yet again. They sued the Guilford commissioners and the company, Weaver Investment Co., developing the property, claiming the rezoning was "arbitrary and capricious" and not based on "rational consideration" of the interests of the homeowners. Home Depot fought back. First, its attorney asked for and received "zoning vested rights" from the Guilford planning board, protecting the retailer from the lawsuit. And Home Depot and the developer threatened to seek damages from the homeowners that might have totaled thousands of dollars under the state's unfair trade laws unless the neighbors backed down. The Brassfield residents, out of money and scared, settled the lawsuit. Home Depot opened a store on the disputed site in November 1994. But the residents still remember what happened and how hard Home Depot fought. Home Depot "will be part of their own downfall by the way they do business," argued David Massey, a family doctor who lives near the store. He vowed never to shop there. "I am going to shop at Lowe's," he said. Despite his assertion, the Home Depot store prospered.

Home Depot isn't alone as a retailer battling neighborhoods and people who live near its proposed stores. In 1994, more than 40 organized groups fought Wal-Mart stores in the Northeast, Midwest, and the West Coast. Al Norman of Greenfield, Massachusetts, gained national attention a year earlier when he successfully stopped Wal-Mart from opening a store in his hometown. Since then, Norman—dubbed the "guru of the anti-Wal-Mart movement" by 60 Minutes—created a monthly Sprawl-Busters Alert newsletter chronicling such fights.

He had a willing audience. People feared that a Wal-Mart near their homes would destroy property values, kill smaller, hometown retailers in the area—some operated by friends or family acquaintances—and increase traffic to dangerous levels. Norman expanded his review to Home Depot, creating a 16-page Home Towns vs. Home Depot pamphlet that detailed battles between citizens' groups and the retailer across the country. He also noted the similarities between Home Depot and Wal-Mart. Founders like Sam Walton or Marcus and Blank are given reverential status among their employees and on Wall Street. There's a customer service focus; Wal-Mart employees are taught that if they come within 10 feet of a customer, they're supposed to say hello. And both have ambitious expansion strategies calling for locating stores as close as 7 miles apart.

Unlike the Wal-Mart opposition, however, where opponents

invoked historical preservation laws and drafted anticompany referendums, Home Depot protesters were loosely organized in the past. That's changing. Norman's newsletter notes proposed Home Depots have been rejected or withdrawn due to community opposition in Yarmouth, Massachusetts, Greenbush, New York, Manalapan, New Jersey, Santa Rosa, California, and North Olmsted, Ohio.

Other fights have not been as brutal as they were in Greensboro. In Home Depot's backyard, the Atlanta suburb of Cobb County, a group called "People Looking After Neighborhoods," or P.L.A.N., convinced Home Depot to move to another street corner away from a neighborhood. Then, the group talked Home Depot into using a duller shade of orange and brick rather than its usual stucco for the store's exterior.

In other areas, Home Depot backed down. On Cape Cod, where Wal-Mart, Sam's Club, and Costco stores had been rejected in the past, Home Depot pulled out of South Yarmouth in March 1997 after it couldn't come to terms on the purchase of a particular site it wanted. A year earlier Home Depot had conducted an extensive advertising and public relations campaign designed to sway local residents to their side. In April 1996, Yarmouth residents voted to give Home Depot a hearing. But after Home Depot backed off from purchasing the site and began looking for another nearby, it paid the state a $10,000 fine for failing to report in a timely fashion how much it had spent in campaigning before the election. The fine was seen by some former Home Depot managers as a sign that the company was no longer conscientious about its expansion.

Marcus, for one, denied that perception and shrugged off the battles as a necessary part of expansion. "I think what has happened is that we're opening more stores," he said. "That's why you're hearing more of it. The amount of restraint against these openings is about what it was years ago. It's just that we're opening more stores. When we were opening 10 stores, you heard about it in 1 store out of 10. Now when we're opening 130 stores, and you hear about it in 5 or 10, then you'd say, 'Well, my God, this is quite awful.'" Marcus said he's been fighting such opposition since Home Depot's early days. "I remember when we were opening in California, and it must have been our 12th store," said Marcus. "We went through just terrible things in Los Angeles, just horrible—about as bad as what we're going through now. It hasn't changed."

Marcus's assessment is accurate. Community activists are more organized against Home Depot today than they were a decade ago. Another change was the identity of some of the backers of the opposition. In some cases, residents have had the support of the most hardened Home Depot opponents—its competitors. In 1995, Home Depot went to court against one, Rickel Home Centers, to stop Rickel from backing a "citizen's group" opposing expansion in New Jersey. The case proved to be one of the most bitter instances of opposition to Home Depot.

In 1946, brothers Al, Mort, and Robert Rickel started a heating contracting business called "Rickel Bros." in Newark—ironically, where Marcus was born and raised. Shortly after the Rickels opened for business, young Bernie Marcus graduated from a local high school. Seven years later, the brothers opened a store on Route 22 in nearby Union. The company grew, and in 1969 it changed its name from Rickel Supermarts to Rickel Home Centers. That same year, the company merged with the Pathmark supermarket chain. Like Handy Dan on the West Coast and dozens of other regional home center retailers, Rickel—on the East Coast—developed the do-it-yourself business in the 1970s. By 1975, it had more than $80 million in sales and a niche as the dominant home improvement retailer in the Delaware Valley. And for most of the first decade of Home Depot's existence and expansion, Rickel was insulated from the growing competitor. Home Depot stayed south of the Mason-Dixon Line.

That changed in 1989. Home Depot opened a 100,000-square-foot store in East Hanover, New Jersey. A year later, Marcus and Blank added 3 more locations in the state—one each in Lakewood, Paramus, and Parlin. Employees at the new New Jersey stores wrote a song used to serenade Marcus and Blank. Part of it was, "When we come to town they say, all the others run away. Channel they ain't got no class; Rickel's we'll just kick their ass." Within three years, Home Depot had 12 stores in the state, including 10 in the northern half where Rickel once dominated.

Rickel was feeling the heat—and losing customers. In 1994, in a bid to cut its costs, Rickel was sold to a New York investment group and merged with another home center retailer, Channel Home Centers. Rickel also looked at other ways of reversing its fortunes. Those moves would lead it into Home Depot's buzzsaw. In 1993, Home Depot applied to local government agencies to build stores in two more New Jersey towns—Pequannock and Bloomfield. As in North Carolina, the new stores received angry criticism from a citizens' group, which called itself "Concerned Citizens for Community Preservation." Marcus and Blank once again moved Home Depot into an adversarial situation.

In Pequannock, Home Depot proposed building its store near the intersection of State Road 23 and Jackson Avenue—near a local park visited by children. The group posted fliers and signs discussing Home Depot's alleged "legacy"—basically, a Home Depot store brought in crime and traffic to an area. "Our kids will be crossing through this deathtrap!" said one of the fliers. A local attorney involved in the group, Frederic Azrak, lined up experts to testify at planning board meetings. At one, Azrak stood up on a chair and rolled out a printout of crimes at a nearby Home Depot. The protest defeated the application.

Undaunted but wary, Home Depot moved to Bloomfield where the retailer was seen as a key in the town's efforts to redevelop a location once owned by the Schering-Plough Corp., a huge pharmaceutical company, near the Garden State Parkway. When Schering left Bloomfield in 1993, it gave the property to the town. A developer bought the land and talked to Home Depot about building a store there.

Quickly, another citizens' group complained. It too was headed by Azrak—even though the attorney was not well known in Bloomfield. As in Pequannock, citizens circulated fliers around town claiming Home Depot attracted car thieves and other criminals. The fliers claimed a Home Depot in nearby Clifton accounted for a high percentage of the crimes, including car thefts, in that town. (The numbers had been grossly inflated, and the Clifton police disputed them. They noted Azrak obtained a crime report for a much wider area than that just around the Home Depot.) Some stores in the town put "No Home Depot" signs in their front windows. Others joined the community group.

Azrak went a step further this time, filing a lawsuit for the citizens' group in late 1994 claiming zoning violations by Home Depot and Bloomfield. However, local officials realized Azrak's main client was Rickel, which had a store in town. And they were angry. "I was deceived," said Bruno Marino, chairman of Bloomfield's planning board. "The way Mr. Azrak was going on wasn't fair to the public." Added Betty Cass-Schmidt, Pequannock's mayor at the time of Home Depot's application: "You should know, in any type of hearing, who the real opposition is. When you use [other people's] names instead of your own, you are intentionally misrepresenting who is concerned and why they're concerned."

Home Depot's attorneys also discovered who had funded Azrak's efforts and the citizens' groups. Azrak, they deduced, had been hired by Randal Langone, Rickel's store manager in Bloomfield, to stop the new store. In July 1995, Home Depot filed a lawsuit in Essex County Superior Court in Newark, charging Rickel with defaming and disparaging Home Depot's name and reputation and with unfair competition practices. Azrak wasn't named as a defendant, but the complaint alleged a Rickel store manager authorized him to "take whatever steps were needed" to stop Home Depot.

Once the Rickel lawsuit was filed, Home Depot reacted with the same anger displayed against the retailer by the so-called citizens' groups. "Home Depot cannot allow its good name and reputation, built up through the hard work of its employees and by delivering on its promises to its customers, to be dragged through the mud in this way," said Larry Mercer, then northeast division president. Mercer said Home Depot was prepared to compete fairly against Rickel any day. "But we will not stand by idly under these circumstances, when lies and distortions are circulated about us," he added.

In turned out Rickel's moves to thwart Home Depot in Pequannock and Bloomfield were the last gasp for a dying company. Agent Orange had already delivered its killing blow. By January 1996, Rickel filed for Chapter 11 bankruptcy protection from its creditors. The chain closed 43 stores and hired a new chief executive, Joseph Nusim, who tried to distance Rickel, with smaller stores between 40,000 and 50,000 square feet, from its orange-colored competitor. "In the past, the company thought of itself as a competitor of Home Depot," noted Nusim. No longer, he added. "Rickel's vision is very simple. Rickel is the neighborhood paint-it, fix-it, repair-it store. We serve the customer that does not want to do a major project. Frankly, if you're going to put a room on your home,...you should go to Home Depot."

Nusim's comment in March 1997 was an astonishing admission that Home Depot had won the war. Despite a heavy advertising blitz using comedian Don Rickles as the "Weekend Warrior," expanded gardening and kitchen departments and open houses with workshops and raffles, Rickel was finished. Within seven months, the fight ended. Rickel shuttered its remaining 49 stores. Although the company was crippled by inept management for the previous decade and a leveraged buyout of its parent company in the 1980s, Home Depot contributed to its problems, kicking it when it was down.

To Marcus and Blank, the end of the battle meant that many of Rickel's customers were soon shopping at their nearby Home Depot. Marcus saw such competitors' closing their stores as verification that Home Depot was giving the customer service, product selection, and low prices that others weren't. "When you look at a graveyard full of the Grossmans and the Ernsts and the Rickels and all of those folks out there, the consumer wasn't very impressed with what they had," said Marcus. "And they blame the Home Depot for putting them out of business. They can't blame the Home Depot. It's not our fault. It's really the consumers who did it. They just didn't want to shop there anymore. They chose to shop at our store because they recognized the values and they recognized all the good things that they got out of it." Marcus's assessment focused on Home

Depot's strengths versus its competitors' weaknesses, but it did have some merit.

This wasn't the first time a Home Depot competitor had gotten involved in community groups fighting Agent Orange's expansion. Nor would it be the last. Two northern California towns, Santa Rosa and Napa, saw such retailers lead the opposition to Home Depot stores in 1997. In Napa, the Coalition for Balance, which included Central Valley Builders Supply and North Bay Plywood, noted county sales figures indicated the area's entire farm and home improvement market totaled $60 million. It was estimated a Home Depot store in the area could garner $54 million of those sales, virtually wiping out all of the local businesses if the market didn't grow after Home Depot opened.

In the Rickel's case, Home Depot had won, just as it had virtually everywhere else, but its reputation had been sullied. Rickel's tactics showed just how far some competitors would go to stop its expansion. With success, realized Marcus and Blank, come those wanting to knock you off your pedestal. Marcus and Blank were retaliating with aggressive moves. At times that meant a nasty—and often fierce—battle.

Ironically, at the same time the battles in North Carolina and New Jersey were beginning, Marcus and Blank were praised in other markets for helping revitalize downtrodden regions.

On the cover of Home Depot's 1993 annual report, there's the slogan, "Good things happen when Home Depot comes to town." Obviously, many competitors and some residents in the towns and cities where Home Depot has expanded disagreed. There is evidence, however, that lends credence to that statement.

In 1993, Home Depot entered the Oklahoma market with two stores in Oklahoma City. Expansion in the state was seen by Marcus and Blank as a logical extension of its growing dominance in Texas and Louisiana. They wanted to add more stores in Oklahoma, but they were having trouble finding sites. One location that interested them was in downtown Tulsa.

The Warehouse Market building had been a landmark in

Tulsa since 1929. Built next to the railroad, the building served in its early years as a center of commerce for farmers who supplied food to a city once known as the "oil capital of the world." But the popularity and prosperity of the farmers' market were short-lived due to the Depression. It later housed Club Lido, where famous musicians like Cab Calloway and Duke Ellington performed. The building became the Warehouse Market in 1938 and operated as a grocery store for the next 40 years before closing in 1978. Before Home Depot became interested in the site 15 years later, it had been used off and on and had fallen into disrepair.

The simple thing to do would be to tear it down and build a new Home Depot. There was one problem: The eastern Oklahoma chapter of the American Institute of Architects included the building on its list of endangered landmarks—buildings considered "vacant, vulnerable and irreplaceable." The building features a brilliant terra cotta facade with a center tower. Two large medallions on a blue background flank the entrance to the building. One of the medallions depicts a goddess holding a sheaf of wheat and cornucopia and the other shows a god wearing a winged helmet with an oil derrick in one hand and a train engine in the other. The work is symbolic of the building's original purpose, and it was well known in Tulsa. Tearing it down would have brought the wrath of an entire city upon Home Depot, and it would have crippled Marcus and Blank's efforts to enter into what they believed was a lucrative market.

They arrived at a compromise. Home Depot's real estate manager, Stephen Lam, struck a deal with city officials. The retailer would spend more than $1 million to preserve the facade. Home Depot would build a store about 500 feet behind the facade. It was a deal even the architects lauded. "We knew that the reuse of the attached building was impractical and it should be demolished," said Elaine Bergman, executive director of the architect's association in eastern Oklahoma. She called the agreement "an impressive demonstration of corporate developers' and preservationists' working together. This is the most significant improvement, both visually and economically, to downtown Tulsa's eastern gateway in contemporary history."

Home Depot's store in downtown Tulsa did more than save a landmark. It was considered the first coup for local authorities in rebuilding a downtown region in disrepair. Downtown Tulsa Unlimited president Jim Norton said the store helped stabilize the area and spur further development. "Home Depot," said Tulsa Mayor Susan Savage, "has demonstrated that its interest in Tulsa extends beyond our strong business climate."

There have been other areas where Home Depot's expansion has been considered a boon for the local folks. In Westchester County, the affluent suburb north of New York City, Home Depot's first store there was seen as the hope that one of its communities was on the rebound.

The retail world can be a cruel place for small towns like New Rochelle, New York, which have small malls anchored by one or two department stores. In many cases, those stores are among the biggest employers in the area, and residents depend on the stores for clothes, furniture, and other items. The stores, quite simply, are a symbol of community stature. But those stores are operated by huge companies pushed by Wall Street to report better earnings and sales numbers each quarter. When the stores close as the parent cuts costs and concentrates on better-performing stores, often in big metropolitan cities, the town suffers. Home Depot is no different, yet Marcus and Blank have for the most part avoided closing stores in markets that rely so heavily economically on Home Depot.

That's what happened in New Rochelle when the Macy's that anchored the New Rochelle Mall closed in 1992. The city suddenly found itself without its major shopping attraction. The mall couldn't attract a new tenant for the Macy's location and itself closed in 1995.

The Macy's pullout was the first of several crushing blows to the community. In 1993, New Rochelle was in the running to become the new world headquarters for UNICEF, the children's relief agency. The group remained in Manhattan. Then real estate mogul Donald Trump proposed developing an area of New Rochelle into a millionaire's retreat, full of mansions and luxury town homes. That fell by the wayside when Trump discovered toxic waste.

Into that void came Price Club, a discount retailer that opened a 103,000-square-foot store downtown on Palmer Avenue in 1994. Then, two years later, Home Depot opened a 118,000-square-foot location on Weyman Avenue. The town's movers and shakers gushed over their good fortune after years of disappointment. "These two stores will bring customers to New Rochelle from a wide geographic area," said the town's mayor, Timothy Idoni. "That's the way it used to be when the New Rochelle Mall was in business. Now people will have a reason to visit us again." Indeed, after The Home Depot opened, a developer bought the New Rochelle Mall and renovated it, adding a multiscreen theater. Local leaders credited that move to Home Depot's entry into town.

To be sure, Home Depot's expansion and its effect on neighborhoods and towns have been controversial. Marcus and Blank have never denied that. And while the company's response in some markets has been to use whatever means possible to protect its position and ensure its expansion, even to the point of appearing to be the big bully intent on taking away milk money from the other kids, it does have a soft spot and realizes that in many instances its store will help a community. The Tulsa example and others like New Rochelle have shown that.

There have been, of course, many other ways Marcus and Blank have helped communities. Many have been behind-the-scenes actions shoppers didn't know about, but that show Marcus and Blank have not forgotten the lessons they learned from their experiences with Sandy Sigoloff. One of those instances occurred not far away from the Tulsa store where Home Depot saved the facade of the old farmers' market. When a terrorist bombed the federal building in Oklahoma City in April 1995, Home Depot employees—taught to act in the best interests of their customers by Marcus and Blank—reacted in a way that made the cofounders proud.

Management Lessons

When Home Depot has been opposed by community groups and competitors, it has addressed the concerns but continued with its expansion plans. Every business, at one point or another, will be faced by someone who doesn't want it to grow. How that business reacts to the situation will impact its future growth rate.

1. Some customers will always resent your expansion plans, and Home Depot knows that. When customers and consumer groups have attacked Home Depot, the company has been firm to stand its ground without hurting its long-term growth plans.

2. Home Depot has been aware and respectful of those that opposed its growth because it realized that some of those people may one day be shoppers.

3. Don't be afraid to fight back for what you feel is right. Home Depot vigorously fought competitors who have tried to stymie its growth using controversial tactics, but in the end its best defense has been the customer service that its stores provided.

4. Home Depot doesn't let competitors get in the way of its goals, preferring to concentrate on its plans. While the retailer watches its competitors, it is more interested in making sure its strategy goes off as expected.

5. Look to expand in markets that need your company. Home Depot has found sites for some of its new stores in areas that desperately wanted an infusion and welcome the retailer with open arms.

GETTING INVOLVED

The thing that strikes me specifically about lots of folks [is] how little they are willing to share with others. And one of the things we have learned is to give back to the community.

—BERNIE MARCUS

It was the most brutal act of terrorism ever perpetrated in the United States.

At 9:02 A.M. on April 19, 1995, a bomb inside a rented truck parked outside the Alfred P. Murrah Federal Building in Oklahoma City exploded. The facade of the building crumbled down, burying scores of people. A dozen children being cared for in a second-floor day-care center were among the first confirmed dead. Eventually, 168 bodies, including those of 19 children, were uncovered in the rubble. Survivors were badly hurt.

The scene was captured on live telecasts carried for hours on CNN and the other networks. Behind the scenes, Home Depot did its best to help the victims and the rescue workers. Marcus heard about the bombing that morning and called the manager of one of the two Home Depots in Oklahoma City. He wanted to know whether any company employees or family members were involved. None were.

The store manager wasn't in. So Marcus called the manager of the other Home Depot. He wasn't in either. Marcus got angry. "If they come in, tell them to call me," Marcus barked into the phone, then hung up.

Thirty minutes later, Marcus got a call from a mobile telephone. It was the two Oklahoma City store managers. As soon as they had heard about the bombing, they had loaded trucks with wheelbarrows, shovels, lanterns, tarpaulins, plywood, and other items needed at the bomb site. And they gave those supplies to the rescue workers. "Everybody has pulled together," said Don Shaw, an assistant manager at one of the Home Depots. A week after the bombing, President Clinton named Team Depot, the company's employee volunteer program, in a ceremony honoring volunteers that helped during the bombing.

That Home Depot workers reacted so quickly and without any prodding was reward enough for Marcus and Blank. The duo has encouraged employees for nearly two decades to make decisions quickly, without checking with a higher-up in Atlanta. "No one ever told them to do it," says Marcus. "If they had had to go to corporate, we'd have been in deep trouble."

That's the way Marcus and Blank want it, and such community-minded moves set Home Depot apart from other companies. "When I talk to other CEOs, they look at me in amazement when I tell them about the things our employees do, about the way we are involved in our communities," adds Marcus. "They are always asking me, 'How do you do that?' The answer is, it's second nature—we live our lives that way. We don't know any other way of doing things."

That's Home Depot's community involvement in action. Instead of relying on corporate giving from headquarters, Home Depot's 700-plus stores decide what they want to give and when they want to give it. When tornadoes ripped through the Florida town of Kissimmee in February 1998, a local Home Depot set up a makeshift lumberyard with its rivals Lowe's and Scotty's near a devastated subdivision. It offered no-interest credit for six months to storm victims, and employees, to help make repairs. "We have tried to teach our people all over the United States to be involved with their communities—that it's not just important for us to write a check," says Marcus. "Anyone can sit and write a check. What happens here is something different. Every store is involved in something in its location."

A good example of Home Depot's involvement is the volunteer work of two employees—Max Gulloti and John Leahy—at Home Depot's store in Nashua, New Hampshire. When they learned in 1992 that a local boy rehabilitating an injured hip couldn't get into his pool to exercise, they spent six days of their own time extending a deck so that it wrapped around the hexagon-shaped pool. After that, the boy was able to walk to the pool's edge and lower himself in. "I wish we could have done more to help," said Gullotti, then the store's manager of building materials. "I felt bad for the kid. I don't know if he'll walk straight or play sports."

Gulloti's not alone. Suzanne Apple, Home Depot's director of community affairs, estimates 30 percent, or nearly 50,000, of the company's 150,000 employees, are involved in community service. That level of commitment is much higher than at other retailers. "It's how we develop our leaders," said Apple, noting that time spent on charitable activities builds morale and team spirit. In 1997, more than 1,300 Home Depot employees got involved in a single charity event. They ran and walked the 3.5-mile course of the Promina Corporate Challenge in downtown Atlanta. No other employer had anywhere near as many workers participating in the event as Home Depot.

To be sure, Home Depot has a huge community activist program at its home office. In the past six years, it has contributed money to more than 300 nonprofit organizations, primarily those focusing on at-risk youths, affordable housing, and the environment. In 1998, the company gave away more than $13 million in grants. In 1999, that figure is expected to be 25 percent higher—nearly $17 million. But more than 50 percent of the money is given to district managers who then attack their philanthropic mission with a passion normally seen in only the most hard-core activists. The result is a community involvement unsurpassed in the retail world.

Home Depot employees—including executives such as Blank—regularly get together to build houses for organizations such as Habitat for Humanity. Through the Christmas in April program, orange aprons help repair homes for the elderly, disabled, and the poor. They build playgrounds in Chicago and teach Girl Scouts in Florida how to make home repairs. Through the national YouthBuild USA program, Home Depot workers teach disadvantaged young people how to build houses while they complete their high school education. And when they're done with school, Home Depot looks to those young men and women to fill jobs at its stores. Home Depot gives away millions in home improvement products to the needy through former President Jimmy Carter's The Atlanta Project. It has kicked environmentally unfriendly products out of its stores, and it has helped some vendors develop new products that are environmentally safe.

Marcus and Blank get involved in causes they feel are important. Marcus, for example, founded a think-tank in Israel promoting democracy and encourages do-it-yourself manufacturers from that country to be more competitive in the global marketplace. Blank has helped the North Carolina Outward Bound school raise money and tutored its students.

Home Depot gets credit for its activism. It has been honored by the Christmas in April USA program with the Community Builder Award. Team Depot earned the 1995 President's National Community Service Award, beating out 3,000 other nominees from across the nation. The company was a winner of the Business Ethics Award by the magazine of the same name for superior corporate involvement. In 1996, Home Depot and wood supplier Collins Pine received the Presidential Award for Sustainable Development at a special White House ceremony.

But winning awards isn't important. "Our philosophy is that we don't need to seek or get credit for all the things we do," says Marcus. "We do it because it's the right thing to do. My experience is that in the end you do get credit within the community— our people talk about it, people hear about it, but we don't necessarily have to go out and get credit in the press." Marcus is overenthusiastic. Studies show that two-thirds of shoppers would switch to retailers associated with good causes. Marcus and Blank are aware of such figures, and they realize philanthropy builds Home Depot's sales.

It's a balancing act, because Marcus and Blank—whose activist attitudes may be a by-product from their Handy Dan firing—see getting involved as a way to give back to the shoppers that made them successful. "Back in 1978, Bernie and I founded the Home Depot with a special vision—to create a company that would keep alive the values that were important to us," says Blank. "Values like respect among all people, providing excellent customer service, and giving back to our communities and society. We serve our customers well because they bring in sales. Because we do the right thing for our customers, they keep coming back."

Home Depot's community involvement is heartfelt—it is not just something Marcus and Blank do to win over customers and boost sales. "It's very hard to go back to the beginning and regroup, to redesign the culture, the morality, the ethics," says Marcus. "We have a very strong advantage over other companies, because we started that way. It's been part of Home Depot since the beginning. If we decided now…that we wanted to put our beliefs into the company, I could spend the rest of my life doing that and we might never get to where we are today. The problem is, it won't work if you don't have it in your heart. You can't fake morality. People watch the titular heads of companies, how they live their lives, and they know they are being sold a bill of goods. If you are a selfish son-of-a-bitch, well that usually comes across fairly well. And it comes across no matter how many memos you send out telling people that you want to change the culture, that you care for your fellow man, that you're making a donation to the United Way."

Such activism, notes Blank, is more important to society than selling hammers and power tools and sinks. But Home Depot's community involvement can't simply be copied by other companies wanting to get involved. "There is no magic formula for being socially responsible," he says. "What works for us may not work for everyone. Yet, we receive lots of calls and letters asking how we do it at Home Depot. They ask, 'Where is the yellow brick road to greater social responsibility?' Who has the directions, and what is the project plan? How do we take steps A through Z to become more socially responsible?"

It's not that easy, adds Blank. "You hold the answer," he says. "But the paradox is this—you must reach out beyond yourself to find it. That is because by giving back to society, each of us confronts our own humanity. Only then can we embrace it, nurture it, act on it, and give it meaning. And what gives our humanity meaning is not the amount of our wealth, our influence, or our talents. What gives it meaning is how we use our wealth and our influence and our talents to build a better tomorrow for our fellow human beings."

That means more than donating money. Take the Oklahoma City bombing. Store managers weren't told to get involved. They just did. "These are our customers, the people that have made us successful," says Marcus. "We owe something to them. So if a tornado hits, an earthquake hits, a hurricane hits, all of our people know that they mobilize and they do what's right."

It's not easy to decide how to get involved and when. A Home Depot district manager sees as many as 500 proposals a month from organizations seeking support. These groups know if Home Depot will help them, they'll get 110 percent support.

The first Earth Day to raise national awareness of environmental issues occurred in the spring of 1970—nearly a decade before Home Depot opened its doors. When the twentieth anniversary of Earth Day rolled around, Home Depot had $2.7 billion in sales and more than $100 million in profits. By that time, some executives, particularly Inglis, were aware that some sales came from environmentally harmful products and could embarrass Home Depot in a culture beginning to pay more attention to how its actions affected the world in which it lived.

Inglis decided that Home Depot should help improve the environment. Soon after the 1990 Earth Day, the company hired Mark Eisen to be its first manager of environmental marketing. "We all live on this planet Earth, and we all have a responsibility," said Blank shortly after Eisen was hired. "He's going to help us get more focused in this area."

Eisen had worked in accounting firm Coopers & Lybrand's retail practice. But he'd lived across the street from a recycling center and had become interested in environmental issues. He had asked the center's owners if they might be interested in working with a retailer. They were. Eisen kept that idea in the back of his mind.

Eisen realized that Home Depot was at a critical point. "Retailers were tiptoeing around what to do about the environment in 1990," said Eisen. "I came in and said that, more than other types of products, home center merchandise is more fundamentally tied to the environment, and Home Depot had a great opportunity that cried out for leadership." Eisen noted that the home, second only to people themselves, has the biggest environmental impact on the world. "When you think of the home, you think of all the materials used to build it and the resources you use to maintain, heat, and cool it."

Eisen first got Home Depot to use recycled materials for store and office supplies, in advertising and signs, and for shopping bags. He established an evaluation process to validate environmental claims made by Home Depot's vendors. And he began working on Home Depot's product mix to make it more environmentally friendly. In 1992, the company stopped selling lead plumbing solder. Eisen also worked with a company called Kleanstrip to develop a product called Klean-Strip Green—an environmentally friendly paintbrush cleaner. "The fundamental most powerful way a retailer can affect the environment is to look at its merchandise," noted Eisen.

Home Depot became the first home center retailer to sell independently certified wood that wasn't stripped out of forests without regard to the environment. One of the first Home Depot products certified—by an outside third-party organization—as being environmentally friendly was wood from the Collins Pine Co. of Portland, Oregon. A company called Scientific Certification Systems conducted an exhaustive study of a 94,000-acre forest run by Collins in northern California. They examined the health of the surrounding ecosystem, the socioeconomic benefits to the community, and the "sustainability" of the forest. "*Sustainability* means using resources today without compromising the ability to provide those resources to future generations," explained Eisen. "We won't run out of resources and harm ourselves or the earth if we help consumers use products wisely. That's a simple message every Home Depot associate can take into their store each day."

Inglis knew that because Home Depot had become the largest home center retailer in the world, it had to be a leader in promoting environmental issues. "The world is changing permanently, and you can lag behind, or you can get out in front and be proactive," Inglis told merchandisers at the 1993 National

Hardware Show. "Our customers expect Home Depot to be proactive and out in front. We think that in the long run green marketing is a business that will be profitable for us. But most important, it's the right thing to do." Still, Eisen had some convincing to do. When he was hired, Blank, Marcus, and others were skeptical that Home Depot needed to be involved in the environment. That would be a battle Eisen would fight and eventually win, and in the process he would garner support for many projects.

Eisen still wanted to merge a recycling center with a retailer. The first Recycling Depot opened on the parking lot of a Home Depot in Duluth, Georgia, in 1993. The recycling center paid do-it-yourselfers and contractors to bring in discarded items like aluminum gutters and copper wiring. The first Recyling Depot lost money, as a drop in aluminum and copper prices led to a decrease in recycling. But Home Depot rolled out the concept to a handful of stores. For some customers, the idea of walking in with an aluminum screen door and walking out with $5 to take into the store to buy a replacement was appealing.

Home Depot customers became more aware of the environment. In 1992, Eisen developed the Environmental Greenprint to help customers be more environmentally friendly with their homes. The pamphlet showed homeowners ways to cut energy waste and garbage. A dripping faucet, for example, can waste as much as 700 gallons of water a year. A ceiling fan can cut air-conditioning costs by 40 percent in the summer. And it explained the health issues caused by certain products. For example, when concerns arose in 1996 about the lead in plastic miniblinds, Home Depot directed its vinyl blind vendors to find an alternative. "This lead issue, in fact, shows how our proactive stance pays off," explained Eisen. "Home Depot voluntarily dropped lead plumbing solder in 1992 and reprinted posters and fact sheets on reducing lead hazards, and it supports numerous nonprofit groups involved in the lead issue." One of those was Consumer Action, an organization that supports the Lead and Poisoning Prevention Project, which helps protect children from lead poisoning.

Naturally, Home Depot supports environmental groups. In

1996, for example, it gave more than $360,000 to them, pushing its contributions to such organizations for the previous four years over the $1 million mark. The company gave money to Keep America Beautiful, Inc., among others, to help fund the Build America Beautiful program, which encourages home builders to prevent litter and reduce waste at construction sites. And it gave money to Global Green USA, a California organization that partners with Habitat for Humanity to educate professional builders, manufacturers, and utilities about creating healthier and more efficient houses.

For some, Home Depot's environmental stance isn't enough. In August 1997, the Rainforest Action Network protested outside a Home Depot in Williston, Vermont, over concerns that the stores sold wood from ancient forests—the equivalent of killing elephants for their ivory, according to the group. Activists claimed that destroying such forests changes the global climate because the trees store carbon dioxide that moderates the earth's climate. Earlier in the year, Home Depot agreed not to sell or buy old-growth redwood lumber. But the company still sold old-growth tropical woods like mahogany and teak.

Home Depot has a strong environmental commitment that none of its competitors, and arguably no other retailer, has displayed. Home Depot knows shoppers are also concerned about the environment. While Marcus and Blank may not have been as involved in Home Depot's environmental movement as they were in other projects, they provided the framework that enabled the company to make a difference in protecting the environment.

President Jimmy Carter returned from his four-year stint in Washington to his native Georgia in January 1981, just as Marcus and Blank were expanding Home Depot into Florida. Although the former peanut farmer had never met the two retailers, they had a lot in common. Carter had an interest in Middle East peace—as did Marcus. And he wanted to find a way to get corporations involved with helping the poor in inner cities. That topic interested Blank.

Carter and Blank, a fellow Democrat, became friends.

Blank once gave Carter and his wife Rosalynn an Outward Bound weekend. By 1991, the former president was raising money for his Atlanta Project, through which he aimed to improve living conditions for Atlanta's poor by creating partnerships between big companies and neighborhoods. One of the first people he went to was Blank. Home Depot's involvement in the Atlanta Project seemed a natural. Carter wanted to improve low-income housing. With Home Depot's cooperation, the project could teach poor people in Atlanta's inner-city neighborhoods how to make repairs and remodel their homes to make them more livable.

With Blank's backing, Home Depot became a sponsor, giving $1 million to the Atlanta Project. But more important, the company also got directly involved. Other corporations sponsoring the project helped a specific neighborhood. Home Depot sponsored projects in all 20 neighborhoods, helping residents make home or building improvements. Each cluster got a $5,000 account at its stores to buy equipment and products. (Home Depot would later also give $300,000 to help renovate some public housing projects.) "The Atlanta Project was an opportunity for partnership that we'd never had before," said Apple, Home Depot's director of community affairs. "It offered tangible ways to channel corporate involvement in the community. We liked the idea of an integrated, businesslike approach—dealing with problems holistically."

Home Depot provided the do-it-yourself products and ideas to help these neighborhoods rebuild. The Southside cluster, for example, took $1,500 of its Home Depot materials to help the Southside High School baseball team build a dugout for the field behind the school so varsity games could be played there. Another $500 in Home Depot supplies helped build a playground for the day-care center operated by the Urban Hope Family, Youth & Child Development Center. In the North Clayton cluster, Home Depot provided materials to refurbish the bathroom for a family with a severely disabled child.

Carter's Atlanta Project contrasted starkly with Home Depot's corporate world. In the world of the poverty stricken, do-it-yourself repairs was a start, but the repair work wouldn't solve all the problems. "You automatically had a land mine," said Apple. "Community development is a long, drawn-out process, and business doesn't understand that. Business works with a time frame. The problems of poverty have no end." That's why Home Depot let each community decide how it wanted to use its Home Depot supplies. "The people in the community have really helped define how they want to live and take control of their lives," said Blank. "They'll make it work because it's their solution."

Giving supplies to poor Atlanta neighborhoods wasn't the only way Home Depot reached out to help. Before the 1996 Olympics in Atlanta, Habitat for Humanity decided to build 100 homes for the needy in the area. Home Depot employees built eight of the homes. "We all have to put our shoulder to the wheel," said Blank one morning while he helped build one of the homes. "Sweating together is important. That's how communities are improved." Home Depot had been involved with Habitat for years. In June 1995, for example, 60 Home Depot employees joined President Carter and his wife to build 20 houses in the Watts area of south-central Los Angeles.

And with Marcus and Blank adding do-it-yourself repair and building expertise to Home Depot stores each day, it became natural to tap into that knowledge with the company's community activism.

In 1972, around the same time Marcus became Handy Dan's president, people in Midland, Texas, realized that a number of their neighbors, particularly low-income, elderly, and disabled people, could not afford to repair their homes. Roofs leaked. Wiring was defective. Steps were rotting. The volunteers worked together each April to rehabilitate the homes. The project spread across the country and garnered a name— Christmas in April USA. Five and a half million low-income homeowners were elderly, and the majority were women. More than one-third lived alone, and half spent 40 percent of their income on housing expenditures. In other words, most of the poor with a home couldn't afford to maintain it.

By 1988, the organization became a national workforce. A couple of years later, its affiliates in California contacted local

Home Depots and asked for supplies. Seeing the retailer's huge response with volunteers and free products, those Christmas in April volunteers told the national office in Washington, D.C. Home Depot became a national sponsor—the organization's first—of the Christmas in April program in 1992. In the next four years, Home Depot partnered with 60 Christmas in April organizations across the country and donated nearly $1.2 million. But they were giving more than free merchandise. Home Depot employees also made repairs. "They provide tools not found on store shelves: caring, skilled manpower, and leadership," said Patricia Riley Johnson, president of the national organization. In Mobile, Alabama, Home Depot employee Rick Hodges established a Christmas in April affiliate. "When I found out about [Christmas in April], I knew my carpentry skills and experience at The Home Depot could be helpful," said Hodges. More than 35 of his fellow employees repaired an elderly widow's home. They remodeled her bathroom and kitchen, and they painted and landscaped. "It's a lot of work, but incredibly rewarding," said Hodges.

It's not always easy for Home Depot to be involved with Christmas in April, noted Johnson. The time, usually in the spring, when her organization is busy repairing and remodeling homes is also the busiest time for Home Depots as customers turn their attention to repairs and gardening projects themselves. "What we do is contact the stores and say, 'How would you like to be involved?'" said Johnson. "'Would you like to adopt a house in the community? Would you like to deliver the supplies?' Home Depot is a definite leader in terms of the involvement." In 1996, Home Depot received that year's Christmas in April USA Community Builder Award.

In 1998, Home Depot upped its contributions to Christmas in April even further, funding 106 affiliates with $334,000 in credits for merchandise, said Johnson. In return, she added, her organization encourages its 150,000 volunteers and others to shop at Home Depot. "We have to be cognizant that Home Depot has to pay attention to its bottom line," she said. "So we say get out there and work with Home Depot and get in the stores purchasing additional supplies from Home Depot. These credits are in no way a reflection of the total spending in Home Depot stores. Typically, on an average, if you're given a $4,000 credit, they will spend an additional $6,000 to $8,000 in the Home Depot store."

That's just the tip of the two-by-four of Home Depot's involvement in community building projects. When another nonprofit national organization called KaBOOM!, which builds playgrounds in housing projects and rundown neighborhoods, asked Home Depot to help build two playgrounds in Washington, D.C., located in federally subsidized housing developments, the company jumped at the chance. (When the playgrounds were finished, the local store manager hired three unemployed men who had helped out with the projects after Home Depot volunteers saw how hard they worked.) They gave the neighborhoods—in typical Home Depot fashion—more than just a new playground. "When I think back to this summer when your Team Depot volunteers showed up in their orange shirts to help build the playground, I can't help but remember the magic they brought with them," wrote KaBOOM! cofounder Darell Hammond to Apple in October 1996. "I'm not sure the residents of the public housing project knew quite what to think when your army returned day after day until the project was finished. And what a surprise when the volunteers showed up later on with planters to spruce up the surrounding area."

Hammond said Home Depot taught his organization a valuable lesson: "Monetary contributions are wonderful, but the power of a volunteer work force is worth more than money can buy."

In 1997, Marcus and Blank extended their involvement with programs that help rebuild homes—and help disadvantaged teenagers—by giving a $1.5 million grant to YouthBuild USA. That, by far, is the largest gift the organization had ever received from a private company. Started in 1988 by Dorothy Stoneman, YouthBuild teaches teenagers to build and repair homes while finishing their high school education. Stoneman, who developed the program in East Harlem in 1978, wanted to give these kids a chance to make a living by giving them skills employers—including Home Depot—want. "It's a good type of pool for them to recruit from," said Stoneman, who oversees 108 YouthBuild programs. Many of these programs were being supported by their local Home Depots before the company gave the grant. Home Depot "definitely wants people referred to them," said Stoneman.

In Atlanta, YouthBuild students are taken to a Home Depot for scavenger hunts. That helps them learn about home improvement products. In St. Louis, Home Depot provided $10,000 worth of building materials to help YouthBuild construct a model home. And Home Depot is doing more than helping train these teenagers to be future contractors and do-it-yourself experts. It's also taking a leadership role in getting other corporations involved in YouthBuild.

Marcus and Blank remember from their childhoods what it was like to grow up in housing projects and with little money for luxury items. Now that they've become successful, they're making sure others have the same chance to make something of themselves.

In addition to the community involvement that Marcus and Blank have encouraged in the markets where Home Depot has stores, they've also become activists in a region of the world that isn't likely to see a bright orange Home Depot store any time soon.

Because of their Jewish upbringings, Marcus and Blank have a long-standing interest in Israel's political and social climate. One day in 1984, Blank had lunch with Kenneth Stein, a professor at Emory University in Atlanta who runs the university's Middle East research program. Later Blank contributed to the program. Stein and Blank became friends, talking frequently about the Middle East and other issues. Eventually, Blank introduced Stein to his business partner, Marcus. "I used to go up to their old headquarters about four or five times a year for lunch, over sandwiches, [to] talk about their feelings about the political situation in the Middle East and the peace process, what vexed them, how their thoughts and problems could be resolved," said Stein. Because of Blank's involvement with the Carter Center, where Stein was also active, Marcus and Blank had seen how well the idea of bringing people together to solve differences had worked. Soon, Marcus would come to Stein with an idea for resolving some of the differences in Israel.

In 1988, elections in Israel split its parliament between the rival Likud and Alignment parties. Prime Minister Yitzhak Shamir formed a coalition government that planned to make a law defining who was a real Jew. They planned to limit the definition of a Jew to a person who had been converted by an orthodox rabbi. That meant, explained Stein, if you were converted by a reformed rabbi, you couldn't be buried in a Jewish cemetery. "When Bernie found out that they wanted to become exclusive, he became very agitated," said Stein. "He thought something must be done to avoid that eventuality." Marcus went to Stein and asked for help. "He wanted to find some vehicle to help Israel, as he said, in spite of itself," remembered Stein. "He thought the country needed some sort of independent voice that would assess the political future."

Stein put Marcus in touch with an Israeli named Arye Z. Carmon, who was developing an organization to look at religious and societal issues in Israel. Marcus, who traveled to Israel often in the late 1980s and early 1990s, wanted to help Carmon. After years of planning and study, the Israel Democracy Institute, a nonpartisan activist think tank, opened its doors in Jerusalem in 1991 with Marcus as its international chairman. The goal: Respond to the need for a restructuring of the Israeli political system that would enable Israel to have strong leadership in the years to come, even as the country deals with waves of immigration, a polarized society, and a developing economy. Marcus started giving it money to achieve those means. In 1992, his foundation gave the institute $240,000. The next year, the institute received $494,766. At the same time, Marcus's foundation was also giving money to other Jewish causes. In 1992, it gave $15,000 to the Anti-Defamation League. In 1993, it gave $100,000 to the Holocaust Memorial Council and $63,000 to the Atlanta Jewish Federation. Marcus's contributions continue today.

The institute arose at a critical juncture in Israeli politics. Because of its youth, the Israeli legislature, called the Knesset, had not accumulated parliamentary experience or political ground rules. The institute helped develop those systems. In September 1993, the Palestine Liberation Organization and Israel signed a dramatic peace accord. There was, however, still turmoil in Israel. In February 1994, a massacre in the West Bank led to riots. "The animosity and hatred between the Palestinians and the Israelis is not going to go away overnight," said Marcus shortly after the peace agreement was signed. "This peace process is obviously very good news for all Israelis. But I view it with some trepidation. There's some risk here."

Marcus and former U.S. Secretary of State George Shultz, whom Marcus recruited to become the institute's honorary chairman, visited Israel months before the peace agreement was signed to discuss the Middle East situation with top Israelis. Marcus said it was then that he realized that Israel's biggest enemy isn't the PLO, but fundamentalist Moslems. "They were the biggest obstacle to peace, and still are," he said. "Islam is not a bad religion. It's the fundamentalist Muslims that are the problem. It feeds on poverty and the desperate plight of people. We need to develop an economy that's viable."

And Marcus was helping the Israeli economy too. In 1991, he lectured Israeli building products suppliers, saying that they needed to improve to compete in the world market. The suppliers responded, and soon Home Depot was buying supplies from some of them. In the past, "it was always a case where you had to buy [from them] because they were laying a guilt trip on you," said Marcus in 1994. "But today, we're finding manufacturers there that are very creative and tremendously responsive, and some of the products we're buying from Israel, we can't buy anywhere else."

One supplier was Keter Plastics, which sold plastic shelving and supply closets. Keter, which vied with companies like Rubbermaid, for Home Depot's business, showed Home Depot's merchant buyers that its five-tier shelf could hold more weight— 1,000 pounds versus 750 pounds for U.S. makers of similar products. Three years after Marcus's lecture, Home Depot had imported $40 million in goods from 11 Israeli firms. Marcus received the Israel Trade Award as a result.

Home Depot store in Tampa, Florida, is typical of the chain's locations: big orange block letters on the front with a sign underneath naming the specific market. In this case, "Florida's Do-It-Yourself Warehouse." Credit: *National Home Center News.*

Pat Farrah (*right*), who was one of the original store employees and who designed the first Home Depot stores, recently returned to the company to help it maintain its culture, talking with Home Depot's Kelly Mauldin (*left*). Credit: *National Home Center News.*

Jim Inglis, former executive vice president, instrumental in CrossRoads, Expo, and international expansion. Credit: *National Home Center News.*

Bernie Marcus (*left*) and Arthur Blank (*right*) in orange aprons, sitting on the boardroom table the day of the announcement that Marcus was stepping down as CEO, May 29, 1997. Credit: *Atlanta Journal-Constitution*/Laura Noel.

Arthur Blank (*left*) rappelling down the Candler Building for Outward Bound, one of the organizations he donates his time and money to. Credit: *Atlanta Journal-Constitution*/Marlene Karas.

Lynette Jennings, host of Home Depot's "House Smart," at a taping of one of the first shows. The television show is one way Home Depot has increased name recognition as it has expanded across the country. Credit: *Atlantic Journal-Constitution*/Phil Skinner.

Inside the CrossRoads store in Quincy, Illinois, part of Home Depot's test to see if its stores could work in rural markets. Credit: *Atlanta Journal-Constitution*/Marlene Karas.

Still, his main Israeli concern was ensuring peace in the country. In November 1995, the institute convened a round-table with Knesset members, journalists, rabbis, and academics one week after the assassination of Prime Minister Yitzhak Rabin to discuss the crisis in Israel's democracy. The meeting was so successful that another one was held the next month on the same topic. Since then, the institute has held other round-tables on topics such as the use of hidden microphones and a referendum on the peace process. In addition, the institute has conducted studies on topics such as how the Israeli media portrayed candidates and political parties in the 1996 elections. It was the first time such a study had ever been done in Israel. While Marcus had no direct involvement in those studies and projects, he participated in the roundtables and obviously lent his financial support to finding solutions to Israel's issues.

In early 1997, the institute brokered a major breakthrough. Knesset members Michael Eitan of the Likud Party and Yossi Beilin of the Labor Party developed what was called the "Beilin-Eitan Document." It outlined the areas of agreement between the two parties to be negotiated in the final talks with the Palestinians. Included in the document were important decisions such as the future of Jerusalem, the future of Jewish settlements, and the scope of Israeli withdrawal from certain areas. The document was significant because it was widely seen as the first consensus among Israelis on what was attainable.

Both the Likud and Labor representatives had approached the institute months before to provide meeting rooms in which to hammer out the document. "They said they wanted to hold these meetings but that they couldn't be held in the Knesset because they would be too visible and there would be too much pressure on them," said Marcus.

During the discussions, one of the Labor members got up with tears in his eyes and said he couldn't believe people with such opposite viewpoints could sit together and talk without yelling and screaming at each other. "It's never happened before in Israel," said Marcus. As a result, the Eitan-Beilin Document provided for a border to run through the West Bank. That was a radical departure from the Likud Party's previous position.

Such results have made the institute well known in Israel, although it's virtually unknown to the non-Jewish community in the United States. "It's not just to put out papers," said Marcus. "We get involved with issues where we try to find a solution and then try to implement that solution. We're trying to improve the democracy and governance in Israel."

Yet at the same time he's been pushing to improve Israel, Marcus has stayed out of the fray, not wanting to have his voice heard, say friends and associates. "Bernie has made it almost a passion," said Stein. "He is deeply troubled by what goes on inside the [Israeli] society, and he feels that only Israelis can solve their problems, but they need the wherewithal. Bernie thinks that if something needs to be changed, he doesn't have to make that change; he can provide individuals with the means to effect the changes they see fit. In other words, he acts as a catalyst to stimulate others. He's been very good about staying out of the political part of it."

By getting involved in helping the poor and the Middle East, Marcus and Blank have become role models for tens of thousands of Home Depot employees, Home Depot's competitors, other retailers, and other U.S. companies. And that's why Home Depot's community involvement has been so successful in helping those who need help. Because Marcus and Blank make it a point to get involved in issues, others have seen that they too can make a difference.

MANAGEMENT LESSONS

Any successful retailer always gives back to the communities where it operates because shoppers appreciate such caring. Home Depot has made it a point to get involved in projects that are related to its stores and business, knowing that can be another way to show the world its home improvement expertise and caring for others. Any business would do well to follow Home Depot's community activism.

1. Give employees the ability to direct community involvement because they are the ones that know the concerns of a local town or city. Because of that philosophy, Home Depot's employees are involved in community projects all over the country.

2. Pick a handful of community concerns and make them company concerns. Home Depot has focused on improving the environment, for example, because it knows that some of the products it sells have an impact on the environment.

3. Be involved in community issues that are related to your business. Home Depot's management realized that its building and repair expertise would work well with projects like building homes for the needy or parks for children.

4. Community involvement should begin with top management, and Home Depot executives like Bernie Marcus and Arthur Blank are heavily involved in such projects, whether it's giving money to foundations to actually helping build a home.

5. Put your money where your mouth is. Give freely to non-profit organizations. Home Depot gives millions each year to hundreds of groups because it believes that successful companies should give something back.

6. Get involved in good causes because you believe in them, not for the publicity. While Home Depot is

involved in hundreds of community projects and programs each year, very rarely does it get any attention for its good deeds. The retailer realizes that the return it will get is from shoppers it has helped.

AT A CROSSROADS

In the home improvement business, we need to be all things to all people.

—Arthur M. Blank

For more than a decade, Marcus and Blank grew Home Depot by concentrating on large metropolitan markets such as Dallas and Los Angeles. In doing so, they became wildly successful. Shoppers marveled at Home Depot's product selection and service. Marcus and Blank even became smart enough to plan urban expansion in a way to improve customer service. By building stores in big markets close to each other and cannibalizing sales, Marcus and Blank eliminated long lines and crowded parking lots—two things frustrating shoppers—by diverting some customers to new Home Depots.

But by the early 1990s, Marcus and Blank wondered what would happen when they had finally built as many stores as they could in those cities. A study determined that by the turn of the century, Home Depot would have saturated those markets with between 1,000 and 1,200 stores. For the shortsighted, that may have seemed like a lot of new stores to go. By 1992, Home Depot still had only 214 stores. With Marcus and Blank's aggressive expansion plans, however, the total could be reached in less than a decade. Marcus and Blank liked to think about Home Depot's future in chunks of 20 and 30 years. If Home Depot's growth was going to slow or even stop in the near future, the stock price would stop its meteoric rise, hurting Marcus and Blank's ability to keep employees happy. If the workers became frustrated with the stock, then they'd stop giving customers excellent customer service. Home Depot's future success in more ways than one was tied to how Home Depot kept growing.

To be sure, Marcus and Blank had begun talking about making Home Depot a national chain of do-it-yourself stores in 1979 when they opened the first location. But they had spent most of the first decade expanding Home Depot into huge metropolitan markets. Although Home Depot had some smaller markets like Shreveport, Louisiana, with a single store, the retailer had never put one in small towns that had no more than 25,000 or 30,000 residents, which was the bread and butter of another successful retailer, Wal-Mart. To address its future growth, Home Depot looked small—small town, that is. The company was putting stores in markets with 120,000 people. With the number of those cities without Home Depots now dwindling, Marcus and Blank set their sites on towns and small cities with 60,000 people.

The decision made a lot of sense. Land was cheaper in smaller cities. Salaries and other operating costs would be lower there compared to San Francisco or New York. Competition was weak. Many of these cities had small hardware stores with limited selection and weak customer service. In addition, discount department store giant Wal-Mart had made billions putting its large stores in small towns like Auburn, Alabama. (While Marcus wasn't a big fan of putting Home Depots in smaller markets, he had seen and talked about Wal-Mart's small-town success with Wal-Mart founder Sam Walton and CEO David Glass, who were friends.) The demographics showed why. The number of people moving into rural counties jumped 2.2 percent between 1990 and 1994, easily outpacing the 1.8 percent growth in migration into urban counties during the same time period. City residents still earned more money than their rural cousins, but income for rural residents had jumped an average of 5.1 percent annually since 1990. That reversed a 20-year trend and beat the growth in cities, where income had grown 4.8 percent annually. Everyone from credit card companies to hotel chains was looking at rural markets with new interest. So Home Depot wasn't alone in wondering about the sales potential in smaller towns and cities.

At first Home Depot considered a smaller version of its

warehouse-sized locations in such rural areas. That wasn't a new idea. Other retailers selling home improvement items like Nashville's Tractor Supply had made a name for themselves by putting stores one-tenth the size of a regular Home Depot in such towns. The idea of a mini-Home Depot was quickly shelved, primarily because the company would have been trying to be something it wasn't. (However, Home Depot now plans to test smaller-sized stores in 1999.) "Depot's expertise was in being a large store category killer," noted Jim Inglis, who by 1994 had become executive vice president of strategic development. "We'd be trying to play a game we weren't used to. You had to come in and own the market." In addition, if Home Depot had put in smaller stores, competitors like Lowe's or Menard's could have come in and overwhelmed the market with larger ones. Explained Marcus to employees in 1990: "The [smaller] prototype takes a whole new strategy of thinking, and I don't think we're prepared for it yet." However, Marcus grudgingly approved Home Depot's small-town exploration, although he wasn't sure it was a smart move for a company that had always concentrated on big cities.

Before Home Depot could build stores in farmlands and rural outposts, however, it had to make changes, slowly and carefully. A normal Home Depot, thought Marcus and Blank, wouldn't play in Peoria because shoppers there want different products than suburban customers. "We could not take a Home Depot as it is and plop it into these areas," said Marcus, showing his skepticism. "They wouldn't be as successful and give us the return we expect." As they had done in the past with other major company decisions, Marcus and Blank picked the best do-it-yourself experts to build the first small-town Home Depots.

Marcus and Blank asked Inglis to assemble a team to study the issue. Another executive examining rural stores was Denny Ryan, a goal-driven guy who had joined the company a decade earlier as a building materials merchandiser. Like most of the company's current executives, Ryan worked his way through Home Depot, playing a key role in its successful northeast expansion in the late 1980s and early 1990s. By 1992 he was senior vice president of merchandising. (Denny's wife Betty also was Marcus's secretary.)

Another was Tom Smith, hired from Wal-Mart where he was vice president of operations. Smith, made director of special projects, was a small-town America retailing expert. His expertise would help Home Depot's planning—even though he sometimes fought to get others to understand smaller market dynamics. Born in Meridian, Mississippi, which has a population of 42,000, Smith had also lived in York, Alabama, and Clarksdale, Mississippi, so he knew small towns, especially in the South. In 1979, Wal-Mart hired him as an assistant manager at its store in Jasper, Alabama—then as far east as the retailer had expanded. Smith moved 14 times during his Wal-Mart career, running stores in West Point, Mississippi, and Savannah, Georgia. In such towns, said Smith, "You put your hand over your heart when they play the national anthem and you treat people right and you don't have to lock the doors."

Smith knew Home Depot's aggressive reputation. In the early 1990s, while running 180 Wal-Marts in Texas, Smith found himself embroiled in a ceiling fan price war with his future employer. In retaliation, Smith bought truckloads of lumber and sold it in some Wal-Marts. That drew Home Depot's ire. When he interviewed with Marcus and Blank in 1993, the company cofounders remembered the incident. "I walked into the meeting and the first words Bernie said to me were, 'So you're that son of a bitch,'" said Smith. "He knew who I was before I walked into the room." Smith had actually been recommended to Home Depot by Wal-Mart's Glass, who suggested he call Blank. Smith didn't know the Home Depot president, but he called him anyway. Immediately, Smith got an interview with the two cofounders in New Jersey, where Marcus and Blank were visiting stores.

Marcus and Blank asked Smith about putting Home Depots into small towns. "I told them I felt that there was a great opportunity for Home Depot to grow in smaller communities," said Smith, who had opened more than 500 Wal-Marts in his retailing career, some in towns with no more than 5,000 residents. "The very first do-it-yourselfer in America was a farmer, not some guy in Atlanta or New York. These county seats or communities through the United States were rural, but they had a need for products. Wal-Mart had proven it. Home Depot had the opportunity to prove it." Smith told Marcus and Blank that in towns of 20,000 people, there were Wal-Mart stores with $40 to $50 million in annual sales. Those numbers convinced Blank that Home Depot needed to explore such markets.

His partner wasn't satisfied. Marcus thought there was still plenty of opportunity in bigger markets. "Bernie said, 'I don't agree with Arthur. I don't think it will work. But Arthur's the president, and he's going to do it,'" said Smith. "I know that Bernie—in conversations I had with him one on one—didn't support the concept." The half of the Home Depot duo, Blank, who didn't have as much retailing experience as the other, Marcus, would be proven right.

Smith, Inglis, and Ryan decided Home Depot should broaden its view of what could sell in its stores. A team of merchandisers looked at products that, for example, farmers and ranchers would buy and traveled from Minnesota to Florida, looking at competitors. "The attitude that the normal Home Depot merchant had was, 'I'm the best,'" said Smith. "That's not a bad thing. But they thought they knew what rural America needs. I told them to forget that and go into the markets and talk to the customers and see what the competitors were selling."

In focus groups, Home Depot asked what farmers and ranchers liked and disliked. A typical response: Give us the large wrench sizes for tractor work and the ability to buy in bulk. They asked for work pants with a 58-inch waist, gloves in handy 12 packs, and 1,500-gallon feed tanks. They wanted Home Depot's how-to book offerings expanded to include titles like "Raising Sheep the Modern Way." Yet the new product offerings upset some traditional Home Depot merchandisers, who didn't like the idea of selling saddles or dog food.

Inglis and the team also decided the stores should have a huge drive-through lumberyard so farmers and ranchers could drive trucks into the store and load up. That was a controversial decision. Blank noted that one of Home Depot's competitors, Payless Cashways, had drive-through lumberyards. Home

Depot had proven it could go into a market and force such Payless stores to close. (Others gave Home Depot less credit, blaming Payless's problems on a leveraged buyout that kept it from opening new stores and improving existing locations.) Blank felt Home Depot's success against Payless showed a drive-through lumberyard wasn't important to customers. Smith also thought the lumberyard should be smaller. Ryan, who was a lumber expert, wanted the bigger lumber area.

Once it decided on a product mix that would attract rural shoppers, Home Depot's rural store team picked a name for the stores—they selected "CrossRoads" from a list of about 250 names one morning during a meeting in the board room that included Smith and Inglis. It conveyed an agrarian setting. Then they went looking for locations.

Quincy, Illinois, is in what Mayor Chuck Scholz calls "the belly-button of Illinois"—where the state protrudes outward and forms a curve that the Mississippi River slowly winds its way around. Quincy is also miles away from any metropolis. It's 120 miles north of St. Louis, 270 miles west of Chicago, and 240 miles east of Kansas City. If you want to go shopping and feel like you're in the big city, you'd better pack a lunch and have a full tank of gas.

"We've been isolated, and there's some value in that," says Scholz proudly. Indeed, despite its small size—about 40,000 live in the city limits and another 20,000 live in the rest of the county—Quincy has attracted such retailers as men's clothier Jos. A. Bank and, of course, a Wal-Mart and Kmart. The clothing store, whose smallest market had been twice the size of Quincy, opened only after two years of letter writing from the locals pointed out that people came from far away to shop in Quincy. "There isn't anything else around us," said Mike Schaffer, who runs the Jos. A. Bank store. In its first year, the Bank store had $1 million in sales, 67 percent more than projected. That led the men's clothier to expand into other small towns.

Quincy, naturally, made the perfect location for a rural Home Depot and drew Smith's attention. The town was surrounded by rolling hills that contained farms. But Quincy had enough old homes and new neighborhoods to create a demand for hammers and nails as well as sinks and bathtubs. The number of houses in Quincy had grown during the preceding 20 years, and 95 percent of the population lived in homes worth less than $100,000. More than half of the households had an annual income of between $15,000 and $50,000. The largest employers were the local hospital and agricultural equipment maker Titan Wheel International. To the Home Depot team exploring smaller markets, the Quincy numbers showed a customer base with enough disposable income to afford its product selection and customer service. "That town of Quincy was wonderful folks," said Smith. "It was our kind of town. It had a great economy and was an aggressive town. It wanted new business."

Other retailers in town told Home Depot it could draw from a population base of 250,000 in a 50-mile radius. This was nothing new for Marcus and Blank, however. Home Depot had experienced the phenomenon of shoppers' traveling great distances to come to its stores. After the first stores opened in Atlanta, people from Chattanooga, Tennessee, drove more than 100 miles to shop. According to the company's consumer research, the shoppers were attracted by—what else—its product selection, customer service, and low prices. The survey results surprised Marcus and Blank, but they also taught them about the power of word-of-mouth advertising. Home Depot didn't run ads in Chattanooga until it opened a store there a decade later.

In early 1994, Smith developed a business plan for small-town locations, projecting that the stores would have $25 million in annual sales. That was less than the Wal-Mart stores Smith told Marcus and Blank about. But it was enough to make Home Depot want to build those stores. Marcus and Blank okayed the rural store test. Everyone, including Marcus finally, had high hopes. "It's an experiment," said Marcus. "If it works, it will be phenomenal, absolutely phenomenal. This is a 10-year project. In 5 years it will be a great business. In 10 years it will be phenomenal." His comments, of course, belied his skepticism. To Mayor Scholz, Home Depot answered his economic prayers. "If a guy gets in his truck and drives 45 miles to make a major purchase at CrossRoads, he's going to eat at our restaurants and go to the mall," he noted.

Two other locations were also picked to test rural stores. Waterloo, Iowa, and Columbia, Missouri, had similar demographics—populations of about 60,000 to 70,000 that had a strong agriculture base mixed in with a strong backbone of homeowners who took pride in keeping their houses in good shape. There were other factors. Waterloo was the location of competitor Menard's No. 1 store in that size market. Menard had always operated stores in smaller markets. And Lowe's was planning a store for Columbia.

But the Quincy store would be the first CrossRoads. Home Depot picked a location on the outskirts of town, at the southeast corner of Illinois 104 and I-72, a four-lane highway completed in 1991 giving surrounding farmers quick access to town. A year earlier, the 20-acre plot had been covered with oats. Home Depot wanted to turn the site into a 117,000-square-foot store with a 100,000-square-foot lumberyard.

Home Depot's CrossRoads store drew a lot of interest. Competitors complained to government officials. They feared the store would affect the town more than the Lincoln-Douglas debate held in oak-lined Washington Park in 1858 or the 1993 floods that damaged its riverfront area. "They're projecting sales of $30 million a year," said Jim Millman of Great Central Lumber in Palmyra, Missouri, just across the river, to the Quincy Planning Commission. "That's business they're going to take away from people such as myself. You owe it to the people of Quincy who have been here for years to look at what this will do." Millman's sales estimate was high, but it was not that far off from the sales estimates for the store. Added Silber Mixer of Mixer Lumber and Construction in nearby Clayton, "We keep hearing that they're going to hire 200 people. But how many are they going to unemploy?" Home Depot was used to such criticism when it went into new markets. In Quincy, it found such feelings weren't confined to urban markets.

Still, people were happy to see Home Depot in town. If the people of Quincy had their way, Home Depot would have hired more than 200 workers. The store received more than 2,600 applications through a state agency. The company scouted local retailers for experts, hiring two dozen. These new converts to the Bleeding Orange philosophy made suggestions to Home Depot about what products would sell—and what wouldn't. One was Ray Deters, who a year before the store opened had farmed the oats on the property. His grandfather had bought the land in 1958. "I'll be roaming these aisles," said Deters, who could point to the spot next to the parking lot where his family had buried two mules. "You're right in my back yard. Back then, you could make a living on 40 acres." Now, Deters would be making a living helping shoppers.

When it opened in July 1995, CrossRoads was unlike any other Home Depot in the country. After 16 years of selling lumber, nails, and paint to do-it-yourself suburbanites, Home Depot had entered uncharted turf. These were different customers, and they wanted different products. This was not your typical Home Depot. Inside the front doors and to the right were bags of dog and cat food and cat litter stacked 6 feet high. Such pet-related products had caused quite a ruckus between some of Home Depot's merchandisers and Smith. "There were many times I would be feeling as if I were the lowest person on Earth because 'over their dead body' would they sell saddles or cat and dog food," said Smith. But he had seen how Wal-Mart had introduced a line of dog food in its stores that quickly became No. 2 in the field. A selection of rabbit houses could be culled over. To the left were rows of car batteries and tractor tires from Goodyear, Michelin, and BF Goodrich. The store would install them in its garage or send workers to fix a flat.

Behind the animal food was a clothing department with overalls, canvas and rubber work boots, reinforced socks, and belts and suspenders. "It's not really fashion," deadpanned Ryan. "People that are workers in the field, this is their clothing. This isn't designer stuff."

Walk down the aisle past the Wrangler and Lee jeans and there were lariats to rope horses for $22.91 and saddles for as much as $827.42. A bit further back was an animal health department stocking nonprescription drugs. There were salt blocks for horses, barn fans, and buckets of barn-red paint. There were culverts and barbed-wire fencing and wagons that could be attached to tractors.

Throughout the store, Home Depot had added products such as Honda and Husqvarna tractors it had never sold before. And it was trying to add others like John Deere. Just as at the first Home Depots in Atlanta in 1979, Home Depot's merchandise buyers had to convince manufacturers their products would sell at its stores. "We had to beg some vendors to do business with us," said Smith.

Out in the lumberyard, the entrance and exit were operated by a remote control. But shoppers could drive in and use their trucks as shopping carts. More than 60 cars and trucks would fit in the yard at one time. This was in stark contrast to the typical Home Depot, where lumber was sold inside—to stack it in the back of your truck you had to park near an entrance. The rest of the store looked like any Home Depot across America. There was a garden center with a greenhouse. The lighting and wallpaper departments were slightly smaller. But the Cross-Roads also contained kitchen and bath displays and stocked refrigerators, ranges, freezers, and washers and dryers.

Ryan downplayed the store, saying, "It's just another Home Depot." That wasn't even close to being true, except that each Home Depot was unique in its own way, offering products for sale other stores didn't have. If someone wanted to build a home from the ground up at a typical Home Depot, it would be difficult. At CrossRoads, with its huge lumberyard and other essentials, that task was much easier to accomplish. The store, which was so big that maps were made available at the front door, sold everything. Marcus and Blank had taken the home center concept and stretched it way beyond its normal boundaries in a bid to seek more customers and more sales.

Ironically, Smith—called Gomer Homer by some at Home Depot because of his rural focus—never saw the Quincy store. He quit weeks before it opened, frustrated over arguments he'd had about the store with Ryan and Inglis. He had wanted a smaller store, and he didn't like Ryan's changing the store's layout. "If you created a one-stop shopping environment for the

farmer, the do-it-yourselfer, and the housewife, you would control the market, and you could do it in a 65,000-square-foot
store," argued Smith. "You didn't need 200,000 square feet."
While he admired Ryan's lumber expertise, he felt that he didn't
know much about rural markets. Inglis, whom he called "one of
the best merchants I have ever seen," was clashing with Blank
over the direction of the company, and Smith—whose office
was next to Inglis's—often felt caught in the middle. Smith
remembers one argument during which Inglis offered his resig-
nation to Blank. Within a year, Inglis would be gone from the
company. When Smith left, the CrossRoads stores lost one of
its biggest champions, foreshadowing its eventual consolidation
back into the rest of the company. To this day, Smith has never
been in the Quincy store, although he's seen pictures of it.
"That was one of my biggest disappointments," he has said. But
his work made the store a success and helped prove to Home
Depot there was a future in small towns.

Down the street from the new CrossRoads in Quincy, competitors were wondering what was going to happen when the
new competitor opened their doors. Walk past the mole traps,
the stacks of baling rope, and jars of udder balm, and you'd
find a healthy dose of worry at the Quincy Farm & Home that
first week Home Depot CrossRoads came to town. "People
don't really want us to be a super center," explained Dan
Henke, director of purchasing for Quincy Farm & Home, trying to downplay CrossRoads' impact. "When you walk in here,
you walk into a traditional farm and home center. We try to
provide a little bit different niche." Still, Henke added, "Our
feeling is that it's going to be a long year. They're a huge tree.
We're a sapling."

Unlike CrossRoads, Henke's store carried farm-related toys,
food, drinks, hunting goods such as fishing rods and houseware
items such as toilet paper, paper towels, and detergent. He felt
Farm & Home could compete by honing its niches. Farther in
town, Gael Baker, manager at Timberline Lumber, prepared for
battle. "I'm sure they're not going to have everything available,
and we'll still be able to supply some of the out-of-town cus-

tomers," said Baker. "I don't know if we can compete product by product. The only thing I know we can do is improve on our customer service." Fighting against Home Depot on customer service was a tough battle, however.

Furrow Building Materials, a store operated by Payless Cashways, hadn't waited for CrossRoads to open before making adjustments. It remodeled its bath and lighting departments and renovated its lumberyard. But it was ironic that the only thing separating the Furrow's store from the CrossRoads parking lot was the Quincy Memorial Place cemetery. Marcus and Blank were taking dead aim at one of Home Depot's largest national competitors. Two years later, Payless would be in Chapter 11 bankruptcy court protection, weakened by Home Depot's entry into its core midwestern markets.

To be sure, rural discount stores carrying a wide variety of products weren't a new concept. There had even been large versions of such stores. Before Home Depot had opened its CrossRoads, Wal-Mart tested a 69,000-square-foot store called Country Farm in Kirksville, Missouri. That store included cattle and horse feed, padded tractor seats, boots, work gloves, and cowboy hats. Country Farm closed after two years. But Wal-Mart incorporated one product category—an expanded line of lawn and garden products—into its larger discount stores. Wal-Mart already had hundreds and hundreds of stores in small towns. It didn't need another store format to cater to those markets. In contrast, for Home Depot to succeed it needed to fill a niche in rural areas for customers who couldn't find such specialized items as engine brackets or irrigation pipes at a general store. At the time Home Depot opened its first CrossRoads store, experts estimated the farm and home supply retail industry had more than 850 stores and sales of $6 billion. It was into this developed market—both in Quincy and through the country—that Home Depot entered.

As in earlier battles with Builders Square, HomeBase, and others, Marcus and Blank prepared the troops for a fight. "Competitors usually don't like us," said Denny as he stood in the Quincy store a week before it first opened. "We'd like their customers to be our customers."

Marcus and Blank wouldn't be disappointed. As soon as the Quincy store opened, customers crowded its aisles. A Home Depot consultant estimated that the Quincy location would have $18 million in annual sales. But privately, the goal of some Home Depot executives, including Smith, was $25 million. The store passed both expectations, selling $27 million in goods the first year. That fall, the CrossRoads in Waterloo opened amid talk that Marcus and Blank had found yet another hot new retail concept with hundreds of new products.

Yet, despite CrossRoads' success, there was reason for Marcus and Blank to be worried by the results. They expected sales at the store to be driven by the new products. To be sure, the pet supplies, culverts, fencing, trailers, boots, and work clothes all sold extremely well. Those were some of the products Smith fought to get into the stores. Tires and livestock feed, on the other hand, sat on shelves. Home Depot realized those products sold better at other stores.

But the Quincy store showed Home Depot that many of the products from its regular stores—and which comprised approximately 60 percent of the product mix at CrossRoads—were also big sellers. Marcus and Blank deduced from the CrossRoads store that regular Home Depots would do well in much smaller markets than they had ever previously imagined. "Because of the success of the CrossRoads store, we found out that a [same-sized] Home Depot store would be successful in rural markets without the new products," said Inglis. "It became exactly what we wanted it to become, and that's the dominant store in the market." Indeed, the Quincy store is now part of Home Depot's growing midwest division, helping the company fill in a gap in its march across the country.

The CrossRoads store, however, also pointed out problems for Home Depot. Marcus and Blank had created a separate division for the rural stores. Ryan was overseeing purchasing agents buying products for those stores. Because there were only three stores, the buyers could visit the markets and determine which products would sell and which ones wouldn't. But there were hundreds of rural markets all over the country.

There was no way the CrossRoads merchandising team could visit all of those markets if Home Depot was to roll out a chain of such stores.

Home Depot did have merchandisers in each of its five divisions scattered across the country. They were already buying products for dozens of different stores and tweaking the assortment based on each market. Home Depot's merchants stocked lots of snow blowers in its stores in Connecticut but not in its stores in the Miami area. It would be easy for them to start buying products that catered to rural markets.

The solution, Marcus and Blank quickly realized, was to roll the CrossRoads stores back into Home Depot, and for each division to explore small, rural markets for expansion. In addition, Marcus noted, by putting the rural stores back under the Home Depot name so well-known around the country, the company could save on advertising. The marketing department wouldn't have to develop separate ads for nearby Home Depot and CrossRoads stores.

Smith, who'd left the company for a job in California by the time the CrossRoads was folded under the Home Depot name, agreed with the move. "I never intended for the Cross-Roads to be a stand-alone chain of stores," said Smith. "I was a proponent to call it the Home Depot. You worked so many years to develop that name—why call it anything else? My intent was to go into these small towns and develop a mix and learn from these rural stores products that could be used in Home Depot stores throughout the United States. I can go into Home Depot stores in Boston and see products that were put into the CrossRoads mix."

Some saw the quick end to the CrossRoads division as a failure by Marcus and Blank to develop a new store concept, and they thought it showed a lack of thorough planning, raising the question about the company's ability to expand other store concepts. Others believed it failed because Marcus never fully supported the idea. But the CrossRoads test stores are open today under the Home Depot name. And they still sell the special farm products. Most important, CrossRoads became a critical part of the evolution of the Home Depot store concept. Marcus and Blank discovered that its ware-house-sized stores could do well in markets much smaller than they had expected. And the rural store test led to the discovery of hundreds of new products that could be rolled into its regular stores.

Less than two years after the first CrossRoads store opened in Quincy, Home Depot opened two new stores in Georgia an hour away from the company headquarters. They were in Rome and Athens, two small cities much like Quincy, Illinois, and Columbia, Missouri, in that they attracted rural shoppers. Five years before, Marcus and Blank would have never added stores into such markets. Today, the stores stock items like dog and cat food, saddles that cost more than $600, work boots, and aluminum truck boxes. All are big sellers.

In addition, for the first time Home Depot put the professional shopper—whether it was a farmer or rancher or building contractor—on equal terms with the do-it-yourselfer. That was an important lesson as Marcus and Blank began looking for ways in the late 1990s to get more building contractors to shop at its stores. "The development of a CrossRoads concept took great power of thought and a tremendous amount of guts on the part of this company," said Marcus, its most vocal critic. Yet in the end, Marcus had realized that expanding into the smaller towns was the right move for Home Depot. He had been wrong about the potential.

Before CrossRoads, Marcus and Blank hadn't thought about rural markets and products. But by exploring areas they previously ignored, they expanded Home Depot's sales in ways they hadn't considered in the past. Today, when Home Depot talks about expansion, small towns are in the plans. Many of the stores earmarked for those towns will stock products first tested at CrossRoads.

In Florida, which was Home Depot's first market expansion outside of Atlanta in the early 1980s, Marcus and Blank approved the opening of 9 new stores in 1999 and another 15 new stores in the year 2000. Some of those stores will be in small towns like Bradenton, Stuart, Weston, Kissimmee, and

Titusville. Many are near farming areas. And a store that opened in Marathon, a town in the Florida Keys, in March 1998 stocked lobster traps and bait freezers. The 88,000-square-foot store was in the best tradition of CrossRoads, containing other products unique to Home Depot such as marine-grade plywood, boat-bottom paints, bilge pumps, and dock-repair kits. In 1998, Home Depot added 10 new stores in Virginia. In the past, the company had focused on adding stores around Washington, D.C. But now, it's putting Home Depots into smaller markets like Hampton, Virginia Beach, and Roanoke.

The saying is that you can't teach an old dog new tricks. But after nearly 30 years of operating home improvement stores, Marcus and Blank continue to learn new ideas that continue to bring them new shoppers.

MANAGEMENT LESSONS

After spending a decade and a half expanding in metropolitan markets, Home Depot began looking at smaller markets. The move was a dramatic shift for the retailer, but eventually showed that a business can to work in virtually any location, whether it's rural or urban.

1. Home Depot has looked to expand in geographic markets it previously hadn't considered. Opening stores in rural markets has expanded the retailer's growth potential and given it new customers.

2. Tailor your product offerings to specific communities even if they're in the same state, because it shows your customers that you're attuned to their needs. A Home Depot in the Florida Keys sells lobster traps, while 50 miles away a Home Depot in Miami carries none.

3. Don't be afraid to ask customers what they want in your stores. Home Depot's market research in the 1990s showed that shoppers in more rural markets would buy products like pet food and work clothes if the retailer stocked them.

4. Challenge how your company has done business in the past. Home Depot's biggest challenge in opening rural stores was its history of expanding solely in metropolitan markets. Yet today a good chunk of Home Depot's growth is in rural markets.

THE EXPO FACTOR

That store's going to give us some vibrant ideas for the future. The key is to stay ahead of your competitors on a constant basis.

—BERNIE MARCUS

CrossRoads was one result of Marcus and Blank's continuous search for new ways to sell goods and services to customers. Indeed, Home Depot's strategy of frequently changing store layouts and product offerings kept its entrepreneurial spirit alive—and its rapid growth escalating at nearly a 25 percent clip well into its second decade of operation. Very few $30 billion companies can maintain such a fast growth rate for such a long time. Home Depot has continued to grow because Marcus and Blank are never satisfied.

The company had reached $2.7 billion in sales and more than $100 million in profits by 1990, spreading its 118 stores into 12 states. And there were still new markets for expansion. But, rather than simply multiplying the number of stores, Marcus and Blank pursued a long-term plan. Home Depot had built a reputation as a do-it-yourself store with tens of thousands of products all under one roof. Marcus and Blank knew that there were thousands of other products they didn't yet offer that homeowners and remodelers in its core urban markets might buy if the retailer could add them to the stores.

To address that idea, Home Depot has tinkered with and slowly refined a decor store concept called "Expo." If Expo pays off, Home Depot can prove that it remains a nimble entrepreneur despite becoming a $30 billion company with a growing bureaucracy. A slow research and development process runs counter to its fast expansion of its regular Home Depot stores. But in some ways, that is one of Home Depot's strengths—it can move at two different speeds with two different store formats. That's one of the secrets to Home Depot's success.

Inglis, who joined the company in 1983 as a vice president of merchandising, first had the idea for Expo. He visited an Ikea furniture store in Toronto a year later and wondered whether "we could do the same kind of decor store with home improvement products." Years later, during a strategy session, someone asked the question: Where is Home Depot vulnerable? The answer, responded Inglis, was if another retailer "took a category of the store and blew it up, out-Depoting Depot. That could be a possible threat."

To thwart that threat, Inglis examined products such as expensive faucets, designer cabinets, oriental rugs, and other items aimed at bringing more fashion to the middle class. He also thought Home Depot might attract more shoppers if they could help people design their home remodeling projects. After internal discussions, Home Depot decided to open such a store, called "Home Depot Expo," to test decor products and services. They picked San Diego as the test site. The market was a natural for a couple of reasons. By the end of 1991, when the store opened, Home Depot would have 11 stores, including the Expo, in the area. By adding the Expo to the area, the company could figure out how well—or poorly—the new products would sell when competing against regular Home Depots.

Inglis knew the San Diego market, having joined the company from Dixieline Lumber, a local retailer with five locations. And a location 1 mile away from an existing Home Depot—the best seller in the entire chain—had become available. Competitor HomeBase wanted the site, but Home Depot got it first. "It was not the greatest location, but it served its purpose," remembered Inglis, who asked Blank for his approval. "It wasn't difficult. A lot of people think Arthur is a brick wall. But he will experiment with damn near anything."

In September 1991, Expo opened. The same size as a typical Depot, the store offered customers free advice from certified interior designers, a service so well received there was often a waiting list. And it differed from other Home Depots by not offering lumber or building supplies. Lora Castellanos, then the vendor relations manager in merchandising, called the store a "laboratory" that "is giving us some new merchandise ideas."

Those ideas came as Home Depot executives walked Expo's aisles, looking at what worked and what didn't. Inglis noted merchandise and services tested in the Expo could find their way into traditional Home Depots. Home Depot remained cautious. Still, the store garnered attention because none of Marcus and Blank's competitors had tried a second store concept. Industry publication *National Home Center News* noted that power tools and lumber, two major Home Depot products, weren't anywhere. The store did have a custom picture framing department and dozens of bath towels.

Store manager Steve Smith brought in new products and threw others out, seeking the right mix for decorators and remodelers. Smith added more refrigerators and stoves. A fresh-flower shop was scuttled, and silk flowers were moved inside from an outside nursery. A custom-order throw pillow department was added. And wood flooring and cabinet offerings grew. The lighting department was remodeled to look like a showroom. After the store had been open for about a year, a professional print counter opened, stocked with limited-edition art prints.

Even early on, Home Depot realized the Expo required more customer service than its regular locations. Expo is "a unique business," said Barry Silverman, vice president of merchandising for the northeast division, instrumental in developing the concept because he had once worked in San Diego. "We were surprised, for instance, how long it took to handle some of the special orders." The store had 50 showroom employees, all trained in other Home Depots in San Diego. It also hired several vendors to work in the specialty departments, a common tactic to gain expert knowledge. A former Thermador sales representative, for example, was hired to sell appliances. In addition, four design experts worked only with scheduled appointments. In a bid to keep service levels high, the number of designers had increased from the two decorators when the store first opened.

Yet, the San Diego store had fewer customers than its

orange cousins. The store had about $35 million in sales versus $45 million for its West Coast counterparts. Said Inglis: "We continued to try to fine-tune the concept, but we realized we needed to start with a clean sheet of paper." The San Diego Expo store borrowed too heavily in its product assortment and layout from Home Depots. For Marcus and Blank to accurately gauge Expo's effectiveness and long-term potential, they would have to develop a store from scratch.

Home Depot did just that. In 1993, they planned to open a second Expo in metro Atlanta about 10 miles from the headquarters. That would give Inglis, by now executive vice president of merchandising and based in Atlanta, as well as Marcus and Blank, a close look at Expo.

The idea was a favorite of the cofounders. Blank wanted Home Depot to "push the envelope" in its merchandise and services, to "be all things to all people." Marcus had said if Expo gave Home Depot the desired return on its investment, it could become a "roll-out chain." This was the first time Marcus or Blank had publicly expressed the notion that Expo could become a separate chain. "The key," emphasized Marcus, "is that these stores have to give us a return on our investment." While Home Depot was expanding its customer service reputation and the number of products that it sold, it did so only when there was a reasonable profit to be made. Marcus wasn't interested in furthering their customer service reputation if doing so cost the company money.

The 117,000-square-foot Atlanta store, which opened in January 1994, was a shrine to lessons learned in San Diego. The Atlanta store was also Home Depot's first serious attempt to change Expo's look from the rest of the company's stores.

Instead of Home Depot's characteristic bright orange shelving, the Atlanta Expo had neutral white shelving. Display cases should blend in, explained Smith, now Expo's vice president of merchandising, and not stand out in a setting where shoppers decide what colors to put on walls. In addition, Expo employees wore subdued yellow aprons, not the loud orange that was Home Depot's signature look. The product mix changed too. A professional contractor in San Diego, for example, bought tile from the Expo store, but bought tile adhesives at a competitor because Expo didn't stock his favorite brands. Once Expo employees found out, the store carried the adhesive.

The Atlanta store also offered more services in a bid to handle more customers. There were 30 designers—up from the 4 at the San Diego store—who made house calls for a fee. Skilled workers built custom-ordered merchandise, such as bathroom and kitchen counter tops, at the store.

Home Depot added a gourmet diner for customers, with food provided by Proof of the Pudding, an Atlanta catering company, and the Buckhead Bread Co., owned by the posh Atlanta restaurant operation Pano's & Paul's. Afterward, Home Depot added Depot Diners to its regular stores, offering McDonald's hamburgers and chicken and biscuits from Mrs. Winner's, a southeast fast-food chain. No other home improvement retailer was catering to the do-it-yourself customer's palate.

Expo's uniqueness—it was radically different from any other do-it-yourself store—was a great leap forward for Home Depot. Competitors such as Lowe's and Builder's Square were evolving in the early 1990s. The Expo store sold products and services others had virtually ignored. Expo's competition came from small bath retailers and carpet stores, but none offered Expo's wide selection.

The Atlanta store's sales were 25 percent, or another $10 million to $15 million, more in annual sales than a regular Home Depot, albeit with more space and with more employees, cutting into profits. That worried some as a rollout was discussed. Blank talked more about expansion, but he noted that Expo would not expand into a large number of stores because customers shopped there less frequently. But Expo customers drove from as far away as 40 miles to shop there. And they were spending more money than the typical Home Depot shopper.

Still, Marcus and Blank endorsed the Expo idea, creating a separate division. Longtime employee Bryant Scott was named president. Scott had helped open the south Florida market and had been vice president of merchandising in the southeast, Home Depot's largest division. Before that, he'd worked in

Home Depots in Los Angeles, San Diego, and Phoenix. Scott was well versed in some of the upscale markets that could support Expos. Investors wanted that. Analysts, noting that Expo exceeded initial expectations, envisioned a chain of 200 to 400 stores.

Initially, they weren't disappointed. In 1995, Home Depot opened two more Expo stores—Long Island and Dallas, two affluent markets that Marcus and Blank believed were well suited for Expo. Long Island's Expo—a gleaming 150,000-square-foot store in Westbury—carried the largest selection of design products and home fixtures available anywhere.

But the Long Island store's September 1995 opening foreshadowed Expo's impending problems. Home Depot invited analysts and shareholders to the store to talk about growth plans. It was the first time Home Depot had organized such a meeting. The goal was to boost Home Depot's stock, stagnating near the $45 mark after being as high as $50 in 1993. At the time, Home Depot's stock was down 12 percent for the year, partly because it missed Wall Street expectations on its earnings for the previous three quarters. The company had also scaled back plans for Canada and Mexico. Some wondered whether Home Depot was exploring too many growth options. Marcus, Blank, and others inside the company felt a face-to-face meeting with analysts would alleviate concerns and show that the company's growth prospects were still strong.

The meeting started well, with a dinner at the store. Marcus and Blank made a few comments. And then Blank called on Scott, who along with the yellow-aproned employees showed the crowd his company spirit.

"Give me an H," shouted Scott, and the employees shouted back. "Give me an O," he added, and continued to spell out Home Depot, with the workers shouting back after each letter. "What a group!" said a smiling Blank after the cheer was over, pleased with the way the meeting had started. The cheer, however, would be the highlight of the two-day event. Home Depot's strategy of meeting with Wall Street analysts exploded in its face like a broken window pane.

The next morning, Marcus made a presentation. "Is that Expo store incredible or what?" he said. "That's what we mean by leading-edge creativity." Then Marcus told the analysts that Home Depot would trim its 1996 expansion so that it could focus on customer service at its existing stores. Specifically, Marcus said the retailer would add 90 to 95 new stores in 1996, 10 to 15 fewer than the company had projected earlier in the year. The news sent Home Depot's stock down $1.75, or nearly 4.5 percent, that day. Many investors and analysts expected better news and came away disappointed. Robinson-Humphrey analyst Dan Wewer spoke to a reporter by telephone on his flight from New York back to Atlanta that afternoon. "You know how fickle Wall Street is," he said. "The stock really hasn't done anything in two or three years. A lot of investors went to the meeting hoping to hear some catalyst to get the stock going up." After trying to coddle Wall Streeters, Marcus and Blank saw the event backfire on their attempts to boost Home Depot's stock.

In fact, Marcus and Blank presented a sound business plan. They discussed new 1996 markets such as Minneapolis, St. Louis, Philadelphia, and Pittsburgh. Marcus talked about international expansion. They said that as many as four more Expo stores could be added in 1996. And they gave the analysts a preview of Home Depot's new rural concept store CrossRoads, scheduled to open its second location later that week in Waterloo, Iowa.

In looking at the health of the U.S. retail industry, the move to cut the number of new stores to be added to the chain to allow the company to concentrate on increasing sales at existing locations was savvy. Store sales in 1995 were weak virtually everywhere. While Home Depot's 1995 sales growth topped 20 percent, it was the company's weakest performance in its history. Marcus and Blank needed to keep a close eye on the performance of their existing stores to keep their sales growing. They made the right move—and the stock got killed.

The Long Island store and the Dallas location, which opened two months later in November, were close in design and layout to the Atlanta store, but they had nearly 20,000 square feet of additional selling space. There were also the typical changes dictated by region. The 3,000-square-foot café in the Long Island store, for example, was operated by New York-based Chock Full O'Nuts Corp., not the Atlanta caterer and restaurant. The Long Island store contained furniture ranging from patio sets to ready-to-assemble pieces to upscale, custom-order upholstery, and prices ranged from $19 for imported wood stools to $6,000 wool rugs from Pakistan. The Westbury store added furniture from Lexington, Lane, Howard Miller, and Sauder.

Home Depot increased the number of Expo employees to 360 to keep its customer service levels high. Color consultants and project coordinators were added. The new stores included wall coverings, doors and windows, art, and mirrors. The Dallas store, for example, included meeting rooms for private sessions between designers and shoppers. It offered special store hours for commercial customers and offered phone and fax ordering services. The Dallas store even offered personal shoppers.

No wonder. The Dallas location on the east side of the Dallas Parkway just north of the Galleria was situated near an upscale clientele. It offered a concierge. The store contained 32 kitchen and bathroom models, and its departments carried everything from Italian linens to a Schonbek crystal chandelier with a $17,500 price tag. There were $4,000 reproductions of a 1920s gas stove made by Heartland, a Ralph Lauren shop, and a Laura Ashley section for bedding. Only about 10 percent of the merchandise in the Expo was also in a typical Home Depot. Thus Home Depot continued to explore new product offerings that could be added to other stores. Marcus was particularly happy with Expo, saying it was "reaching out to the underserved decor market" and adding that "each store is merchandised according to its geographic location, and customers come from a wide area."

At the Dallas store opening, Scott said, "There's very little cannibalizing" by Expo of Home Depot sales. "We know it really creates new business for us," he added. People come into the locations to get ideas—the way some might tour model homes—and are inspired with ideas for a remodeling project, said Scott. Expo "is the perfect interior design resource—whether you want to redecorate a single room or remodel an entire house," added Rob Houghtlin, the Dallas store manager.

The Expo stores were a great resource for ideas and products. But some cracks were forming in its walls, giving Marcus and Blank one of their sternest retailing tests.

Suddenly, Marcus and Blank stopped talking publicly about Expo's potential. There was good reason. Inglis lost an internal battle to improve Expo's training and computers. Because a big bulk of Expo's sales—more than 50 percent—came from special orders and installations, the stores needed computer systems completely different from regular Home Depot's. And many Expo employees who worked in the aisles simply restocked shelves and didn't know how to handle customers with unique project needs. Since costly new software and specialized training weren't needed for the bulk of Home Depot stores, Expo—for the time being—suffered.

Indeed, progress at Expo was being stifled due to the lack of movement in Home Depot's stock price. It had been stuck near or below the $50 mark since 1992. Marcus and Blank felt that the stock price, key to the company's success because a higher stock price provided an incentive to employees, would grow again if they concentrated more on the core stores. Some at Home Depot felt that the regular stores were being ignored while other projects were explored. While the move to slow down projects like Expo, CrossRoads, and international expansion seemed smart given the tough retail environment in 1995, by early 1996 Expo still needed a remodeling job.

There were problems with special-order and installation sales. Said Inglis, who left the company shortly after the Long Island and Dallas stores opened: "You had to have computer systems to track purchases by customers and special orders from vendors and [to] track installation." Customers placed orders, and the different pieces were delivered to the store. But often the stores couldn't tell when the entire order had arrived and was ready to be installed. Only after irate customer calls would employees track down the various parts.

The computer problems were long-standing at Home Depot. Its first computer system was a disaster, and it was often overridden or ignored by store managers.

Blank, who took a special interest in Expo, gave Scott a mandate to fix the problems before Expo blemished Home Depot's customer service reputation. Soon after, Blank said they were "still working on that model," but he added that no more Expo stores would open until 1997 at the earliest—taking back the projection at the Long Island meeting that four new Expos could open by the end of 1996. "There's lots of things I like [about Expo], far more than I dislike," he added. Blank conceded service was a struggle. "It takes an inordinate amount of time to give the right level of service," he said. "The more different [Expo stores] are from a Home Depot, the more successful they are."

Ironically, someone complaining about Expo's service was Wall Street analyst Wewer, who sat next to Blank at an April 1996 investment conference as the Home Depot executive talked about the service problems. Wewer had bought ceiling fans and kitchen counter tops from the Atlanta Expo location and then had them installed in his home. "On both of them, they've had to come out and rework the project," said Wewer. The counter top was cut wrong, and a worker broke Wewer's attic ladder when he was installing the fan. In addition, Wewer noticed screwdriver marks on the fan. "And my case, from what I've heard, is not unusual. In their defense, they responded quickly." However, when Wewer thought about carpeting his basement, his wife nixed the idea of using Expo. "They need to make sure when they say they'll install something, it will be done correctly the first time," said Wewer. "It kind of taints their reputation. It just takes a lot of tender loving care to run that business."

In a catalog sent to shoppers in Atlanta that summer, the Expo store boasted of "professional installation." It continued: "When you choose Expo, you've chosen a team of hand-picked professionals with the latest information in new products, techniques, and materials—and, of course, The Home Depot philosophy of providing uncompromised service and installation."

For kitchen and bath projects, Expo promised "on-site visits to verify layout, measurements, and job conditions," as well as "pre-job conferences, continued site visits, and building code compliance." On carpeting jobs, Expo offered an "in-home site visit to verify flooring measurements" as well as "delivery of new and removal of old carpet and pad" and "haulaway of old carpet and vacuuming." Clearly, based on Wewer's experience and other customer complaints, Expo's standards weren't being met.

Home Depot moved quickly. Within months, Scott was saying, "We've made some strong strides. We've got those things done a little bit quicker than we thought." It helped that the problem was confined to the small, four-store Expo division. A widespread customer service issue in the main Home Depot stores could have taken years to correct—as struggles with the installation and delivery services showed.

Scott added project managers at each Expo. Their task was to visit a job site at least three times during a project to oversee the work done by subcontractors—addressing the issue Wewer complained about. Expo stores began naming their best installers during monthly sales meetings. But Scott added, "We need to continue to work on the quality" of the subcontractors.

He decided, and Blank agreed, to open a new Expo store. They picked Miami—far enough away from the other Expos so no one would know about the other stores but close enough to Atlanta so they could watch its results. Scott examined demographics, including household incomes and housing prices, before picking south Florida, a market he knew from the 1980s when he worked in its first Home Depot stores. The location is 5 minutes from highbrow Coconut Grove and 10 minutes from tony Miami Beach. Fort Lauderdale and Boca Raton, other high-income regions in south Florida, were 30-minute drives away, which was also factored into the location's selection. Scott also wanted a market with warm weather throughout the year so that the store would have a constant customer flow. The CrossRoads stores had run into problems with outdoor lumberyards during the winter.

It wasn't the location of the Miami store that raised eyebrows of those watching Home Depot tinker with Expo. It was the size. The location was only 80,000 square feet—just more than half the size of the Long Island and Dallas locations. "It continues the Expo tradition," explained Scott to a group of visitors soon after the store opened. "The New York store is different from the Atlanta store. And the Atlanta store is different from the San Diego store."

The Miami location was also radically different from other Expos. The store rid itself of the last vestiges of a regular Home Depot and took on the appearance of a true design shop specializing in bath and kitchen remodelings. The Miami employees dropped the yellow aprons worn by their counterparts. Instead, they dressed in khakis and polo shirts, or skirts and blouses. "It's a little bit more professional," said Scott. "There's no need for them to wear an apron. They're walking around with ladies dressed very nicely telling them about Ann Sacks tile." (There was virtually no way to get dirty in this store. Only one worker mixing paint actually needed an apron.)

The storefront's stucco facade was a cross between peach and pink—not Home Depot's trademark orange hue. And the name on the front downplayed Expo's connection to Home Depot. Previous locations had used the name "Home Depot Expo." But the Miami store was called "Expo Design Center," with the letters spelling E-X-P-O being orange, pink, dark green, and navy blue, respectively. Below that, in much smaller letters, was the phrase, "A Home Depot company." Explained Scott: "We think there's a tremendous amount of brand equity" in the Home Depot name. "We don't want to take away from that. But we want a different image. To go after the same customer doesn't make sense." Internally, Scott argued Expo needed to distance itself from the Home Depot name—a strategy some considered a rebuke of the company's overall success since it wasn't cannibalizing sales from its orange cousins.

Inside, the Miami location looked totally different from a Home Depot—and from other Expos. There were no checkout counters at the front door nor was there a high, warehouse-type ceiling. The cash registers were located in an island in the middle of the store, designed in an oval racetrack format. And the ceiling was dropped, a remnant of its previous tenant, a Kmart. The lower ceiling allowed for better signs and improved visibility. The store had a more consistent look and didn't try to fit a design showroom into a warehouse size. The smaller size and the oval aisle made for a more navigable shopping experience.

Scott consciously sought to create a chasm between Home Depot's ubiquitous warehouse-type, do-it-yourself sites and the upscale designer stores tested for the previous five years. Past Expos, he admitted, kept some Home Depot trappings that customers expected, such as roving assistants, a low-cost warehouse atmosphere [Expo's past slogan had been "Expo style, Depot prices"] and in-supply hardware items that could be bought off the shelf. Before Miami, Expo spoke to two sets of customers with the same store, giving it a split personality.

The Miami store catered to affluent homeowners and interior decorators with large projects taking as long as two months from planning to installation. Special orders took as little as three days, or as long as six weeks. Customers were encouraged to schedule appointments with design specialists. And many offerings became special order because of the limited products actually for sale inside the store due to the smaller selling space. Dropped products included lawn and garden, a picture frame shop, ready-to-assemble furniture, showcase areas for Laura Ashley and Fieldcrest linens, and a 24-foot-long working showerhead display. The showerhead display required a lot of maintenance, and "We weren't getting a lot of sales from the products it offered," revealed Smith. Ralph Lauren became the only paint line sold. Even the diner was eliminated, replaced by an espresso bar.

Customers wanting Home Depot prices could still find $2-per-square-foot tile and $20 faucets. But Expo stocked $3,000 wood-paneled refrigerators that resembled armoires and 300-year-old tile from Israel costing $40 per square foot. And the display was different. At a Home Depot, lamps are stacked on a floor. At Expo, they sat on shelves or on tables—where they'd be in someone's house. Tile is displayed on shelves at a Home Depot. At Expo, it was set into the floor so customers could walk over it. The idea at Expo was to get shoppers sampling the goods and seeing how they'd fit into the decor so that they'd buy more. "We think we're a project store," said Scott after the Miami store opened. "We want to offer a one-on-one experience. If you're doing kitchen jobs, bath jobs, tile jobs, inherently the ticket will be higher. We learned so much in the last year and a half. There's a lot less overlap of product. This is stuff you won't get in a regular Home Depot. We've decreased a lot of the on-hand offerings." Scott said the Miami store is "more reflective of where we're headed."

Before the Miami store opened, Scott conducted focus groups and customer interviews. And he and Smith had visited design centers around the country. "Our goal is to be the best design firm in the United States," said Scott. The result was a store aimed at far fewer customers, but higher average purchases. (One of its first customers bought $6,000 worth of kitchen appliances.) Such a strategy is highly unusual in the retail world, which typically tries to increase customers. But Home Depot felt that going against the grain would work for one critical reason. By making the store unique, Expo customers would spend more. The Miami store focused Expo's offerings on seven core, high-ticket areas—kitchen, bath, appliances, carpeting and rugs, ceramic tiles, lighting, and window decorations—and then Scott and Smith told workers to set Expo apart from other design boutiques with its product offerings.

Indeed, no other design boutique offered those seven core product areas together. For example, Home Depot hired Pat Shaw, who ran carpet stores in Dallas, to run the carpet department. "We're trying to play up pattern carpet, which hasn't been done in a long time," said Shaw. "It's a little different tack than what the competitors are doing. We're trying to have every taste available." In oriental rugs, Scott and Smith hired Ricky Ramnarian, who had more than 20 years' experience in the field. Scott and Smith made it a point to hire workers with extensive knowledge in their departments. Many came from small design stores in the Miami area, attracted by Home Depot's higher salaries.

Unlike the Long Island debacle, when Home Depot's long-term growth plans overshadowed the store's opening, the

Miami store took a low-key approach during its opening, and it paid off. To attract customers, Expo sent direct-mail publications to 15,000 south Florida residents living in high-income zip codes. And it advertised in *Florida Design,* an interior design publication, with a slogan that read, "The perfect home exists only in your mind. And here."

This Expo spoke clearly to the target audience. After a store visit, one Wall Streeter lauded Scott's ability to "step outside of the Home Depot shell and to bleed pink instead of orange." *National Home Center News* executive editor John Caulfield said he "came away with a new appreciation for a company as large as Home Depot that's willingly tinkering with a new format in ways in which other retailers would never dream." While Caulfield noted that the Miami layout wasn't likely to be the final word on what a national Expo rollout would look like, he added that "Expo is that rare animal in a risk-averse retail universe: a work in progress." The latter's comments particularly stood out considering the sometimes terse relationship between Big Orange and the industry publication.

Two startling points stood out about the Miami Expo. While most retailers wanted bigger stores—Tandy's Incredible Universe and Wal-Mart Supercenters are two prime examples—Home Depot was the first with a smaller format. By design, the Miami store, unlike the other Expos, is not surrounded by other so-called Big Box retailers. It's located in a strip mall between a grocery store and an Eckerd drug store—an unconventional Home Depot location. A smaller store and lower rent means lower capital investment for the Expo concept, making it easier to roll out into new markets.

In addition, by breaking from the Home Depot mold, the upscale Expo concept finally shifted away from the mass appeal the company's original stores have. The Expo store concept, as it now stands, is a radical departure from a Home Depot, and the income gap between shoppers at the two stores has widened. You're likely to see BMWs and Lexus, not the pickup trucks that are a common sight at a Home Depot, in its parking lot. That move was intentional. With the new Miami store design,

Marcus and Blank broke Expo away from the Home Depot mold to see if it could stand on its own—and withstand the rigors required for a national rollout.

They got results. Expo's sales by the end of 1997 were increasing by nearly 20 percent. Home Depot opened two more Expo stores in Florida in 1998, and Scott is optimistic about their performance. One of the new stores, located in Davie, is ironically a former Builders Square location and about 40 minutes north of the Miami store. As in Miami, the Davie store is located in a strip shopping center with a grocery store near the interstate.

But like the other Expo stores, it evolved the concept. The Davie location has a lighting department that shows lights on a wall, ceiling or table, resembling how they would be used in a home. Antique sideboards adorn a room with Tiffany lamps. The art and mirror framing department, which had been removed from the Miami store, was put back in at Davie. And it has an expanded outdoor lawn furniture department. "We took what works in other stores and created a hybrid," said Scott.

The new other new Expo store in Florida, located in Boynton Beach, shares a parking lot with a Home Depot to see how much its sales will be affected. Another Expo store is slated to open in 1999 in Atlanta. And Home Depot now believes Expo will eventually grow to 200 stores in the next seven years. "We try to keep learning," said Scott. "Maybe the next one will be 5,000 square feet smaller or 5,000 square feet larger. We've got to test it. We need to be cautious. At the same time, we're excited about it. We'll get customers in, and we'll ask them what they think."

To be sure, Expo has remained true to its original purpose—a laboratory to try out new products that could then be rolled out into regular Home Depot stores. In February 1996, Home Depot opened a new store in the posh Buckhead area of Atlanta that included a selection of Ralph Lauren paints originally tested in Expo locations. The Buckhead location also included blue and green bathtubs and toilets originally sold in Expo. Many Home Depots now offer some of the installation services first provided at Expo.

But under the direction of Marcus and Blank, the store con-cept has evolved into much more than a "laboratory" for new products and services. Expo's future is to have more stores and to be a stand-alone chain. The company has more than 700 reg-ular Home Depots. And while those stores are now entering smaller markets that a decade ago the company would not have even considered, eventually Big Orange will tap all the possibili-ties for its flagship retail outlet. The Expo store, with an empha-sis on big-ticket remodeling projects managed by designers and architects, provides Home Depot with an alternative expansion path into metropolitan markets long after it has built dozens of its regular stores in these areas.

Still, the company won't meet rosy earlier forecasts for Expo. One Wall Streeter predicted in 1995 that there would be 40 to 50 Expo stores open by the end of 1998. Yet, the slow exploratory process of Expo—in contrast to the fast growth of Home Depot—was the right strategy for the tough retail envi-ronment of the 1990s. That evolutionary strategy means that Expo one day could become the company's second retail chain, with hundreds of locations dotting the landscape and billions in sales. And it's likely to be successful because of the slow tinkering and refining that strengthened the format. Think of the customer service snafus that might have occurred had Home Depot decided to immediately add dozens of Expo loca-tions after the initial success in San Diego and Atlanta.

If they can make it work, Expo is a tremendous growth vehicle that gives Home Depot a head start on the competi-tion. But Marcus and Blank had better hurry with their roll-out. Rivals are already competing with new stores of their own. In February 1998, Sears opened a 120,000-square-foot store called "The Great Indoors" with similar kitchen and bath departments. Expo's success, despite some of its problems, has attracted attention.

Management Lessons

Home Depot has also tinkered with its store design to come up with another retail format. The move shows that the retailer is constantly searching for ways to find layouts, products and other items to attract customers into a pleasant shopping experience. And it showed how a business can continually refine a format to make it suitable for a national rollout.

1. Home Depot began exploring new store formats to draw the attention of new customers nearly a decade ago. That strategy has allowed it find a way to attract more remodeling business, showing that Home Depot is able to think outside of its traditional store format.

2. Home Depot has expanded with new stores in ways that will prevent competitors from stealing sales; it eventually changed its Expo stores so that they look nothing like a traditional Home Depot store. That gave Home Depot another store that doesn't compete against itself, but rather other retailers.

3. Make sure problems have been corrected before expanding a service. Home Depot learned with the installation service it was providing at its Expo stores that bad service can thwart growth.

4. Constantly tinker with your store format to entice customers. Home Depot's Expo locations were refined into a smaller store with a calm, soothing interior emphasizing a handful of product lines that customers wanted.

5. Slow growth for new projects helps refine the concept, as Home Depot learned with Expo. Because its other stores were growing so fast, Home Depot was able to take its time with Expo until it found the right product mix and format.

HOME DEPOT
GOES GLOBAL

It's a good idea to find out what the rest of the world is like.

—BERNIE MARCUS

Marcus and Blank had made Home Depot's do-it-yourself product selection, customer service, and low prices legendary in markets throughout the United States. But how would Big Orange fare overseas?

In 1990, Marcus told some employees, "We have a lot to do in the United States first. [International expansion] takes a lot of energy and a lot of time." He did, however, say at the same meeting, "We feel there is a market overseas." By 1992 Marcus and Blank looked harder overseas as they realized they could exhaust domestic expansion possibilities in the next 20 years. As they looked at how and where the company would grow in the next century, adding Home Depots around the globe made sense. International expansion would complement domestic growth plans for CrossRoads, Expo, and delivery and installation services.

To be sure, Marcus and Blank realized that international expansion couldn't carry Home Depot's growth any time soon. And entering unfamiliar markets meant radically changing the store's products to cater to home building techniques. In many countries brick or cement blocks, which were foreign to their merchandisers, are used to make homes instead of wood. There were also pitfalls to doing business overseas like currency exchanges and export protocols. Such a move would not be as easy as picking a site, getting zoning approval, and building a store. Home Depot saw, however, dozens of emerging do-it-yourself markets where consumers embraced home remodeling and repairs. If Marcus and Blank could expand Home Depot into those markets, they'd be able to once again lead a retailing revolution.

Inglis, already traveling the world to examine new do-it-yourself products, looked into expanding Home Depot overseas. He had befriended top international home center experts in his travels. And the company received proposals nearly every week to franchise its stores somewhere in the world. Those deals were turned down because Home Depot would have lost control over the stores. So Inglis visited every continent where home center retailers were developing and looked at the possibilities. "International just sort of evolved," said Inglis. "There was never a time where we sat down and said, 'Let's roll out internationally.'" Still, he added, "It wasn't a tough decision." Marcus and Blank knew if Home Depot could be successful in the United States, it could work elsewhere.

The exercise gave Home Depot some of its sternest tests, teaching it how to evaluate foreign markets and reminding it of the pitfalls of acquisitions. As with its experience with Cross-Roads and Expo, Home Depot moved carefully and slowly—too slowly for some executives. But Marcus and Blank had never experienced the problems they faced in foreign countries. The workers spoke different languages and in many cases had never been exposed to ideas like warehouse assortment. And there were dozens of legal requirements.

The most promising international markets, Inglis discovered, were in Europe and Latin America. In Europe, Inglis received a green light in 1994 to enter Europe. In France, however, there were laws against building Home Depot's 100,000-square-foot stores. And the market had entrenched home center retailer Castorama. Despite France's $12 billion do-it-yourself market, Inglis turned to England.

There, he found home center retailer B&Q who had small stores but who was beginning to build large, warehouse-sized locations that looked like Home Depots. Inglis was impressed with B&Q's leader, a friendly Brit named James Hodkinson. By early 1994, Inglis convinced Hodkinson to leave B&Q to oversee

Home Depot's international growth. The move was considered a coup. Hodkinson was well known in the British market. With him leading the charge, Home Depot could quickly gain entry into markets and access to home center products manufactured in England. Marcus and Blank had confidence in Hodkinson because he knew the industry. Hodkinson, in turn, was impressed with Home Depot. "It was a good operation full of vision," he said. "One always likes to work for the best."

The do-it-yourself market in England at that time was a $7 billion industry—small by America's standards. Still, Inglis and Hodkinson felt there was room for Home Depot. B&Q was the largest player, with about $1.5 billion in sales in 1993. Growth in new homes was declining, meaning that people were refurbishing and remodeling older homes. Expanding into England "would have shaken the whole European market, which is geared more to builder's merchants and [has] stores with no service," said Hodkinson.

Hodkinson came to Atlanta for training with the understanding that he would spend six months plotting strategy and learning the culture and then return to England to open stores there and possibly also in Germany. After a couple of months, however, Hodkinson quit—his wife was homesick and didn't want to move to Atlanta—and returned to B&Q, where he opened Home Depot–like stores all over Great Britain. When Hodkinson informed Inglis and Blank of his decision to return to England, they were understanding. But Marcus was upset with Hodkinson, yelling at him during a phone conversation. "When Hodkinson came over, we all loved him," said Don Campbell, vice president of imports at the time. "When he went back, Europe went off the horizon." After losing Hodkinson, Home Depot couldn't find anyone with the experience and knowledge to lead an entry into Europe.

Inglis began looking again, this time, south of the border. Other American warehouse-sized retailers such as Wal-Mart were expanding into Mexico. With its growing economy, low labor costs, and expanding middle class, Mexico was an attractive target in 1994. The country already had more than 7,000 hardware stores, but the business was shifting away from traditional retail venues such as the Calle Corrigedor, a street in Mexico City where stores filled with hardware, plumbing, and lighting products dominated the sidewalk. Larger home center stores had entered the market. Retailer Del Norte opened three stores in Ciudad Juarez as big as 50,000 square feet with another 40,000 square feet for lumberyards. Domestic competitors Grossman's and Payless Cashways established joint ventures with Mexican companies to open stores. Home Depot wanted in before competitors got too much of a head start.

Again, Inglis hired in February 1994 someone familiar with the market to lead Home Depot's charge. This time, the executive would stick around to expand the retailer into a foreign market, just not the one originally intended. Bill Pena, a former HomeBase senior vice president and a native of Ballinger, Texas, spoke fluent Spanish and knew the Mexican market—50 percent of Mexico's residents were under the age of 19. "One of the reasons we find this to be a great market is that it's a young market," said Pena. "There's a lot of growth potential." Together, Inglis and Pena developed a merchandising team to create a new product mix—more cement and concrete blocks and less lumber. And they began looking for sites in Mexico City, Guadalajara, and Monterey. They were within weeks of buying land to build stores.

Then, the Mexican economy crashed in December 1994. The peso lost 40 percent of its value almost overnight. Home Depot put its Mexican expansion plans on hold and looked elsewhere. Yes, Marcus and Blank admit, they got lucky, and if they had bought land in Mexico sooner, Home Depot's international plans might have been scarred. But Inglis and Pena took a methodical approach. And that meant Home Depot was able to stop before it was too late. Today, Marcus and Blank still see Mexico has a viable market for Home Depot, but they are also concentrating on other markets.

In May 1993, Home Depot announced it would open its first Canadian store, just across the border in Vancouver. While the move was an extension of its expansion in the competitive Seattle market, it was also symbolic. Marcus and Blank planted Home Depot's orange flag in a new country for the first time.

The Canadian market was a prime Home Depot target. First, the do-it-yourself market was big, with $13 billion in annual sales at that time. Second, 80 percent of the country's population lived within 100 miles of the U.S. border, making expansion easy to watch. And the market had its first warehouse-sized home center stores—Home Depot copycats called "Aikenhead's Home Improvement."

Aikenhead's was run by Stephen Bebis, the former Home Depot executive who was once so moved by an Outward Bound class that he cried. Bebis left in 1991 to help the giant brewer Molson develop Aikenhead's. "We weren't too happy when he left," said Marcus. "We'd never lost an officer before to a competitor." After assessing the Canadian market and Aikenhead's, Marcus and Blank didn't lose Bebis for long. Aikenhead's stores were similar to Home Depot's size and stocked similar merchandise. Molson had given Bebis a blank check to build a chain before Home Depot entered the market.

However, Molson later decided it wanted to sell its retail interests and concentrate on its brewing operation. Less than a year after announcing plans to enter Canada, Home Depot bought 75 percent of Aikenhead's from Molson for $150 million and gained the right to buy the other 25 percent. At the time, Aikenhead's already had five stores in the Toronto area and had plans to open four more stores in Ontario and British Columbia. "We are totally opposed to acquisitions," said Marcus. "But this was a unique opportunity to enter Canada quickly and profitably. These stores are clones of ours. Plus Aikenhead's is in markets we want to be in. This accelerates by four years our plans in Canada."

Shortly before the deal was announced, Bebis and Blank met again. "We hugged," said Bebis. "When Arthur walked through the door, I felt as though I were home." The feeling was mutual. "The orange blood runs thick," said Marcus. "He has done an absolutely outstanding job on opening these stores." Bebis stayed on after the acquisition and helped convert the Aikenhead's teal stores into Home Depot orange.

Marcus and Blank's foray into Canada wasn't smooth, however. The stores lost money that first year, primarily because of a slump in the Canadian economy along with Home Depot's adjusting to its unfamiliar market surroundings. Within a year, Marcus and Blank cut back expansion in Canada, adding one fewer store in 1995 and five fewer in 1996. In 1995, Home Depot's Canada operations turned a small profit and the company had 19 stores. By the end of 1996, there were 24 Home Depots north of the border. "There was a lot of pain involved in Canada," said Marcus.

There was a reason that Marcus didn't like acquisitions. A deal struck a decade before the Canada purchase had hurt the company. In March 1984, Marcus and Blank bought land for stores in the Los Angeles area—returning to the market where they had been running Handy Dan just six years before. They also announced plans to move into Houston, San Diego, San Francisco, and Detroit.

The decision to expand into Detroit turned heads because it would be the first market for Marcus and Blank outside the Sun Belt that stretched from California through Arizona to Florida. That meant Home Depot would have to change the stores, stocking more cold-weather–related items like insulation and snow blowers in those stores. Changing the products wouldn't pose a problem because Home Depot was already tinkering with its assortment. However, they did need to learn what cold-weather products like snow shovels might sell well and who were the manufacturers.

Marcus and Blank were also looking at purchasing competitors, including the Home Club in California and the home center division of Bowater, the huge forest products company. The California deal never panned out. But the Bowater Home Center, division, based in the Dallas suburb of Plano, had opened its first stores in early 1983, and by late 1984 it had nine locations, including six in the Dallas market. Buying the chain would give Home Depot an immediate presence in Dallas and address a growing concern the company was having in finding new store sites. Bowater stores in Baton Rouge and Shreveport would complement their New Orleans locations. In

addition, by buying Bowater, Marcus and Blank would eliminate a competitor in a crowded field. The transaction seemed
to have only positives.

In October 1984, Marcus and Blank struck a $40 million
deal for the Bowater stores. But the stores fit into Home
Depot like a screwdriver inserted into a live electrical outlet—
the result was a big shock. Changing the Bowater locations to
an orange motif, training its employees in the Home Depot
way and adding such company staples as do-it-yourself classes
proved easier said than done. "We bit off more than we could
chew," said Rick Mayo. "It helped us determine that a 25 percent growth rate was about our maximum effective rate."

Home Depot compounded its mistake. Instead of closing
the stores during a renovation, Marcus and Blank kept them
open so they wouldn't lose the revenue. But the construction
confused customers and frustrated employees, and Marcus
and Blank admitted that it was wrong to try to operate the
stores under those circumstances. In addition, "it took us
more than a year to change the consumer's mind and convince
him we weren't just Bowater under another name," said
Blank. The usually loquacious Marcus, for once, was more
succinct, calling the Bowater stores "a used car."

The lemon Marcus and Blank bought, however, soured the
rest of the company too, causing concern about Home Depot
as a whole. "When you're very busy opening stores, there are a
lot of little things you don't do, and you soon outdistance the
talents and the abilities of your people," said Marcus. Home
Depot couldn't handle new stores being opened and the
Bowater conversion at the same time. The Bowater acquisition taught Marcus and Blank—and the entire company—a
valuable lesson. Home Depot was riding high in the early
1980s. Bowater was its first big failure. The Bowater stores
diverted attention away from the 19 stores Home Depot had
at the beginning of 1984 and the dozen that would open in
the next year. While the company's overall sales grew the next
year to $700 million, profits fell for the first time ever. The
stock price fell to about a third of its price from three years
earlier. Tails tucked between their legs, Marcus and Blank got

the company's focus back on the stores and off the Bowater problems.

They slowed expansion. In February 1986, Marcus and Blank sold their four unopened Detroit locations to Pace Membership Warehouse—a deal that also boosted Home Depot's bottom line and assuaged the fears of Wall Street, which had grown concerned that Marcus and Blank were about to destroy the company by growing too fast. After opening 19 new stores in 1985, Home Depot scaled back to just 10 new stores in 1986. The Snow Belt would have to wait for its first Home Depot. It was a move Marcus and Blank didn't want to make. But it was the right move for Home Depot's future. Although they were correcting a much bigger mistake than simply buying a product that didn't sell in their stores, Marcus and Blank had learned that when errors occur, it's better to correct them immediately rather than let it fester.

Despite the problems with Bowater and some unrelated hiring snafus, Home Depot grew and returned to its pre-Bowater profit levels. The company passed the $1 billion sales mark in 1987 and nearly hit $2 billion in sales in 1989. By 1991, the company had $3.8 billion in sales. Net income rose from $23.9 million in 1987 to $163.4 million in 1991. Marcus and Blank had created an organization that could churn out ever-increasing profits and sales.

Despite Marcus's aversion to acquisitions, in many respects Home Depot committed the same mistakes with Aikenhead's that had occurred with Bowater a decade earlier. The Aikenhead's stores weren't a good fit with Home Depot. The operation had used different computer systems and had retained more employees than they needed at many stores. To cut workers, Home Depot had to move slowly and carefully so they wouldn't invite union intervention. As with Bowater, employees had to be retrained, displaying once again the value of Home Depot's training practices. And there was the difficult task of introducing the company's culture into a foreign country.

There was one major difference between the Bowater and Aikenhead's deals, however. By 1994, Home Depot was a huge company, with $12.5 billion in sales, more than $600 million in net income, and 340 stores in 28 states. Marcus and Blank had built a retailer able to withstand the pain of integration. The Canada problems barely raised a blip on Home Depot's financial performance. With Bowater, Home Depot was crippled for a year.

Still, Marcus and Blank made some changes. After a year in the market, they realized it would help Home Depot if it could find a native Canadian to run its stores. "Retailing is dependent on local customs," observed retail consultant Kurt Barnard. "If you operate in a foreign country, it's to your advantage and to the advantage of the business to have someone acquainted with local custom, lifestyles, and language." Bebis, despite his Home Depot ties, had to go. He was not Canadian.

Blank looked for a successor. He found Annette Verschuren, a 39-year-old who was running the Canadian operations for Michael's crafts chains. While she didn't have any home center experience, she knew Canadian retailing. What she didn't know was Home Depot's culture. So Marcus and Blank put her through an extensive, four-month training program. "She worked in a variety of capacities in our stores, in different positions in the stores, worked in different departments in the stores," noted Blank. "She spent time in every key functional area of the company, spent time with our senior merchants, strategy meetings, understanding how we were structured from a merchandising standpoint, what our positioning was in terms of our customer segments, spent time in marketing."

That training paid off. Verschuren returned to Canada, put on an orange apron and visited the stores, just as Marcus and Blank did in the beginning and still do today. "I think leaders today have to stay connected to the customers," she said. "That is my philosophy and what I'm all about." Marcus and Blank couldn't have said it any better.

Verschuren turned around what had been Home Depot's weakest division. She customized the stores to fit markets, adding French signs and a bilingual staff to Home Depot's stores in Ottawa and a large Chinese staff to its store in Richmond, British Columbia, where half the customers speak Chinese dialects. Today, Canada is one of Home Depot's fastest-growing and most successful markets. It had 32 stores by the end of 1997, with plans to double that number by the end of the year 2000. An Expo store might be opening in Toronto and Vancouver in the next couple of years. Sales in Canada grew by more than 40 percent in 1997, the average purchase price grew by 7 percent, and Home Depot's Canadian profits grew by more than 90 percent.

Marcus and Blank passed on a chance in 1997 to expand Home Depot further into Canada, giving up its right to buy 11 Reno Depot stores in the Quebec province. Perhaps they didn't want to repeat the cultural problems resulting from Bowater and Aikenhead's. The Reno Depot stores were in the lone Canadian province where a majority of residents speak French. Those employees might have been the most difficult of all to retrain and teach the Bleeding Orange culture. They were also unionized, and Marcus is adamantly antiunion. French home improvement chain Castorama bought the stores. But a year later, in April 1998, Marcus and Blank bought the remaining 25 percent interest in the Home Depot stores there from Molson for $262 million. Marcus and Blank, with a lot of help from people like Verschuren, had figured out the Canadian market.

Marcus and Blank still wanted to expand Big Orange overseas.

Their first opportunity came in China. In 1994, the Tianjin North Building Materials Trade Company proposed opening the country's first warehouse-sized home center store in Tianjin, China's third-largest city and a major center for building material and trade. The Chinese company had developed an import and export network for do-it-yourself products. Together with Chinese government agencies, the consortium of suppliers asked for Home Depot's help.

China wasn't high on Home Depot's list. "But we realized the opportunity and began establishing relationships in order to research potential business and lay a foundation for the future," said Rick Chavie, then Home Depot's director of strategic planning. Home Depot didn't offer any monetary support. But Marcus and Blank agreed to lend their expertise in developing relationships with vendors and training employees. (And the next time Inglis went to China, he visited Tianjin to see the store.) Home Depot already was importing Chinese ceiling fans and rugs, and they saw their involvement with the store as a way to find more products. Home Depot would also learn about the Chinese market and its consumers.

While China's 1.2 billion population was five times that of the United States, its home improvement market was dramatically smaller, having grown from $1 billion in 1990 to $6 billion in 1994. Despite the smaller market, Home Depot was curious. "It is one of the fastest-growing economies in the world and will be one of the largest in the next century," said Chavie. "We are proceeding carefully, not calling this a joint venture, but a lesson in building relationships and learning how to go into other countries successfully."

Marcus, for one, was interested in China. "We're going to watch them very carefully," he said. "It gives us a clue as to what will happen in undeveloped markets. It's a way for us to find out if there is a market for Home Depot. If Home Depot is going to be an international company, it's going to have to make a move somewhere." While Marcus wasn't sure the Chinese venture would work, he saw it as a way to test Home Depot's strategies in a faraway land. Having the Chinese government as a partner was also appealing. Because the government issued licenses to foreign companies operating in the country, Home Depot would have an easy entryway into the market through the store. The store would also have an import-export license, giving Home Depot greater ease at getting products in and out of the country.

The proposal went before the Home Depot board. Sales growth at Home Depot stores open a full year slowed from 15 percent in 1992 to just 3 percent, the lowest rate ever for the company, in 1995. Part of that drop was due to Home Depot's cannibalization of some of the store's sales to keep customer service levels high. Marcus and Blank, who felt Home Depot should spend more time focusing on improving the results in the domestic stores, never signed the formal agreement.

The Chinese store, called Home Way, opened in late 1996

with a strong Home Depot resemblance. Employees—trained at Home Depot stores in the United States—wore orange aprons and offered product advice for more than 40,000 items. The store also offered Home Depot staples: everyday low prices, free delivery to locations near the store, project seminars, and installation services.

There were differences. About 70 percent of the store's merchandise was manufactured in China, including concrete products and stainless-steel stairway railings unique to the market. But other products in every category, from lumber to kitchen and bath supplies, were imported. And to entice Chinese shoppers to buy special-order imports, the store built a 3,000-square-foot, two-story American-type home inside the store. The home, a traditional Cape Cod design, looked as if it had been lifted off a street in suburban Boston. Home Way's consortium of suppliers is trying to add more stores in cities like Beijing and Shanghai. Into those new markets, they'll be taking many of the products and services Home Depot first made famous in the United States.

Marcus and Blank are watching Home Way's progress—even though Home Depot isn't involved in the project anymore. Because the store looks so much like a Home Depot, the company can test its retail concept in one of the world's biggest markets without having to spend its money or time.

Still trying to apply what they had learned from their missteps in England and Mexico, Marcus and Blank wanted to place a true Home Depot store outside of North America. After the Mexican expansion was shelved, Pena worked on Home Depot's latest, and biggest, version of its warehouse-sized stores. He returned to the international job in late 1995. "Once we identified international as a growth avenue, Bernie and Arthur asked me to invest quality time over a nine-month period to look at the retailing environments of developed regions around the world," said Pena.

Pena examined how other big retailers had entered foreign markets. Wal-Mart, for example, was not the first retail entry into South America, Mexico, or China. But it got into those markets early and emphasized its low prices and customer service. Toys R Us grabbed an early lead in Europe, Hong Kong, Japan, and Singapore.

Pena also tapped the expertise of Keough, a former Coca-Cola president who had helped the soft drink company successfully expand across the globe and a present Home Depot board member. By the end of 1997, Coca-Cola held a 50 percent share of the worldwide soft drink market, including a 71.9 percent share in Chile and a 62 percent share in Argentina, two markets Pena liked. From Coca-Cola, Pena learned about business practices in different countries. "Don told us that to succeed internationally required the strong support of senior management," said Pena. "We've had that management support from the beginning."

Pena visited 15 countries in 1996, including South Korea, Japan, China, France, Great Britain, Argentina, Brazil, and Chile. He discovered that Home Depot was well known around the globe. When he arrived at his hotel in South Korea, Pena had 10 messages waiting for him. And he was getting calls that first night as late as 1 A.M. "The word was out that I was there representing Home Depot, and everybody wanted to set up an appointment to discuss our business," said Pena. "It was relentless. The Home Depot name is well accepted around the world. Business people know that name. They have read about us. We had the red carpet rolled out."

It was time for Home Depot to take advantage of that international name recognition. Pena assessed each market's do-it-yourself industry, the economy's growth rate, existing competition, household spending, inflation, labor costs, taxes, and political climate. Developed countries offered a higher chance of success because the business environment to support Home Depot was already in place. "In a developed country, you have favorable economies and stable government, which helps minimize risk," explained Pena. "In emerging countries, there will be higher initial investment and a higher degree of risk involved."

By 1996, Home Depot's international strategy focused on taking sales away from existing home improvement stores rather than creating a demand from scratch in a country. "We want to go into developed markets where the home improvement industry is starting to take hold," said Pena. "Then, we'll bring it to its next higher level. A common thread we find is that everybody wants good customer service, everybody likes to find the products they want in stock, and to be served well. And for the most part, the industry is underserved today. That gives us the opportunity to provide a higher level of service, and that will be our edge."

Pena also discovered that the home improvement market in most countries was dominated by professional builders and contractors. Many consumers hadn't yet grasped do-it-yourself projects. That profile was in contrast to Home Depot's domestic business, which is about 75 percent consumer and 25 percent contractor. Home Depot would have to change its strategy to be successful overseas. Its focus became how the international home center business caters to professionals.

Pena traveled for more than a year around the globe, crisscrossing Inglis's earlier travels. "The good news is that we believe we could put our type of store almost anywhere in the world," said Blank. "There's a need for the products and services that we provide. The bad news is, we had to pick a place to start. That was the hard part."

Although Japan and Germany were the two biggest international do-it-yourself markets, government restrictions and trade barriers made expansion there difficult. Pena steered Home Depot to South America, where there were fewer problems. Another factor in favor of a South American location: A treaty signed between Argentina, Brazil, Chile, Paraguay, and Uruguay meant that it would be easier to import products into those countries and easier to ship merchandise between them. It also influenced Pena that most of the region spoke Spanish, a language he knew and could use to converse with local manufacturers and potential hires.

In December 1996, Blank led a group of executives on a South American trip. They gave Pena the OK to move forward. Pena struck a deal with Falabella, a big department store chain in Chile. The 100-year-old retailer was the country's biggest, with annual sales of $1 billion. Through a joint venture, Home

Depot would open stores in and around Santiago. Falabella would provide computer systems, a credit card operation, warehouses, and a fleet of trucks. Home Depot could send mailings, for example, to consumers who had a Falabella credit card, which made up about 17 percent of the country's population. "Conceivably, we could start off with a customer base of 2.2 million people," said Pena. And Falabella also owned large shopping centers, giving Home Depot easy access to retail sites. Finally, its computers handled more than 60,000 products from nearly 4,000 suppliers. Falabella was to Chilean department stores what Home Depot had become to American home centers. The strengths of the two retailers meshed as well as Marcus and Blank. "We looked at all the South American countries, but we felt like Chile would be easier for us," said Ron Brill, who went on the trip with Blank. "They've got a growing middle class. They've got a stable government."

About 85 percent of Chile's 14 million residents live in urban areas—similar to those that for nearly two decades had been Home Depot's core markets domestically. And its economy is the most dynamic in Latin America. Between 1991 and 1995, its gross domestic product had increased at a healthy annual rate of 7.4 percent. That growth led to retailers adding stores in Chile. During 1995, retail sales in Chile increased a healthy 8 percent—twice as fast as in the United States. Most of that growth was in furniture and appliance stores, leading Pena and Home Depot to believe the country was ready for its warehouse home center stores. Chile already had the most developed do-it-yourself market in Latin America. Home Depot wanted to take that a step further.

No other South American country had home center retailers as big as those already operating in Chile, making Home Depot's acceptance with shoppers easier. On a typical Saturday in Santiago, nearly 10,000 customers were jamming into the 38,000-square-foot Easy Homecenter, and more than 70 percent were buying something. Not far away, a 74,000-square-foot Sodimac Home Center was filled with 28,000 shoppers that same weekend. Sodimac, with 40 stores and a half billion dollars in annual sales, was holding a commanding lead in the market. Bracing for the arrival of Home Depot, Sodimac remodeled its original store in the Santiago upscale suburb of Las Condes, and it planned to add one store a month to the market. And Sodimac hired Inglis, who had left Home Depot in 1996, as a consultant, helping it prepare for its new competitor. Competition never stopped Marcus and Blank, however. Pena hired a Sodimac executive, Julio Campos, to be general manager of Home Depot's Chilean operations. "He's well aware of Sodimac's ability," said Pena. "They're a company that's been successful for a long period of time. But there's been no competition. Our intent is to be the dominant market leader in Chile."

Home Depot picked three sites for its first stores, two in Santiago and one outside the city. Pena also reviewed other sites. The stores, Home Depot decided, would be typical 130,000-square-foot locations but with smaller garden sections. "Home Depot will not look exactly the same, because we will embrace market differences," said Pena. "But, we will keep our principles of excellent customer service, broad assortment and low prices. This is the know-how we bring, which has been forged over the years by our associates in North America. Their day-in, day-out commitment built our customer service culture and makes it possible for us to look beyond our shores." And he picked two Spanish-speaking executives, Ramon Alvarez and Rick Vasquez, to direct store operations and merchandising. The operational strategy was the same as in the domestic business: Put the infrastructure near the stores and don't run the business from Atlanta.

Home Depot hired workers from Chile to staff the store, although a handful of company experts provided know-how and developed the culture. "We need to adapt to and understand the local culture in order to best serve our customers," explained Pena. A group of core workers—who spoke Spanish and English—for the Chilean stores trained in Home Depot locations in Miami, San Antonio, and Dallas. They also went to Atlanta and visited stores there, met with Marcus and Blank, and even went on an Outward Bound excursion. They were treated just as any other Home Depot employee.

Home Depot invited some Chilean vendors to Santiago to

hear a presentation by Pena and Marcus. And Pena met with U.S. vendors in Chicago. The focus, however, was to develop new vendor relationships so that the store's products would come mainly from that country. The move was smart because it reflected a strategy of hedging against currency fluctuations, catering to Chilean's attachment to local brands and avoiding the expensive cost of shipping do-it-yourself products overseas. Marcus and Blank wanted to limit the potential problems as much as possible that they would be faced with trying to operate a store so far away from Atlanta. The drawback for this strategy was that developing such relationships took time, which slowed Home Depot's international expansion.

Home Depot's first store in Chile opened in August 1998, and its second was ready by the end of the year. Home Depot ran an advertisement in Chile for rank-and-file store employees in February 1998 and received an estimated 5,000 applications in the first five days, an indication that the Santiago market was well aware of Home Depot and a good barometer that the first stores would receive a lot of customer traffic. Marcus and Blank were confident that the stores would eventually become as successful as their other locations.

Home Depot saw Chile as the platform upon which to expand into other South American countries like Argentina and Peru, where Falabella has stores. The first Home Depot store in Argentina is expected to open in Buenos Aires in 1999 or 2000. "We're not saying Chile is better, but it gives us a great platform to grow into other markets in the region," said Pena. Once successful in South America, Home Depot could then expand to other continents. Pena's team is already compiling a list of Home Depot employees who speak another language. "This is part of our long-term approach for knowing which of our associates have other language skills and are interested in the international arena," said Pena. "Then, when the opportunity does come along, we might know someone inside our company who can help us."

Marcus and Blank, despite having stubbed their toes in England and Mexico, know international expansion is vital to Home Depot's future growth and success. While it took the company a while to get itself in gear, it is now going full steam ahead. In 1998, they hired a European consulting firm to look at other countries outside the United States. "One of the lessons we've learned from others is that you can wait too long to develop international business," said Pena. "We are not going to wait five years. We are going to start now. We need to get moving in order to gain priceless experience and under-standing of local business practices. That will give us the momentum we need to succeed."

MANAGEMENT LESSONS

Expanding internationally is not for the faint of heart, as Home Depot has discovered during the past decade. While it's just now adding stores outside of North America, the retailer went through numerous missteps before it finally made the right moves. Its trials and tribulations with overseas expansion shows that every business must cater its offerings to the specific markets.

1. Home Depot began looking at expanding internationally nearly a decade before it opened a store on foreign soil. It wanted to keep its sales increasing and realized there is the potential to put its locations in many markets outside the United States.

2. Acquisitions are good when the cultures are similar, and Home Depot realized for the second time, when it expanded into Canada, that acquisitions can be painful.

3. International economies can make overseas expansion risky, and that's why Home Depot has treaded carefully into markets outside North America. The retailer has been forced to radically change its stores so that it will be successful in these new countries.

4. Established international markets provide the best possibilities, Home Depot found after initially exploring emerging countries. Established economies and a growing middle class provide stable sales when expanding overseas.

5. Adapt your stores and products to international markets, because while customers in some overseas countries may like the United States, they live in vastly different environments. Home Depot stores in Chile don't sell the same items that are sold in Home Depot stores in Chicago.

THE NEW HOME DEPOT

As good as this is, worlds of opportunity are ahead for Home Depot and each one of us. We have only just begun.

—ARTHUR M. BLANK

Robert Tillman is surveying the battlefield. Tillman, Lowe's chief executive officer, stands in a parking lot just outside Athens, Georgia, and stares across the street at the enemy he has fought for a decade—Home Depot. Lowe's had a store in this college town about an hour northeast of Atlanta that garnered most of the do-it-yourself shoppers for nearly two decades. But Home Depot opened a store here in July 1996, taking sales away.

Tillman responded with a move reminiscent of how Marcus and Blank built Home Depot. He opened a larger, 118,000-square-foot store across the street. "Everything they took from us, we'll gain back, and even more," boasted Tillman. He is immaculately dressed and coifed, with pleated slacks and a white dress shirt that looks as if it has been pressed a half-hour earlier. His black loafers look freshly shined. Tillman is ready to sell some lumber and lawn mowers himself.

Billy Ergle, assistant store manager at the Home Depot across the street, seems unworried. "Having them close is good for us," said Ergle, who began working for Home Depot in his teens. "It makes us more attentive. We're going to continue to take care of the customer, continue to offer the best service and the lowest prices."

The lessons Marcus and Blank teach assistant store managers during training classes stuck with Ergle. Their rival, Tillman, says, "I have a lot of respect for what they've done. They are an outstanding company. Bernie and Arthur, nobody's more deserving of their success." Earlier, Tillman had been the keynote speaker at the National Hardware Show in Chicago where he stated that "one of the best things that ever happened to our company was the Home Depot. As the saying goes, 'A good scare is worth more than good advice.'"

Tillman, who also walks around his stores wearing an apron with his name on it, narrows his eyes as the sun bears down on him in the parking lot and gets to his point. "Home Depot made us what we are today," he said. "We know we can compete against them and be successful. They created the segment. We didn't copy it. We think we made something better."

As Marcus and Blank begin their third decade of building Home Depot, an old competitor is back to do battle again. Under Tillman, Lowe's expanded into metropolitan markets like Dallas and Home Depot's home turf of Atlanta. In April 1998, Tillman announced that Lowe's would open stores in markets such as Los Angeles, San Diego, and Phoenix by the end of 1999, locations that have been Home Depot strongholds for a decade. In Tampa, Lowe's built a store less than 1 mile from Bruce Berg's office at the southeast division headquarters. That's a defiant move many competitors expect from Home Depot. And Lowe's has grown as a result. Its sales have gone from less than $5 billion in 1994 to more than $10 billion in 1998. Its stock price, at $7 a share in April 1993, had zoomed to $46 five years later. Home Depot is not the only one reaping benefits from the growing do-it-yourself market.

In Tillman, Marcus and Blank have their most formidable foe. A life-size cutout of Home Depot mascot Homer—with a target drawn on his chest—once sat in his office. And as he walks through a Lowe's, Tillman makes statements like, "We think they're the best stores in the industry" and "We like to think we're better merchants" and "Everything we do is focused on the customer. Some people pay lip service to it, but we mean it."

Those are fighting words to Blank and Marcus, who for the past two decades waged a winning war on the rest of the home center retailing business and even other retailers like Sears. They hear the footsteps behind them and argue that they're still the industry's leader. "Lowe's is a very strong competitor," says Blank. "I still would submit to you that the level of product knowledge and the shopping and sales experience is better at Home Depot. We think there's a significant gap between Home Depot and Lowe's, and we plan to expand that gap."

Home Depot has responded with its typical competitive aggressiveness. At an Arlington, Texas, store, employees set up a display featuring a mangled toy car with the Lowe's logo on it. And in a presentation to Wall Street analysts in April 1998, chief financial officer Marshall Day showed investors a recent Home Depot newspaper ad for a wheelbarrow that read: "If you buy the manure Lowe's has been spreading lately, you'll need one of these." Added Day: "I've not heard anyone say [Lowe's has] gotten tougher. Our competitors can walk our stores and copy our signs, but they can't copy our culture."

Two of Blank's favorite sayings are "There is no finish line" and "Those that don't make dust, eat dust." For Home Depot, there is no finish line. And nowhere is that seen better than today with Blank pushing the company to keep reinventing itself and find new ways to capture more sales and please more customers.

Marcus and Blank know they can't relax now, even though Home Depot had $30 billion in sales in 1998 and nearly $2 billion in profits. They must find new ways to keep customers walking through their doors—and not the Lowe's across the street.

If they slip just once, they lose a customer. So what are they doing to maintain their momentum and win more shoppers as Home Depot heads into its third decade of being one of the world's most innovative retailers?

Marcus and Blank have come a long way from relying solely on good ole boy Ludlow Porch, a folksy Georgian who was featured in their initial advertising. Now, Home Depot runs slick full-page ads in national magazines like *Sports Illustrated, Time, Newsweek,* and *Life*. Television commercials run on ABC-TV's *Monday Night Football* with the slogan "America's Home Improvement Coach." A catalog for contractors has been expanded across the country. And Home Depot sponsors a 16-city home and garden show by *House Beautiful* magazine. Those are just a few examples of how Home Depot is building nationwide name recognition with consumers, letting them know its stores are the place for their do-it-yourself needs. "We're in the dream business, fulfilling dreams," said Hammill, Home Depot's senior vice president of marketing. "We're putting Home Depot in early into the process."

Home Depot's carpet commercials are a good example of that strategy. Home Depot sells more floor covering—including hardwood floors, tile, and vinyl flooring—than anybody else. In 1996 it expanded its carpet departments to attract more sales. Marcus and Blank admit Home Depot could have done a better job selling carpet in the past, despite their lofty sales. They are continually trying to do better. So the spots use Lynette Jennings from *HouseSmart* and the slogan "Wall to wall, coast to coast, nobody covers more floors."

The same strategy is used with power tool advertising. Home Depot discovered professional contractors buy more tools at their stores than anywhere else in the country. So tool commercials emphasize that point while trying to get do-it-yourselfers to also look at Home Depot as a store where they too can buy tools by using the slogan "Where people who know their stuff buy their stuff."

Home Depot emphasizes in advertising its relationship with brands such as Vigoro fertilizer and Husky tools sold only at its stores. A Vigoro commercial shows a man spreading fertilizer and singing "Vigoro" in an operatic-like tone—an obvious take-off on *The Barber of Seville.* A Husky commercial shows rough-looking mechanics and the phrase "The toughest name in tools, and only at Home Depot."

Home Depot also goes beyond traditional ways to market to its customers. During a *Monday Night Football* telecast, ABC showed a chart of the youngest NFL coaches. In the upper left hand corner was Home Depot's orange square logo. Commercials during Christmas dub the stores "The Toy Store for Big Kids"—an obvious invitation to come in and shop for dads.

Home Depot now goes far beyond television commercials

and newspaper ads to attract customers. In 1996, the retailer tested in Atlanta and Chicago a 1,000-page catalog geared toward professional contractors. The catalog contained about 16,000 of the 45,000 items normally sold in a store and allowed professional builders to place orders by facsimile and have the products delivered to any site. The catalog had new items such as larger size drainpipes, motors, pulleys, and safety cabinets for chemical storage. The catalog was aimed directly at competing publications many contractors and builders kept handy in their trucks. But it was also designed to attract business from maintenance supervisors in hotels, hospitals, and grocery stores, as well as small-business people. "It's not a J.C. Penney catalog going to the consumers," explained Hammill.

By the end of 1997, Home Depot had expanded the catalog, called the *ProBook,* into other markets. It had brought the company more sales in Atlanta and Chicago from contractors and other professionals. They wanted to see how well it would work in other parts of the country. "It will grow the business, but it will also take better care of our existing customers," said Eric Johnson, who helped develop the catalog.

The *ProBook* catalog was just one move to attract more contractor sales. By the end of 1997, Home Depot had garnered a 17 percent market share of the $140 billion home improvement market. It's next closest competitor, Lowe's, had only 7 percent. That's a big lead, but Marcus and Blank looked at market share for discount department stores and saw that Wal-Mart had 50 percent, Kmart had 20 percent, and Target had 17 percent. Why couldn't Home Depot get as large a share of sales among home center stores as Wal-Mart had among discount stores? "The environment we are in today provides opportunities for the strongest competitors," noted Blank.

Blank asked everyone at Home Depot to look past the do-it-yourself and remodeling businesses that had made the company so successful and explore new markets. The do-it-yourself business has $100 billion in annual sales, and repair and remodel work brings in another $40 billion in annual sales. Blank wanted Home Depot to boost its business in the builder and general contractor market, which has $75 billion in annual sales, the $15 billion property maintenance market, the $50 billion heavy industrial market, and the $85 billion market that encompassed licensed plumbers, electricians, and other tradespeople. The last segment, the trades were already shopping Home Depot stores in increasing numbers. But Blank realized those shoppers had different requirements than the weekend do-it-yourselfer. They wanted more products and better customer service.

While other home center retailers look at how they can expand their sales within a $140 billion market, Blank has seen Home Depot's potential in a $365 billion field ripe with opportunities. Single-family home construction in 1996 alone totaled $127.5 billion. In early 1997, Home Depot made its first big move to tap into those other markets.

San Diego–based Maintenance Warehouse was founded in 1973 by Lucille and Ron Neeley. The Neeleys struggled early on—just as Marcus and Blank did when Home Depot started. Their attorney and accountant weren't optimistic. "They told us two things," remembered Ron Neeley. "'Put a padlock on the business. And walk away because you two are broke.'" Neeley bought a San Diego hardware store from his father in 1966, but the shop struggled. By late 1973—three years after they had been warned by their lawyer and bookkeeper—they were nearly broke. They sold their house and began renting. Lucille Neeley thought about becoming a hairdresser. Ron Neeley made calls to apartment managers, looking for a job.

One of the calls Neeley made was to a management company that had recently assumed the responsibility for a large apartment complex. The new managers were refurbishing the apartments, and they decided to buy their equipment from the Neeleys. Due to the success of that account, which grew from $30 monthly to a peak of $10,000 monthly in sales, the Neeley's closed the store and started selling via a catalog to apartment managers.

The Neeleys, like Marcus and Blank, persevered, slowly building their mail-order hardware business, which attracted hotels, hospitals, nursing homes, and office buildings. They decided early on, as did Marcus and Blank, that their success was due to their service to customers. They had no sales force, but they guaranteed next-day delivery to most cities and offered a no-hassle return policy. Twice a year, the Neeleys mailed a phone-book size, 1,300-page catalog to more than 100,000 customers across the country. With a team of more than 50 telephone operators, they fielded more than 5,700 calls a day. More than 90 percent of those calls resulted in orders. Those orders were then sent to a dozen warehouses, from where the products were shipped out.

By 1996, Maintenance Warehouse had $130 million in annual sales—roughly 1 percent of the $15 billion property maintenance market and equal to the sales at two well-run Home Depot stores. But Marcus and Blank saw its potential; Maintenance Warehouse's sales had been less than $70 million five years earlier. In January 1997, the same day Home Depot opened its 500th store, Marcus and Blank bought Maintenance Warehouse for $125 million. "It adds a high-growth direct-mail channel to our business," said Marcus. "It complements the business we are presently in."

Lucille Neeley noted that Maintenance Warehouse had other suitors wanting to buy the company. "Our selection of Home Depot was because of their emphasis on operational excellence and their emphasis on their employees," she said. The Neeleys shared the same philosophy as Marcus and Blank. "We have very optimistic natures," said Lucille Neeley. "We look at something and say, 'We can do that.'" The Neeleys had also spent a lot of time training workers in customer service— 80 percent of all the calls coming into Maintenance Warehouse are answered within 20 seconds.

This time, Marcus and Blank—having been stung earlier by their purchase of the Bowater stores and saddled with Aikenhead's stores in Canada in 1994 that needed changes— bought a company that fit well into their strategy and expansion style. The two companies easily meshed. Marcus and Blank, finally, learned that it was just as important to have the cultures and styles mesh as the business operations in acquisitions. In the first catalog published after its purchase by Home Depot, more than 2,300 items sold in Home Depot stores were added to Maintenance Warehouse's offerings. And Maintenance Warehouse gave Home Depot access to maintenance supervisors and janitors for apartments and hotels—two customer groups that have traditionally avoided its stores.

Marcus and Blank have aggressive goals for Maintenance Warehouse. They want to build it into a $1 billion operation that is the leader in the mail-order hardware business. That may seem hard. But Maintenance Warehouse is competing against local suppliers, niche distributors, and small retailers. And customers such as hotel operators are shifting purchases to national suppliers like Maintenance Warehouse that can handle all of their locations.

Maintenance Warehouse is expanding its product offerings so that it can accommodate those customers. By the end of the year 2000, the company plans to offer more than 13,000 different products, up from just more than 7,000 when it was bought. As a Home Depot company, Maintenance Warehouse now can access products and merchandise it previously wasn't selling through manufacturers that sold their products to Home Depot stores. And it's expanding its customer base by attracting military posts, government buildings, and colleges and universities.

Marcus and Blank are looking at other ways to attract professional customers and contractors. In late 1997, Home Depot began testing in its Austin, Texas, stores ways to improve customer service to professional contractors. At the Austin stores, black and yellow banners and signs mark off reserved parking for contractors near the lumber department entrance. Inside, contractor products are packaged in so-called Pro Packs. The company has added more workers whose responsibility is to help professional builders and remodelers. In the past, such customers were limited to a $5,000 credit line. But Home Depots in Austin offers lines of credit as large as $50,000 so that professionals won't be limited in their purchases. They also installed phone lines and same-day or next-day delivery service aimed specifically at builders and contractors. In early 1998, Home Depot expanded those offerings to Las Vegas, and so far the results look promising. "The pro customer wants more face-to-face customer service, people that know them," explains Brill, now Home Depot's chief administrative officer. "This doesn't take brain surgery to do; you've just got to know what your customer wants."

In another test, Home Depot is renting tools. By the end of 1998, it expected to have 200 tools—everything from saws to electric screwdrivers—available for rent in 50 stores. Tool rentals had been successfully tested in 7 stores in the Nashville area.

Of course, some contractors aren't yet convinced and don't believe that Home Depot, after nearly two decades of primarily catering to do-it-yourselfers, can handle their business. "It will be tough for them to service me the way I need to be serviced, and I wouldn't want to deal with the crowded stores," says V. Michael Rossetti, president of Atlanta-based Ravin Homes. But the moves show Home Depot is addressing the concerns of such customers and will expand their business in ways to attract them. In November 1997, it bought National Blind & Wallpaper Factory, a Detroit-based mail-order supplier, with plans to expand the business. With the acquisition came software systems that will help Home Depot stores provide better customer service to professional designers and remodelers.

And in New York stores, Home Depot added a plumbing service counter with sprinkler systems, boiler repair parts, and a separate cash register to give contractors the chance to get in and out of the stores quickly. At the Home Depot in Flushing, a licensed plumber staffs the counter from 6 A.M. to 3 P.M. during the week. It's no wonder Marcus and Blank tested such moves there: It had $121 million in sales in 1996, making it Home Depot's biggest store in terms of sales.

Then, in April 1998, Home Depot went one step further to cater to professional building contractors. It opened an 80,000-square-foot store in Colma, California, just south of San Francisco, targeting professional housing contractors who told Home Depot they would like the convenience of stores designed just for them. The store is across the street from a 115,000-square-foot Home Depot that opened in 1996 to replace the smaller store, which had opened in 1986. But the larger store still couldn't handle all of the business in the area, primarily because of the number of contractors shopping there.

The contractor store sells more lumber and other building materials than do regular Home Depots, and it features a tool rental center instead of kitchen and bathroom design areas. So far, there are no plans to open Home Depot Pro stores elsewhere in the country, as the retailer did with its Expo and CrossRoads stores. But with Blank at the helm looking for every possible way to expand Home Depot's reach in the home improvement business, that idea isn't so far-fetched.

To be sure, Marcus and Blank haven't been ignoring their core do-it-yourself customers. At the same time they have been improving their services that cater to professional contractors, they have been making changes in the stores that help the weekend putterer.

There is good reason for Marcus and Blank to focus on the do-it-yourselfer as well. Between 1994 and 1997, the number of homeowners in the country increased by 3.4 million. New homes have been built at a rate exceeding 1 million per year since 1991. If anything, their core market has been expanding.

To make sure they could handle what these new customers, and old Home Depot fanatics, wanted, the stores were re-designed yet again. Kitchen and bath displays, for example, were expanded. "We know that many home improvement projects begin with a kitchen or bath renovation and progress naturally to other upgrades," noted Berg, the southeast division president, as he opened Home Depot's largest southeast store in St. Petersburg. "By grouping related products together, we've made home improvement projects less complicated and the shopping experience more enjoyable."

Marcus and Blank also added new products to its store shelves. In Atlanta, the two replaced a smaller store in the tony Buckhead area with a larger location around the corner. About 20 percent of the products—nearly 7,000 items—were new to the store when it opened. The store had a broader array of home security systems and light sensors. It stocked a wider variety of designer items such as blue and green bathtubs and toilets. The store sold a new line of bathroom mirrors. For older homes, the store offered more ornate trim moldings and more styles of brick and stone for remodeling. After nearly 20 years in business, the Home Depot team still was changing the product mix of their stores to cater what the customers wanted.

Such changes have been common in recent years as the company has assessed how much shelf space it devotes to products. Marcus and Blank have taught their disciples to constantly challenge how the company is operated and what it sells. That has led to some major moves—some aborted and some implemented. For a while, Marcus and Blank flirted with adding a full range of appliances—from refrigerators to washers and dryers—to its stores. They hired Don Galloway, a former executive of furniture and appliance chain Roberds to explore product lines, talk to manufacturers, and negotiate prices.

Such a move would have put Home Depot in direct competition with appliance chains such as Best Buy, Circuit City, and even Sears—already a big Home Depot rival in the tool and hardware area. After a couple of months of study, however, Marcus and Blank determined they didn't want to sell appliances. Sure, Home Depot carries a limited line of ovens, dishwashers, and refrigerators for shoppers remodeling kitchens. But the appliance business wasn't growing, and too many other retailers were trying to grab sales. Still, the appliance exploration shows that Marcus and Blank are willing to look at anything if it boosts their sales. "Our business has changed constantly," said Marcus. "Our stores don't look the same every year. We're always in the position of having to go back and redo older stores. If you're not moving and you're not changing, you're basically going backwards. Everybody here is entrepreneurial."

Two other ideas—24-hour stores and truck rental—proved wildly popular with Home Depot shoppers. In 1992, Marcus and Blank kept all but one of Home Depot's stores in New Jersey open around the clock during the Memorial Day weekend. The results were encouraging, but they needed to figure out how to staff stores in the middle of the night. Three years later, Marcus and Blank opened the Flushing store as a 24-hour outlet, and that location became the company's biggest sales producer. Then, in 1997, the store in Secaucus, New

Jersey—surrounded by highways and fast-food restaurants that bring in people at all hours—stayed open 24 hours.

Customers had things break at their homes in the middle of the night and wanted to make the repairs then. Some just wanted to avoid shoppers during the day. "If I come in Saturday morning, I have to waste an hour and a half with parking and crowds and lines," said Bill Arnold, in the Secaucus store at 1 A.M. one night. "This takes me 15 minutes." Another shopper, Leona Newell, was at the Secaucus store to save her wedding reception. The workers redoing the wallpaper at her mother's house, the site of the party, had run out of glue at midnight. She drove 30 minutes and bought a tube of glue. Others couldn't shop during the day because of work schedules. "It's not as though sleep has become less popular," explained Gerald Celente, director of the Trends Research Institute in Rhinebeck, New York. "Our society is so geared toward work that we've become crunched for time." Indeed, people are working 180 hours per year longer than they did 20 years ago. People want to shop at 2 A.M. because they have no choice.

By early 1998, Marcus and Blank expanded around-the-clock, do-it-yourself shopping to stores in Los Angeles, Houston, Chicago, and Tampa. Berg wanted a 24-hour location in Tampa after buying glue at a Wal-Mart at 1 A.M. because that was the only store he could find open at the time. "People are working in the store all night anyway," he said. "It's just a matter of letting customers know you're open." The extra hours were noted in shopper catalogs and with big balloons flying above the stores.

Another change they implemented stemmed from a simple request from customers who wanted to transport riding lawn mowers and stacks of fencing posts to their homes, but they couldn't do it because their own car or truck didn't have enough space. Too often, a Home Depot employee loaded the purchase in his or her own truck and took it to a customer's home. In 1995, Marcus and Blank tested trucks for customers to rent at stores in Nashville and Atlanta. The trucks, with flatbed backs, were in immediate demand. A year later, they expanded the trucks to other Atlanta stores and then to the rest of the chain.

The trucks, called Load 'N Go, work like this: With $19, a

major credit card, a valid driver's license, and proof of auto insurance, a Home Depot shopper may rent one of the trucks for 75 minutes. Extra time costs $5 for each additional 15 minutes. Gas and mileage are included in the fee.

Of course, Home Depot has used the trucks as a competitive advantage against its competitors. Rental trucks were added to its Dallas stores shortly before Lowe's opened locations there. A survey by Home Depot found that 97 percent of the truck renters would use them again. And the trucks lessened the number of smaller, more expensive orders Home Depot was trying to eliminate from its fledgling delivery service.

Load 'N Go's success posed a problem, however, according to some shoppers who complained to Marcus and Blank at the 1997 shareholder meeting. The trucks were so popular—Friday, Saturday, and Sunday rentals accounted for more than 50 percent of the trucks' use—that they often were on the road when many customers wanted them. Some shoppers wanted a reservation system. Marcus told the complainers that he'd look into it, but that sometimes shoppers don't show up after they've made reservations and the trucks just sit there. It was a nice position to be in. Marcus and Blank were defending Home Depot for having more business than it sometimes could handle. In early 1998, Home Depot bought Load 'N Go, which had previously been operated independently. "With every change we make, we keep in mind that the customer relationship, not just the transaction, drives our business," said Blank.

In early 1997, Marcus and Blank moved to a new headquarters complex in north Atlanta. The compound is actually called the "Store Support Center," a name suggested by a store employee, "so everyone who walks into the building knows what their job is, to support the stores," said Marcus. Marcus's office on the 21st floor of one of the buildings overlooks the city's skyline—and a nearby Home Depot store. To Marcus, a view of an orange-colored Home Depot store was the best thing he could look down upon.

The sprawling 43-acre complex, which one day may have five buildings but now contains three, is testimony to Home

Depot's success over the past two decades. (It opened with the ceremonial cutting of a board by Langone, Blank, and Georgia Governor Zell Miller.) Encased in glass in the lobby, however, are not-so-subtle reminders of how far Home Depot has advanced the home repair and do-it-yourself business in the past two decades.

The cases contain tools. Some of them are more than 100 years old. But many look as if they might have been in use as recently as 20 years ago when Marcus and Blank opened the first Home Depot. There's a Stanley No. 45 metal plow and combination plane from the turn of the century. The Stanley No. 45 is the most common combination plane worldwide and still in use today.

There's a wood parallel clamp—such general-purpose clamps are also used today—from before 1900. There's a black Chesterman steel tape measure from before 1925 and an early cast claw framing hammer that look as if they might have come out of a modern workroom. There's a Simonds nine-point handsaw from 1867 that looks as if it could cut down a tree tomorrow.

Advances in tool design due to consumer demand fueled by Home Depot's expansion mean that these tools now serve as a reminder of how far the do-it-yourself business has come in the last 20 years. And Home Depot's new headquarters is a monument to that success in promoting frugal do-it-yourself repairs and remodeling.

In building the headquarters, the company that has helped millions of homeowners with construction projects followed the advice it gives to many do-it-yourselfers. It oversaw the design and made suggestions, but it let someone else handle the construction. Inside is a huge auditorium where Marcus and Blank train employees from around the globe. There's a gym so that workers can exercise before or after work or during lunch. (Blank, who has run marathons, has always encouraged Home Depot employees to stay physically fit.) A 300-seat cafeteria, dubbed "Homer's Café" after the company's cartoon-like mascot, helps feed the Bleeding Orange masses.

The buildings are the by-product—in more ways than one—

of the Home Depot system that has made its stores so popular with cost-conscious shoppers. Instead of using $30-per-square-foot granite in the lobby floor, the company opted for cheaper $8-per-square-foot ceramic tile that looks like marble. The carpet came from Home Depot vendors. And approximately 50 bathroom counter tops came from Home Depot's nearby Expo store. Marcus and Blank made sure the principles of low prices and excellent customer service that made Home Depot successful were used in building their new fortress.

Inside the offices, Marcus and Blank and everyone below them are plotting the strategy to keep Home Depot growing. To handle the products needed for such growth, they opened a $90 million distribution center—it's big enough to hold 13 Home Depot stores—in Savannah in 1997, and they plan to open another on the West Coast in late 1998. Besides overseeing international expansion, new stores, new products, and new services, they're constantly building—or in one instance rebuilding—their team.

Old friend and cofounder Pat Farrah returned in 1995 after a decade away to bring back some of the entrepreneurial spirit that fueled Home Depot's early days. Another early employee, Dan Tsujioka, also came back to the company around the same time. "To have them back now and be very objective about what they see can only help us," said Marcus. "Pat is a merchandising genius, and Dan is one of the best operations people I've ever seen." Tsujioka, however, would soon leave again.

When Farrah left, he got involved in a sporting goods company called SportsClub, which was run by friend and former HomeClub chief executive Robert McNulty. Like Farrah's earlier Homeco venture, SportsClub went bankrupt and was liquidated. "I'm definitely not an operator," laughed Farrah.

Farrah's skills were in home center retailing, however. Shortly after retiring in 1985, he visited a Home Depot store in California. "I see shopping carts all over the parking lot," said Farrah. "So I go to the store manager and say to him, 'I thought we taught you better than this.'" Managers and lot workers had been taught to quickly get the carts back inside so that other customers could use them. Farrah eventually bought a bankrupt lighting manufacturer, M.G. Products, Inc., that sold lights to home center retailers, and he poured millions into the company. Ken Langone and Marcus had even backed a company loan. But the company lost millions. By 1995, Farrah wanted to return to Home Depot. "Marcus and Blank needed me, and I needed them," said Farrah.

Home Depot's growth had made the company so huge that managers and executives weren't getting to the stores as often as they had in the past. When he rejoined the company, Farrah's job was to change that. He began a whirlwind store tour with Bill Hamlin, executive vice president of merchandising, to train merchandisers. Farrah didn't like what he saw in many stores. "One thing we've got to fix is [executives'] distance from the stores," explained Farrah. "Even merchants have gotten away from the stores a little more, and it's hurting them. If you don't stand there and look at what customers see, you don't understand what they go through in the store."

Farrah went to one meeting with merchandisers where selling shovels was discussed. Farrah asked at what prices the shovels were being sold. "They said, 'Well, we have one at $3.47, one at about $7, and one at about $12,'" recounted Farrah. "Okay, fine, and we went out on the floor and instead find the shovels prices at $3, $13, and $20." He made his point clearly. "Unless we go to the store and see the merchandise, we're going to make pricing errors and selection errors, and we'll confuse the customer," added Farrah. "It frustrates store associates. It frustrates customers."

Farrah also reviewed the products sold in stores, picking what would remain and what would go, as Marcus and Blank were growing the stores' profits. Farrah wasn't alone in rebuilding on Home Depot's strengths. People such as Hamlin, hired in 1985 from Payless Cashways, had worked their way through the company and, by the mid-nineties, were considered Home Depot's leaders for the next generation. Shortly before Inglis left the company in 1996, Hamlin began overseeing Home Depot's merchandising. Scott, head of the Expo division, and Martineau, president of the western division, were two others playing increasingly important roles. Like Farrah, Scott and

Martineau knew what had worked and what hadn't since the first stores opened. Another was Larry Mercer, who also started his career at one of the first stores and had since become executive vice president. Many consider Mercer to be the heir apparent, the person who will eventually assume the president's role.

Steve Messana, an executive at the Young & Rubicam ad agency in New York, was hired as senior vice president of human resources after Don McKenna retired and moved to Hilton Head Island. Messana, in turn, hired a new vice president of training, Pat Cataldo, in 1997. Both are considered important pieces of Marcus and Blank's commitment to maintaining the company's focus on hiring good people and training them in the culture and customer service so vital to Home Depot's success.

On May 28, 1997, the torch was passed. Marcus stepped down as chief executive, and Blank assumed a greater role in shaping Home Depot's future. He's moving Home Depot into rural markets and developing the Expo stores. And he's pushing Home Depot into new fields that will expand the do-it-yourself retail business beyond its traditional boundaries.

When asked shortly before Home Depot opened its 500th store what accomplishment made him the proudest, Blank replied, "We've been able to maintain the magic in our stores. When customers leave the stores, they feel as though they've been cared for. People have a lot of passion for our company, not for the products or the pricing, but for the service."

"It's one thing to do that with one store or four stores," added Blank. "But to do it with 500, that's an incredible task. Bernie and I have been on a shooting star. And the ride isn't even over."

MANAGEMENT LESSONS

Despite its unbelievable success in the past 20 years, Home Depot isn't resting on its laurels. The retailer is searching for ways to keep its business from slowing down for another 20 years and is expanding in ways that are stretching the limits of the home improvement industry. That strategy shows that any business can keep growing if it is innovative and adapts to the changing marketplace.

1. Home Depot is always looking for ways to keep growing, whether it's by changing its advertising, introducing catalogs or buying mail-order businesses. The company is always looking for new ways to help customers doing repair and remodeling jobs, and is never satisfied with what it's doing.

2. As it grew and expanded, Home Depot realized the importance of developing and building brand name recognition. By making people aware of the Home Depot name, they were more likely to shop its stores when one opened nearby.

3. Home Depot has learned that expanding into similar businesses with similar customers helps grow the business and boosts its growth potential by increasing the number of shoppers.

4. While Home Depot has expanded by offering services that attract new customers, it hasn't forgotten about the customers who made it successful. For those shoppers, it has continued to listen to their needs and wants.

5. Home Depot has built and rebuilt its management team as it grew, looking for people that had the skills that would help it grow effectively. The company has also brought back former managers to maintain some of its entrepreneurial spirit.

6. No matter how much it's grown, Home Depot realizes there's still more that can be done. The company is constantly searching for new products, new services, and new store formats to grab more sales in the home improvement market.

ARTHUR'S COMPANY

By May 1998, a full year had elapsed since Bernie Marcus handed over Home Depot's reins to partner Arthur Blank. Home Depot was not the same company it was the year before when Marcus stepped down as chief executive. That would be expected for a company constantly changing its store format and the products on its shelves so that its sales would continue increasing.

Blank stepped up to the podium at Home Depot's annual meeting, and he had plenty to report to the company's shareholders. In the 12 months since he had become chief executive, Home Depot's stock price had increased 82 percent. The company's sales had risen 24 percent, and its earnings had jumped 30 percent. The numbers were a sign of a healthy operation: Its profits were rising faster than its sales, meaning that it was becoming more efficient.

Home Depot's sales had become more than double that of Lowe's, and its sales were more than its top seven competitors' combined. It was now one of the 10 largest retailers in the United States and one of the 25 largest in the world. More than 500 million customer transactions were held inside its stores every year, a number of transactions equal to twice the entire U.S. population, including children.

There were more reasons to be happy, Blank added. The retailer pointed out that four competitors were "at risk," a term he used to describe struggling rivals. Combined, they had $8 billion in sales. Home Depot had stores in 70 percent of those markets, and it was adding locations. Home Depot planned to have more than 1,300 stores by the end of the year 2001. That would be double the 660 stores that Home Depot was currently operating. And an American Express retail study showed that consumers planned to spend more and shop more often at stores like Home Depot. "We feel good about our ability to grow," noted Blank. "We will continue to work hard as a team. The outlook for the company is not only good, it's great."

To achieve that growth, Blank had made dramatic changes in his first full year in total control of Home Depot. The company had acquired other operations, expanded across the country, plotted an international strategy, and added key personnel. It had made as many important moves in that time period as it had in nearly all of its previous 18 years. "We see the moon as being the potential for us," said Blank.

And while Blank gushed over Home Depot's growth potential in courting more business from professional contractors, through its design Expo stores, its smaller convenience stores that will be tested in the northeast in 1999, and through international expansion, he also noted that Home Depot's future success would be based on how well it continued to emphasize its regular stores. "Many companies run after the sexy new things they're involved in and forget about their core business," noted Blank. "If you take your eye off the ball, someone takes the ball away from you."

That wasn't going to happen at Home Depot, Blank assured his shareholders. Home Depot had taken its eye off its base stores in the past when it opened rural stores, revamped its Expo format, and dipped its toes into international waters. Blank, with his intense focus on the bottom line, would make sure the company didn't make the same mistake again.

Some things hadn't changed during the transition year at Home Depot. The company still treated its shareholders to chocolate chip cookies and Cokes at the annual meeting, again held at the Cobb Galleria Centre near Home Depot's headquarters. And Marcus, who would remain a company figurehead as chairman, stole some of Blank's thunder by announcing a 2-for-1 stock split shortly after his partner finished his presentation. Marcus's announcement led to a standing ovation. (One minor detail had been changed at Home Depot's annual meeting, however. The table where Blank, Marcus, and other board members sat had been placed at the other end of the ballroom from where it was the previous year, Marcus's last as CEO. To some, the change was a symbol of the 180-degree difference in how Marcus and Blank operated—while still achieving the same results.)

But for Home Depot's shareholders, shoppers, and employees, the new stores and new ideas overseen by Blank to keep the company growing were more important in the long run because those plans would be what would drive the stock price in the future. And with Blank as its reserved leader who understood the reasons for Home Depot's success, the company would keep growing. As he stood there as the leader of a company that had, and would continue to, revolutionize an industry through vision, empowering employees, and the relentless pursuit of growth, Blank gave credit to the hundreds of thousands of Home Depot employees who made sure customers were happy every day. "I am just the messenger of all the good news," said Blank. "The real magic is in the hands of the 152,000 associates who are there every day to serve the customers. You are great, and we love you all." To ensure that culture continues, in June 1998 Blank hired Faye Wilson, already a board member, to be senior vice president of value initiatives.

Home Depot has only just begun to build itself into a retail power. With each customer that enters its orange-colored doors and walks its vast aisles, buying do-it-yourself items to repair roofs and fix leaky faucets, Home Depot grows a little more.

Arthur Blank has grabbed a toolbelt and strapped it around his waist. He's got work to do to keep Home Depot's culture and management style the same as it has been for 20 years. He'll have some help.

NOTES

In the preparation of *Inside Home Depot,* dozens of people were interviewed at length, including former Home Depot board members, former executives, former store employees, people who knew Bernie Marcus and Arthur Blank at one point or another, and many others. In addition, the author had at his disposal notes from dozens of interviews he conducted with Bernie Marcus, Arthur Blank, and other Home Depot executives prior to beginning work on the book. In addition, the author was also able to obtain copies of transcripts or tapes of speeches made by Marcus and Blank. The best ones were:

Bernie Marcus at the *BusinessWeek* Presidents Forum, January 1996

Bernie Marcus at the International Council of Shopping Centers' Spring Convention, May 1996

Arthur Blank at Business for Social Responsibility conference, October 1996

Bernie Marcus, with introduction by Ken Langone, at National Sales & Marketing Hall of Fame, October 1997

The following people were interviewed on the record. Many of them were interviewed more than once, and some were interviewed as many as five or six times:

John Bevilaqua, Don Campbell, Jeffrey Chanin, Peter Cleaveland, Nick Einfeld, Mark Eisen, A. D. Frazier, Jim Hodkinson, John Huie, Patricia Johnson, Jim Inglis, Ned Lenox, Rick Mayo, Bill McCahan, Robert McNulty, Michael

Modansky, Alan Schwartz, Sanford Sigoloff, Thomas Smith, Ken Stein, Dorothy Stoneman.

Although Bernie Marcus, Arthur Blank, and Home Depot did not cooperate with interviews specifically for this book, the author was able to draw on notes from earlier interviews with Home Depot executives, employees, and board members. Much of the information in the interviews was previously unpublished. Those interviews included:

Arthur Blank in December 1996

Kevin Braunskill in July 1995

Ron Brill in January 1997

Marjorie Buckley in January 1997

Lora Castellanos in July 1995

Craig Denton in July 1995

Marian Exall in March 1997 and April 1997

Rob Hallam in September 1995

Dick Hammill in May 1995, July 1995, and March 1997

Jim Inglis in February 1995

Ed Kaminski in July 1995

Ken Langone in December 1996

Bernie Marcus in December 1995, December 1996, and April 1997

Bernie Marcus and Arthur Blank in May 1997 and September 1997

Bill Pena in February 1995 and January 1997

Denny Ryan in July 1995

Bryant Scott in October 1996 and December 1996

Ken Smith in March 1997

Bea Swanson in July 1995

Other people, including former managers and former store employees of Home Depot, were interviewed off the record. In addition, some current employees also talked off the record, despite the company's urging that no worker have any contact with this project. The author did not actively seek to talk to current employees, but many sought him out.

The author reviewed and read thousands of pages of documents, including Securities and Exchange Commission filings for Handy Dan Home Improvement Centers and Home Depot, and court filings, particularly depositions given by Bernie Marcus, Arthur Blank, and other top Home Depot executives in *Vicki Butler et al. v. Home Depot, Inc.* The author also reviewed literally hundreds of magazine and newspaper articles written about Home Depot, including articles in Home Depot's company newspaper, which has been distributed to reporters who covered the company. Articles in Home Depot's newspaper are the source of most of the employee comments used in the book.

Dozens of tapes from *Home Depot Television* were reviewed and used to provide first-person accounts of conversations and events. Some of these tapes were copyrighted by Home Depot, but many others contained no copyright mark. Those that were not copyrighted and were used in providing anecdotes and details in this book include:

"Breakfast with Bernie and Arthur," *Home Depot Television,* March 18, 1990

"Welcome Aboard," *Home Depot Television,* March 27, 1990

"Breakfast with Bernie and Arthur," *Home Depot Television,* June 3, 1990

"Welcome Aboard," *Home Depot Television,* September 5, 1990

"Breakfast with Bernie and Arthur," *Home Depot Television,* September 16, 1990

"Breakfast with Bernie and Arthur," *Home Depot Television,* November 18, 1990

"1990 Managers' Meeting," *Home Depot Television*

"1991 Hardware Show," *Home Depot Television*

"Managers' Meeting," *Home Depot Television,* January 11, 1993

"Import Vendor Meeting," *Home Depot Television,* September 24, 1993

"Respecting our Home Depot Family," *Home Depot Television,* February 25, 1994

"1995 Manager's Meeting," *Home Depot Television,* March 6, 1995

"Issues and Answers," *Home Depot Television,* August 30, 1995

"1995 Vendor Briefing," *Home Depot Television,* November 14, 1995

For the chapter on how Home Depot teaches its customers, the author visited many of the retailer's stores in the metro Atlanta area and attended some of the classes that are offered. No store employee attempted to stop him from attending a class even though the author always identified himself. In one case, his son Andrew attended a Kids' Workshop.

Finally, the author used a number of Internet Web sites for research. They included:

The America Project (http://www.emory.edu/CARTER_CEN-TER/PUBS/tap_corp.htm)

American Hardware Manufacturers Association (http://www.ahma.org/)

Christmas in April*USA (http://www.pdi.com/cina-usa/index.html)

Home Depot (http://www.homedepot.com)

Israel Democracy Institute (http://www.idi.org.il/)

Lowe's (http://lowes.com)

National Home Center News (http://homecenternews.com)

Sprawl Busters (http://www.sprawl-busters.com)

YouthBuild USA (http://www.youthbuild.org/ybusa.html)

PROLOGUE: THE BEGINNING

Bernie Marcus, Arthur Blank, and Bryant Scott were interviewed in December 1996 about Home Depot's beginnings. Marjorie Buckley was interviewed in January 1997. Rick Mayo was interviewed in September and November 1997. Don Campbell was interviewed in November 1997. Jeff Chanin was interviewed in December 1997. Nick Einfeld was interviewed in November 1997. Sanford Sigoloff was interviewed in November 1997. Ken Langone was interviewed in December 1996 about Home Depot's beginnings. Bob McNulty was interviewed in January 1998. Alan Schwartz was interviewed in January 1998.

Information on Sanford Sigoloff and Daylin, Inc., came from:

"Unscrambling Daylin's Affairs," *BusinessWeek*, March 17, 1975.

"The Sigoloff Surgery That Saved Daylin," *BusinessWeek*, November 15, 1976.

John Quirt, "Ming the Merciless Loses His Prize," *Fortune*, May 7, 1979.

Nancy Yoshihara, "Sandy Sigoloff: Private Man in the Limelight," *Los Angeles Times*, August 18, 1985.

Nancy Yoshihara, "Ming the Merciless is on the Prowl," *Los Angeles Times*, July 27, 1986.

Information on Bernie Marcus and Arthur Blank's firing came from:

"Breakfast with Bernie and Arthur," *Home Depot Television*, September 16, 1990.

Securities and Exchange Commission 10-Q filing for Daylin, Inc., May 28, 1978.

Securities and Exchange Commission 10-K filing for Daylin, Inc., December 6, 1978.

Ken Langone speech, National Sales & Marketing Hall of
Fame Induction, October 1997.

CHAPTER 1: HOME DEPOT BOOT CAMP

Ned Lenox was interviewed in December 1997. Jim Inglis was
interviewed in November and December 1997. Bernie Marcus
and Arthur Blank discussed training in numerous interviews
and in "Breakfast with Bernie and Arthur" shows.

Information about Home Depot's training programs came
from:

"Missionary Zeal Permeates Manager Training Sessions,"
National Home Center News, December 1986.

Walecia Konrad, "Cheerleading, and Clerks Who Know Awls
from Augers," *BusinessWeek*, August 3, 1992.

"Pyramid-Style Training Fosters Eternal Growth," *National
Home Center News*, December 14, 1992.

Stacey Levitz, "Management Training Facility Opens," *Doings
at the Depot*, May/June 1995.

Information on Home Depot's formation and first stores came
from:

Securities and Exchange Commission prospectus filing for
The Home Depot, Inc., September 22, 1981.

"Everything You Wanted to Know about Depot's History,"
National Home Center News, December 1986.

"Name Evolves from Bad Bernie's Buildall to Home Depot,"
National Home Center News, December 1986.

"Former Exec VP, Pat Farrah, Sets Sail for Life after Home
Depot," *National Home Center News*, December 1986.

Russell Shaw, "Bernard Marcus," *Sky Magazine*, April 1991.

"Store 101: The End of the Beginning," *Doings at the Depot*,
June/July/August 1994.

Patricia Sellers, "Can Home Depot Fix Its Sagging Stock?" *Fortune,* March 4, 1996.

Chris Roush, "500 Stores and Counting," *The Atlanta Journal-Constitution,* January 12, 1997.

Chris Roush, "First Site Was a Cramped Proving Ground," *The Atlanta Journal-Constitution,* January 12, 1997.

Information about Home Depot's Outward Bound programs came from:

"White Knuckles on White Water Test Team Spirit," *National Home Center News,* December 1986.

"Outward Bound Program Shows Employees Benefits of Team Work," *National Home Center News,* December 14, 1992.

Maria Saporta, "Homeward Bound," *The Atlanta Journal-Constitution,* June 1, 1993.

Information about the 360-review program came from:

Camille Thompson, "360 Feedback Is Going Around the Depot," *Doings at the Depot,* January/February 1996.

"Can Home Depot Fix Its Sagging Stock?" *Fortune,* March 4, 1996.

Ashley Goldsmith, "360 Feedback Gives Direction for Growth," *Doings at the Depot,* July/August 1996.

Information about Home Depot employee changes came from:

"Breakfast with Bernie and Arthur," *Home Depot Television,* September 16, 1990.

"Everything You Wanted to Know about Depot's History," *National Home Center News,* December 1986.

"Former Exec VP, Pat Farrah, Sets Sail for Life after Home Depot," *National Home Center News,* December 1986.

"Executive VP, Kelley, Brings Professional Management to

Entrepreneurs," *National Home Center News*, December 1986.

"Will Depot Survive Pro Management Switch?" *National Home Center News*, December 1986.

Mark Albright, "On the Go for Home Depot," *St. Petersburg Times*, June 20, 1994.

CHAPTER 2: BLEEDING ORANGE CULTURE

Bryant Scott was interviewed in October 1996 and December 1996. Bernie Marcus and Arthur Blank were interviewed in December 1996. Mike Modansky was interviewed in November 1997. Ned Lenox was interviewed in December 1997. Peter Cleaveland was interviewed in January 1998. Alan Schwartz was interviewed in January 1998.

Information about Home Depot's culture came from:

"Welcome Aboard," *Home Depot Television*, September 5, 1990.

"'Culture' Based on Serving Customers, Workers," *National Home Center News*, December 14, 1992.

"Marcus: People Development Is Key to a Successful Company," *National Home Center News*, December 14, 1992.

Graham Button, "Keeping in Touch," *Forbes*, November 22, 1993.

March 11, 1997, deposition of Bernie Marcus in *Butler v. Home Depot.*

Arthur Blank, "Living Our Values," *Doings at the Depot*, May/June 1997.

Leslie Kaufman, "There's No Place Like Home," *Newsweek*, August 4, 1997.

CHAPTER 3: GOING FOR THE GOLD

Bernie Marcus and Arthur Blank spoke about Home Depot's Olympic sponsorship on August 13, 1992, at a "Breakfast with Bernie and Arthur" taping. Dick Hammill was interviewed in July 1995. Lora Castellanos and Bea Swanson were interviewed in July 1995. Kevin Braunskill, Ed Kaminski, and Craig Denton were interviewed in July 1995. A. D. Frazier, Bill McCahan, and John Bevilaqua were interviewed in March 1998.

Information about Home Depot's Olympic sponsorship came from:

Melissa Turner, "ACOG Takes over Brick Marketing," *The Atlanta Journal-Constitution*, February 23, 1995.

Melissa Turner, "ACOG Hopes 'Logical Approach' Will Put Brick Sales on Track," *The Atlanta Journal-Constitution*, February 24, 1995.

Melissa Turner, "Incentives to buy: Replica bricks," *The Atlanta Journal-Constitution*, April 7, 1995.

Melissa Turner, "A Lot Riding on Success of Tickets," *The Atlanta Journal-Constitution*, April 28, 1995.

David Greising, "Javelins are Already Flying at Billy Payne," *BusinessWeek*, July 22, 1996.

Information about Home Depot's Olympic job program came from:

Paul Kaplan, "Employer Remodels Home for Worker Now Paralyzed," *The Atlanta Journal-Constitution*, August 16, 1992.

Melissa Turner, "Local Firm Nails Games Partnership," *The Atlanta Journal-Constitution*, August 22, 1992.

Melissa Turner, "Home Depot on Board as Games Backer," *The Atlanta Journal-Constitution*, August 24, 1992.

Chris Roush, "On the Job Training," *The Atlanta Journal-Constitution*, August 25, 1995.

Chris Roush, "Home Depot Big Winner in Hiring Olympic Athletes," *The Atlanta Journal-Constitution*, August 25, 1995.

Chris Roush, "A Very Fast Employee," *The Atlanta Journal-Constitution*, August 25, 1995.

Kelly McHugh, "On the Job Training," *Doings at the Depot*, November/December 1995.

Kent Ferguson, "The Flame to Fulfill my Dream," *Doings at the Depot*, July/August 1996.

"Saluting Our OJOP Athletes," *Doings at the Depot*, September/October 1996.

Information about Home Depot's Olympic employee programs came from:

"What It Takes to Win an Olympic Spirit Award," *Doings at the Depot*, November/December 1995.

David Henry, "Our Olympics Begin," *Doings at the Depot*, July/August 1996.

"Show That Coaching Spirit," *Doings at the Depot*, 1997–98 Olympic Edition.

Mickey Gramig, "Home Depot's Olympic Ad Working Magic on Viewers," *The Atlanta Journal-Constitution*, February 21, 1998.

CHAPTER 4: BLEEDING ORANGE ATTACKED

Bernie Marcus and Larry Mercer spoke about the gender discrimination allegations during a *Home Depot Television* taping in March 1997. Bernie Marcus was interviewed in April 1997. Bernie Marcus and Arthur Blank were interviewed in September 1997. Attorneys for the women were interviewed in March 1997 and September 1997.

Information about discrimination complaints at Home Depot came from:

Max Boot, "For Plaintiff's Lawyers, There's No Place Like Home Depot," *Wall Street Journal*, February 12, 1997.

Chris Roush, "Home Depot Bias Case Advances," *The Atlanta Journal-Constitution*, March 4, 1997.

Chris Roush, "Home Depot Says It Won't Settle Suit without a Hearing," *The Atlanta Journal-Constitution*, March 4, 1997.

John Caulfield, "Depot Digs in against Charges of Gender Bias," *National Home Center News*, April 14, 1997.

Ronette King, "Bias Lawsuit Has La. Roots," *New Orleans Times Picayune*, April 27, 1997.

Information about the EEOC came from:

Chris Roush and Jeanne Cummings, "Hooters Win EEOC Skirmish in Sexual Bias Battle," *The Atlanta Journal-Constitution*, May 2, 1996.

Vera Dobnik, "Suit: Women Hit 'Glass Ceiling' at Home Depot," *Associated Press*, March 24, 1997.

Chris Roush, "EEOC Seeks to Join Suit Challenging Home Depot," *The Atlanta Journal-Constitution*, March 25, 1997.

"Fawell Questions EEOC Litigation Strategy, Reasons to Intervene in High-Profile Cases," *Bureau of National Affairs*, April 10, 1997.

Chris Roush, "Home Depot Wants EEOC out of Suit," *The Atlanta Journal-Constitution*, April 17, 1997.

Information about the settlement came from:

Chris Roush, "Home Depot Oks Sex Bias Settlement," *The Atlanta Journal-Constitution*, September 20, 1997.

Chris Roush, "Analysts Praise Bias Settlement," *The Atlanta Journal-Constitution*, September 20, 1997.

Chris Roush, "Lawyer's Skill a Major Tool in Home Depot Settlement," *The Atlanta Journal-Constitution*, September 23, 1997.

Vera Titunik, "Facing Hammer, Home Depot Decides to Deal," *The American Lawyer*, November 1997.

CHAPTER 5: CUSTOMER SERVICE IS JOB NO. 1

Arthur Blank was interviewed in December 1996. Jim Inglis was interviewed in December 1997 and in March 1998. Ken Langone discussed Home Depot's customer service at the National Sales & Marketing Hall of Fame dinner in October 1997. Peter Cleaveland was interviewed in January 1998 and February 1998. Bernie Marcus and Arthur Blank discussed customer service during numerous *Home Depot Television* tapings.

Information about Home Depot's customer service came from:

Roger Thompson, "There's No Place Like Home Depot," *Nation's Business*, February 1992.

Ellen Neuborne, "Home Depot Scores Big with Service," *USA Today*, July 23, 1992.

Deborah Royston, "Don't Want to Do It Yourself? Home Depot Has a Solution," *The Atlanta Journal-Constitution*, September 19, 1992.

"Customers Ask for Installed Sales Program and Get It," *National Home Center News*, December 14, 1992.

Chris Roush, "Shopper Survey Shows Strengths of Home Depot," *The Atlanta Journal-Constitution*, August 9, 1995.

Kipp Rix, "The Orange Rule: Customer Service Is Our Responsibility," *Doings at the Depot*, May/June 1997.

Steve Sapsford, "Ben Hill: Helping Customers Help Us," *Doings at the Depot*, July/August 1997.

Ken Bradner, "Top Ten Customer Complaints," *Doings at the Depot,* July/August 1997.

Information on changes in Home Depot stores and operations came from:

Chris Burritt, "Home Depot to Be Own Rival," *The Atlanta Journal-Constitution,* September 27, 1990.

Chris Burritt, "Home Depot Not Waiting until It's Broken to Fix It," *The Atlanta Journal-Constitution,* June 23, 1991.

Chris Burritt, "Home Depot Reports Bigger Profit; Bigger Garden Shops Tested," *The Atlanta Journal-Constitution,* November 20, 1991.

Chris Burritt, "Can Home Depot Build a Marriage?" *The Atlanta Journal-Constitution,* January 6, 1992.

CHAPTER 6: TEACH THE CUSTOMER

Dick Hammill was interviewed in May 1995. Lynette Jennings was interviewed in May 1995. Rob Hallam was interviewed in September 1995. Rick Mayo was interviewed in September and November 1997. Ned Lenox was interviewed in December 1997.

Information on how Home Depot teaches customers came from:

"Home Depot Scores Big with Service," *USA Today,* July 23, 1992.

Chris Roush, "A New Show on the Home Front," *The Atlanta Journal-Constitution,* May 31, 1995.

Chris Roush, "Home Depot Building up Its Visibility: Magazine, Book, CD-ROM on Tap," *The Atlanta Journal-Constitution,* June 1, 1995.

Chris Roush, "Home Depot Reference Book to Go on Sale," *The Atlanta Journal-Constitution,* September 16, 1995.

Chris Roush, "Home Depot Takes to TV with HouseSmart," *The Atlanta Journal-Constitution,* September 25, 1995.

"1-2-3 Ranks as Top Seller," *Doings at the Depot,* July/August 1996.

Chris Roush, "Home Depot to Nail Young Shoppers with Kids' Tool Time," *The Atlanta Journal-Constitution,* June 24, 1997.

Karen Parham, "Cultivating Future Customers: Home Depot Kids Workshop," *Doings at the Depot,* September/October 1997.

Jim Hanley, "Home Depot Cars Race to Victory," *Doings at the Depot,* September/October 1997.

Olivia Bell Buehl, "Partners in Design: What You Can Expect When the Home Depot Helps Plan Your Kitchen or Bath," *Kitchen & Bath Design and Remodeling Magazine,* 1997.

CHAPTER 7: HOME DEPOT'S FOES

Information on Home Depot's competitors came from:

"Elmont Stores Wreak Havoc on Local Outlets," *National Home Center News,* December 14, 1992.

Rod Riggs, "Home Depot Steps Forward to Fill Emporium's Shoes," *San Diego Union-Tribune,* August 29, 1993.

Chris Burritt, "Rivals Dig in against Home Depot," *The Atlanta Journal-Constitution,* November 21, 1993.

Peter Grant, "Invasion of Superstores Taking Toll in New York City Area," *New York Daily News,* February 12, 1995.

Greg Hassell, "Home Depot Hammers Another Foe; Competitor's Houston Stores to Close," *Houston Chronicle,* August 21, 1997.

Jennifer Mann Fuller, "Advertising Claims Fuel Home-Improvement Feud in Kansas City," *Kansas City Star,* August 22, 1997.

"NAD Announces 'No Substantiation' Received Regarding

Advertising by The Home Depot Inc.," Better Business
Bureau, Inc., press release, March 10, 1998.

Information on Frank Denny and Builder's Square came from:

Brad Altman, "Entrepreneurial Enthusiasm. Home-Pro Warehouse Style," *Chain Store Age Executive,* March 1984.

"Warehouse Home Centers: Kmart, Service Mdse. Vie for
Leadership," *Discount Store News,* March 18, 1985.

"Builders Square Squares off Against the Competition," *Chain
Store Age Executive,* December 1984.

"Handy City is Closing its Six Atlanta Area Stores," *The Atlanta
Journal-Constitution,* June 9, 1987.

Ann Wead Kimbrough, "Handy City Stores May Close as Other
Retailers Expand Here," *The Atlanta Journal-Constitution,*
April 8, 1987.

Ann Wead Kimbrough, "Do-it-Yourself Retailers Building a War
Here," *The Atlanta Journal-Constitution,* September 9, 1987.

Chris Burritt, "Builders Square Decided to Call it Quits in
Atlanta," *The Atlanta Journal-Constitution,* August 6, 1991.

Information on Home Depot's fight in Greensboro and other
communities came from:

"New Construction: It's a Duel of Stores on I-40," *Greensboro
News & Record,* February 6, 1993.

"Home Depot Gets Approval to Build Store, Objections Not
Heeded," *Greensboro News & Record,* July 15, 1993.

Jessica Morton, "Home Depot Construction Will Make Street
Unsafe," *Greensboro News & Record,* July 28, 1993.

"Behind Enemy Lines: Home Depot Chairman Spotted
Visiting Lowe's," *Greensboro News & Record,* September 13,
1993.

"Residents File Suit to Stop New Store," *Greensboro News &
Record,* October 22, 1993.

"Home Depot Gets Vested Rights," *Greensboro News & Record,* January 13, 1994.

"Brassfield Residents Drop Fight Against Home Depot," *Greensboro News & Record,* June 10, 1994.

Chris Burritt, "Grass-Roots Protest: Critics Claim Home Depot Uses Heavy-Handed Tactics as it Expands into New Communities," *The Atlanta Journal-Constitution,* November 24, 1994.

Chris Burritt, "Big Stores Tend to Find a Warmer Welcome in South," *The Atlanta Journal-Constitution,* November 24, 1994.

James Kinsella and Mike Karath, "Home Depot Scuttles Site," *Cape Cod Times,* March 5, 1997.

Mike Karath, "Home Depot Will Pursure New Cape Site," *Cape Cod Times,* March 6, 1997.

"Home Depot Plan is Opposed; Unanimous Vote by Cedarville Committee," *Quincy Patriot Ledger,* March 17, 1997.

"Home Depot Settles Campaign Violation Charge," *National Home Center News,* July 9, 1997.

"Bernie Marcus Q&A: Keeping the Revolution Alive," *National Home Center News,* December 1997.

Kathy Mulady, "Developer Taking Steps to Stop Home Depot," *Spokane Spokesman-Review,* December 4, 1997.

H. M. Cauley, "Woodsman, Spare That County!" *Atlanta Magazine,* January 1998.

Information on Rickel's involvement in fighting Home Depot in New Jersey came from:

Donna Mancuso, "Home Depot Sues Rickel, Charging Smear Campaign in New Jersey," *Bloomberg News,* July 5, 1995.

Chris Roush, "Home Depot Sues Competitor, Alleging Circulation of Derogatory Information," *The Atlanta Journal-Constitution,* July 6, 1995.

"Home Depot Alleges Defamation in Lawsuit Filed Against Rickel," *Wall Street Journal*, July 6, 1995.

Eleena de Lisser and Anita Sharpe, "Home Depot Charges a Rival Drummed up Opposition to Stores," *Wall Street Journal*, August 18, 1995.

Lauren Coleman-Lochner, "Rickles to Plug Rickel," *Bergen Record*, March 18, 1997.

Adam Geller and Kevin G. DeMarrais, "Rickel Reaches 'End of the Road,'" *Bergen Record*, October 7, 1997.

Information on Home Depot's impact on communities came from:

"Home Depot Announces Plans to Save Art Deco Landmark," company news release, September 8, 1993.

Lore Postman, "Home Depot's Arrival Hasn't Hurt Business for Smaller Rivals in Carolinas," *Charlotte Observer*, August 20, 1996.

Eve Heyn, "Home Depot Opens, Draws Scores," *Westchester Today*, October 20, 1996.

Mary McAleer Vizard, "New Rochelle Hopes Home Depot Sparks a Revival," *New York Times*, October 20, 1996.

CHAPTER 8: GETTING INVOLVED

Ken Stein was interviewed in February 1998. John Huie was interviewed in February 1998. Mark Eisen was interviewed in September 1997. Jim Inglis was interviewed in December 1997. Bernie Marcus discussed Home Depot's reaction to the Oklahoma City bombing at a January 1996 *BusinessWeek* conference. Arthur Blank discussed social responsibility at a speech in October 1996 at the Business for Social Responsibility conference. Dorothy Stoneman was interviewed in January 1998. Patricia Johnson was interviewed in February 1998.

Information about Home Depot's involvement in The Atlanta Project and other community programs came from:

Maria Saporta, "Executives Get a Taste of Project for the Poor," *The Atlanta Journal-Constitution*, May 21, 1992.

Elizabeth Kurylo, "Carter to Host Clinton, Gore at Habitat Site," *The Atlanta Journal-Constitution*, August 19, 1992.

Maria Saporta, "Local Businesses Line up to Help Atlanta Project," *The Atlanta Journal-Constitution*, October 17, 1992.

Maria Saporta, "New Campaign Aims to Improve Inner-City Housing," *The Atlanta Journal-Constitution*, February 8, 1995.

Arnold Hamilton, "Leaders Trying to Ensure Relief Aid Used Properly," *Dallas Morning News*, May 1, 1995.

Stacey Levitz, "100 Homes Project: Officers and Associates Building Atlanta Legacy," *Doings at the Depot*, May/June 1996.

Christine Jaworsky, "Christmas in April: 'Thank You' Has New Meaning," *Doings at the Depot*, May/June 1997.

Michelle Hiskey, "18,000 to Run 16th Corporate Challenge," *The Atlanta Journal-Constitution*, September 10, 1997.

Information about Home Depot's environmental programs came from:

"Recycling Depot Makes Being 'Green' Profitable, *National Home Center News*, December 14, 1992.

"President Clinton Honors Collins Pine and The Home Depot," company news release, March 7, 1996.

"Up Front with Mark Eisen," *Doings at the Depot*, May/June 1996.

"Home Depot Commits Environmental Grants to 47 Agencies," *Doings at the Depot*, May/June 1996.

"Home Depot Recognized for Environmental Contributions," *Doings at the Depot*, September/October 1996.

Neil Ulman, "A Maine Forest Firm Prospers by Earning Eco-Friendly Label," *Wall Street Journal*, November 26, 1997.

Information about Bernie Marcus and his involvement in Israel came from:

Maria Saporta, "Marcus Cautious on Breakthrough in Middle East," *The Atlanta Journal-Constitution,* September 11, 1993.

"Where Consensus Was Nurtured: Think Tank Launched by U.S. Businessman Helped Give Birth to Likud-Labor Agreement," *Jewish Exponent,* January 30, 1997.

Joshua Mitnick, "Israel's Keter to Supply Closets to Home Depot," *Bloomberg News,* January 29, 1998.

CHAPTER 9: AT A CROSSROADS

Denny Ryan was interviewed in July 1995. Jim Inglis was interviewed in November and December 1997. Tom Smith was interviewed in January 1998.

Information about Home Depot's small-town stores came from:

Chris Burritt, "Home Depot Takes New Look at Small Markets," *The Atlanta Journal-Constitution,* December 23, 1992.

John Webber, "Home Depot Officials: Quincy 'Perfect Site' for Prototype Store," *Quincy Herald-Whig,* October 12, 1994.

Tom Saul, "Building Dealers: Slow Down on Home Depot," *Quincy Herald-Whig,* October 13, 1994.

Susannah Vesey, "Home Depot Chooses 3 Sites for Stores Aimed at Rural Areas," *The Atlanta Journal-Constitution,* October 21, 1994.

Gary Ruderman, "Home Depot Expansion Now at a 'Crossroads,'" *National Home Center News,* November 7, 1994.

Chris Roush, "Home Depot Reaches a CrossRoads," *The Atlanta Journal-Constitution,* July 16, 1995.

Chris Roush, "Midwest City Awaits Impact from Home Depot's New Tack," *The Atlanta Journal-Constitution,* July 16, 1995.

Chris Clayton, "Home Depot Opens with Fanfare," *Quincy Herald-Whig,* July 21, 1995.

"Customers Rave about CrossRoads," *Doings at the Depot,* September/October 1995.

Chris Roush, "Home Depot Drops Rural Store Concept," *The Atlanta Journal-Constitution*, December 9, 1995.

"CrossRoads Concept to Continue to Grow Faster as Home Depot," *Doings at the Depot*, January/February 1996.

CHAPTER 10: THE EXPO FACTOR

Bryant Scott was interviewed in October 1996. Jim Inglis was interviewed in November and December 1997. Bernie Marcus spoke about the San Diego Expo store at the 1991 National Hardware Show.

Information about Home Depot's Expo stores came from:

Chris Burritt, "Different by Design, Home Depot Will Open Upscale Store," *The Atlanta Journal-Constitution*, November 18, 1992.

"Expo Caters to Home Decor Demands," *National Home Center News*, December 14, 1992.

Cynthia Mitchell, "Home Depot Chooses Site for Upscale Expo Store," *The Atlanta Journal-Constitution*, January 1, 1993.

Susannah Vesey, "Home Depot Plans a Finer Diner for Customers at New Expo Store," *The Atlanta Journal-Constitution*, October 23, 1993.

Susannah Vesey, "Do-It-Yourself Chain Drawing upon Its Experience with San Diego Store," *The Atlanta Journal-Constitution*, January 20, 1994.

Susannah Vesey, "Home Depot Ready to Start Expo Chain," *The Atlanta Journal-Constitution*, April 15, 1994.

Susannah Vesey, "Home Depot to Expand Its Line of Expo Stores," *The Atlanta Journal-Constitution*, May 18, 1994.

Chris Roush, "Home Depot Fails to Soothe Wary Wall Street," *The Atlanta Journal-Constitution*, September 13, 1995.

Maria Halkias, "Expo Units Add Finishing Touch for Home Depot," *Dallas Morning News*, November 13, 1995.

Henry Howard, "N.Y. Expo Store Weaves Furniture into Home Offerings," *Furniture/Today*, March 4, 1996.

Chris Roush, "Home Depot to Decide on Overseas Plans by End of '96," *The Atlanta Journal-Constitution*, April 19, 1996.

Chris Roush, "Home Depot Tries Another Tweak with Expo in Miami," *The Atlanta Journal-Constitution*, July 31, 1996.

Chris Roush, "Home Depot's Expo Chain Seeks a Fresh Design," *The Atlanta Journal-Constitution*, October 18, 1996.

Chris Roush, "Expo's Evolution: High-Ticket Home Depot Spinoff Remodels Itself," *The Atlanta Journal-Constitution*, October 18, 1996.

John Caulfield, "Expo: Depot's Showroom in Progress," *National Home Center News*, October 21, 1996.

John Caulfield, "Depot Opens Streamlined Expo Design Center in Miami," *National Home Center News*, October 21, 1996.

Patti Bond, "Home Depot's New Expo Not a Warehouse at All," *The Atlanta Journal-Constitution*, April 4, 1998.

CHAPTER 11: HOME DEPOT GOES GLOBAL

Jim Inglis and Bill Pena were interviewed in February 1995. Bernie Marcus was interviewed in December 1995. Pena was interviewed again in January 1997. Inglis was interviewed again in November and December 1997. Peter Cleaveland was interviewed in January 1998. Jim Hodkinson was interviewed in March 1998. Don Cambell was interviewed in December 1997.

Information on Home Depot's international expansion came from:

Susannah Vesey, "Home Depot to Begin Push into Canada," *The Atlanta Journal-Constitution*, May 19, 1993.

Susannah Vesey, "Home Depot Welcomes Back Departed Executive," *The Atlanta Journal-Constitution*, February 9, 1994.

Chris Roush, "Home Depot Continues Laying a Foundation to Enter Mexico," *The Atlanta Journal-Constitution*, February 14, 1995.

Chris Roush, "Home Depot Curbs Mexico, Canada Plans," *The Atlanta Journal-Constitution*, June 23, 1995.

Chris Roush, "Home Depot Joins Others in Venture into China," *The Atlanta Journal-Constitution*, December 6, 1995.

Chris Roush, "Home Depot Wants Exec for Canada Home-Grown," *The Atlanta Journal-Constitution*, December 22, 1995.

Stacey Levitz, "Home Depot Again Looking International," *Doings at the Depot*, January/February 1996.

Carol Tice, "New President Gears up Home Depot Canada for Growth," *National Home Center News*, September 23, 1996.

David Henry, "Why Home Depot is Building an International Focus," *Doings at the Depot*, January/February 1997.

Chris Roush, "Ready to Nail Chile," *The Atlanta Journal-Constitution*, January 29, 1997.

"China's Home Way Opens to Throngs: Echoes of Home Depot," *National Home Center News*, March 3, 1997.

Chris Roush, "Home Depot Won't Buy Quebec Chain," *The Atlanta Journal-Constitution*, March 11, 1997.

Don Longo, "International: Giant Dips its Toes in Foreign Waters," *National Home Center News*, December 1997.

"Home Deport Execs See EPS Estimates 'in Range,'" *Reuters*, April 1, 1998.

Information on the Bowater acquisition and 1980s expansion came from:

"Everything You Wanted to Know about Depot's History," *National Home Center News*, December 1986.

Tom Walker, "Home Depot Plans Detroit Stores as First Outlets Beyond Sun Belt," *The Atlanta Journal-Constitution*, August 30, 1984.

Keith Herndon, "Home Depot Acquiring 9 Stores," *The Atlanta Journal-Constitution*, October 31, 1984.

Lisa M. Keefe, "Do-It-Yourself Debacle," *Forbes*, May 4, 1987.

CHAPTER 12: THE NEW HOME DEPOT

Robert Tillman was interviewed in August 1997. Dick Hammill was interviewed in March 1997. Arthur Blank was interviewed in January 1997.

Information about Home Depot's strategy to boost sales during the next decade came from:

Chris Roush, "At Home in Buckhead," *The Atlanta Journal-Constitution*, February 27, 1996.

Chris Roush, "Home Depot Branching out into Catalog Sales," *The Atlanta Journal-Constitution*, May 18, 1996.

Chris Roush, "Home Depot Takes on Ambitious Construction Project in Cobb County," *The Atlanta Journal-Constitution*, November 6, 1996.

Chris Roush, "Do-It-Yourself Stores Practice Playing Santa," *The Atlanta Journal-Constitution*, December 15, 1996.

Chris Roush, "Home Depot to Buy Mail-Order Company," *The Atlanta Journal-Constitution*, January 17, 1997.

Craig Rose, "Going for Broke: Risks Pay off in Hardware Company's Sale to Home Depot," *San Diego Union-Tribune*, January 22, 1997.

Chris Roush, "Home Depot's Growth Strategy," *The Atlanta Journal-Constitution*, February 26, 1997.

Chris Roush, "Home Depot Ad Spending to Rise by 40%," *The Atlanta Journal-Constitution*, March 14, 1997.

Nicole Harris, "Home Depot: Beyond Do-It-Yourselfers," *BusinessWeek*, June 30, 1997.

Chris Roush, "More Competition Across the Board," *The Atlanta Journal-Constitution*, August 24, 1997.

Cheryl Hall, "Ideas at Work," *Dallas Morning News*, September 7, 1997.

"Home Depot to Expand Number of 24-Hour Stores," *National Home Center News*, October 9, 1997.

Tom Moran, "More Places to Shop Round the Clock," *Christian Science Monitor*, October 17, 1997.

"No Rollout Planned for Home Depot Pro Store," *National Home Center News*, April 13, 1998.

Christine Overholt, "Home Depot Plans to Open California Pro Supply Store," *Bloomberg News*, April 13, 1998.

INDEX

ABOUT THE AUTHOR

Pulitzer Prize–nominated journalist Chris Roush is currently a business reporter for Bloomberg News. He became an expert on the inside operations of Home Depot while a reporter for *The Atlanta Journal-Constitution* where he covered Coca-Cola and Home Depot, as well as the whole retail industry. It was his reporting on consumer issues that won him a Pulitzer Prize nomination in 1993 by the *Tampa Tribune*. He was also nominated for the Livingston Award by the *Atlanta Journal-Constitution* for his reporting on business issues. Roush has also worked for *Business Week* and the *Sarasota Herald-Tribune*.